TWENTY YEARS AT ST HILARY

BERNARD WALKE

TRURAN

First published in the UK
by Methuen and Company Ltd in 1935
© in that edition Methuen and Company Limited 1935

©This edition first published in the UK by Truran
under licence from Oxfam GB, 2002
© in this edition Oxfam GB 2002
Oxfam GB is a member of Oxfam International and is a
registered charity, number 202918

Truran, Croft Prince, Mount Hawke, Truro, Cornwall TR4 8EE
http://www.Truranbooks.co.uk www.Truranbooks.co.uk

ISBN 1 85022 164 2(p/b)
ISBN 185022 170 7 (h/b)

Introduction© AM Allchin

Printed and bound in Cornwall by R Booth Ltd,
Antron Hill, Mabe, Penryn, Cornwall TR10 9HH

To
Annie Walke

INTRODUCTION

Canon AM Allchin
Honorary Professor in the Theology Department of the
University of Wales, Bangor

It is a great thing that *Twenty Years at St Hilary* should be in print again. Many of those who have read and loved the book have been looking forward eagerly to its reappearance. It tells us the story of a generous, humorous, deeply caring man, a man of many-sided, unexpected character, as his friend Frank Baker put it 'a good man who could never be dull.'

Readers have valued the book for a great variety of reasons. Some have cherished the picture it gives of the life of the farming community in west Cornwall in the days before agriculture was mechanised. Others have been captured by the insight it gives us into the perplexities of a pacifist towards the end of World War 1, and of the subsequent collaboration between Quaker and Anglo-Catholic in the social and economic crisis of the inter-war years in Cornwall. The growing number of those who admire the paintings of the Newlyn School in this period, have been attracted by the vivid glimpses which we find in these pages, of the social and leisure life of this community of artists, into which Bernard Walke and his artist wife Annie fitted so easily. But perhaps above all it is those who have been fascinated by Bernard Walke's way with birds and animals, to be found for instance in the chapter called simply 'Donkeys', who have been most anxious to see the book in circulation again.

Yes, Bernard Walke was a many-sided man with a gift for making friends in very different places and very different circumstances. Before he ever came to St Hilary, he already had more than a decade of pastoral experience in

Cornish parishes, first at St Ives, and then for a longer period at Polruan. In both places as a young unmarried curate he determined to get to know the working life of his parishioners at first hand. So he would go out regularly with the fishing boats from St Ives; he would sign on in Polruan for a tour of duty on the little cargo ships which sailed from the Fowey harbour in the service of the china clay industry. Like others in England at the turn of the century he was powerfully influenced by the example of St Francis, in his identification with the poor, his love of the world of animals and birds, his total disregard for ordinary conventions. This was a new kind of priesthood which attracted many and repelled others.

In his book, *English Christianity in the Twentieth Century*, Adrian Hastings writes about two even more unconventional missionary priests of this period, Arthur Shearly Cripps in Rhodesia, and C.F. Andrews, Ghandi's great friend, in India. Their lives were marked, he says, by 'the sheer quality of their religious commitment, love of neighbour, intellectual integrity, and a flow of poetry affecting every aspect of life.' Outwardly of course their circumstances were very different from those of Bernard Walke, yet how well the description of their quality of life fits with what we learn of the writer of this book.

Inevitably in its final chapters there is a note of sadness and failure, as Bernard Walke comes up against the sheer destructiveness of sectarian bigotry as it manifested itself in St Hilary in August 1932, and at the same time has to come to terms with the breakdown of his health, a breakdown which sends him into the TB Sanatorium at Tehidy. It was in the enforced leisure and isolation of that hospital that this book was written. It is no wonder that some have spoken of Bernard Walke at the end of his life as a 'broken man'. Physically speaking at least that description is true. But if his life was broken it was broken open through generosity and care for others, broken open in a way which proved life giving and indeed healing for those who came into contact with him. Still today the tenacity and vitality of people's memories of him at St Hilary and even at Polruan is a witness to that fact. Many of those memories are linked to the plays, which Bernard Walke wrote for the people of the parish to perform in the church at St Hilary, and which were broadcast by the BBC for almost a decade from 1927 onwards. It was the Christmas play *Bethlehem*, which made the most effect nationally; it was a truly pioneering piece of religious broadcasting, and recognised as such by John Reith. But at St Hilary itself it was the way in which the whole community got involved which people remember: actors, singers, dancers, bellringers, those who made the costumes and those who provided tea and cakes for afterwards. It was something which belonged to all, in which priest and people were united.

If in some ways the man you find in this book is a man of the past, firmly rooted in the England of the late nineteenth century, in other ways he seems still to elude us, still to be ahead of us. We need to hurry to catch up with him.

Note
The book has been reset but the spelling, punctuation, grammar and paragraphing are as in the original edition.

CONTENTS

1 LEAVING POLRUAN

I lie beneath the veranda at the sanatorium looking at Carn Brea and listening to the talk of the men in the beds around me. There are men here of many trades - a tumbling clown, flying men, a diver, a steeplejack, soldiers and sailors, miners and farm labourers. We are all TB men under sentence, who find consolation in being together. I would like to share more than I do in the intimate talk that goes on. I do not want to be always a listener. My difficulty is that, compared to these men, I have so little to say. I have never travelled the world as a tumbling clown, flown an aeroplane across the deserts of Mesopotamia, worked in a salt mine as a prisoner or war, or had any of kind of adventures which make the talk so full of interest. And yet any life, however uneventful, if told truthfully, is a valuable human document. My intention in this book therefore is to put down, is if I were talking to these fellow-prisoners who lie in the beds around me, all that I can remember of my thoughts and doings during the last twenty years of my life at St. Hilary. Life in a sanatorium with its insistent routine of temperatures, rest and meals, has a tendency to blot out the past as if it never existed; possibly the writing of these memories will call these years back to life and give them meaning and coherence.

I had an experience of this kind a short time ago through a letter I received from a listener to the broadcast of my play, *The Little Ass*. The letter was from an old farmer in Sussex writing for his wife, who was paralysed, to say that as a girl she was in service in Wiltshire with a clergyman's family named Walke, and whilst she was with them a child was born whom they called Bernard. Was I the Bernard Walke that she had nursed as a baby? How well I remembered this old nurse, who was called Thursa and whose father was a gamekeeper, although she must have left our service before I had reached the age of four.

How well I also remembered their cottage in a sandy lane by the side of a fir-wood where, as a treat, she would sometimes take me to tea, and where I first saw Canterbury bells. I do not know whether it was the name 'Canterbury Bells' that took my fancy as a child or whether it was the sight of the flowers themselves; there was something magical about them as they grew in my old nurse's garden that I have never forgotten. It delighted me to recall these days, but my real interest in that letter lay in the words, 'where a child was born whom they called Bernard'. I had been told that I was born at 10.45 in the morning on the fifteenth day of June, and that they were cutting the hay in the meadows when the mowers heard the cry of a baby. Like every one else I had always been and still am interested in my birthday, but never before had I realised so vividly the importance of that event for myself. The simple statement, 'a child was born and they called him Bernard', gave me an intense sense of my own identity such as I have rarely experienced.

We - that is my wife Annie Walke and I - lived in Polruan. I will call her Annie Walke in these pages as I have in life, for the name Annie by itself suggested her so little to me that I have never succeeded in calling her Annie. It has always been Annie Walke, and Annie Walke she must remain.

Polruan is a little seaport across the harbour from Fowey with derelict shipbuilding yards, and houses struggling up the hill to the coastguard look-out and the ruins of the old church of St. Saviour. Here Annie Walke had a studio in a sail-loft overlooking the harbour. Men would come running down the street from the lookout on the hill, loose a boat and away to the mouth of the harbour to pilot a ship up to the jetties. Steamers from the Clyde, little schooners that had battled across the North Atlantic with fish from Newfoundland, Italian barques and trim brigantines from Denmark were all to be seen moored alongside each other beneath the hill, waiting their turn to load. There was the constant coming and going of the ferry, and at all times of the day men walking up and down the quay, groups of women standing and talking outside their doors. To Annie Walke, Polruan presented a pageant of life which she might watch from the window of her studio.

For myself, there was the new Church of St. Saviour on the hill, where I said my daily Mass, and a thousand or more people to whom I could minister, and who, if they did not come often to the church, were always willing to stand on the quay, sing hymns and listen to my preaching. There were the cliffs, where I worked at making gardens which the rabbits destroyed. There were the jetties, where from our boats we might watch, high overhead, railway trucks tip and empty a stream of white china clay which would come roaring down a shute to the ships below; and at the water's edge, alive with the chatter of boats at their moorings, as they swung to meet the incoming and outgoing tide, stood our queer little house.

No account of our life there would be complete without the history of the cat to whom we gave the name 'Little Soul'. There is a tradition that cats were introduced into Europe from Egypt by the Fathers of the desert, who risked their lives in taking them out of the country rather than be parted from the companions of their lonely vigils. What treatises might not be written on the companionship of these hermit saints and their cats! Wiser perhaps than St Antony, who chose a pig to remind himself of the sensuality of human nature, these other saints desired as their companions creatures from whom they might learn the ways of contemplation.

In their ancient home cats were sacred to the Gods, and as a race they have never forgotten their high origin; for, while they are the most domesticated of the animals, they have never surrendered their independence. Independence is not the right term, for independence implies a conscious effort and cats are too aristocratic to make any claim to superiority.

This cat of whom I am writing wandered down as a kitten from the farm-place where her mother lived in a half-wild state, and attended my Mass at the church on the hill for three mornings in succession. As no one claimed her I picked her up and took her home. After a time she took to accompanying me each morning with those short runs and stops which a cat adopts in going for a walk, to the church where I first discovered her. Sitting on the step, she would gravely me-ow when I turned to say *Dominus tecum* and go before me to the vestry when Mass was ended. Later she took to coming to the Sunday evening service, walking sedately before me to the pulpit where, from the book rest, she looked down on the people.

One Sunday evening a Miss Mahon, an old lady of Polruan, was sitting in the front pew. The glistening sequins that decorated her mantle proved an irresistible attraction to Little Soul that evening, for, springing from her place in the pulpit, she landed in the lap of the old lady. The following day I received a letter from the Vicar enumerating my many extravagances concluding with the monstrous behaviour of my cat on the previous night. One phrase remains in my memory - 'Your performing cat has made religion stink in the nostrils of the best people in Polruan.' In answering, I advanced the example of St. Philip Neri, whose cat always attended him at his devotions; but our little cat was forbidden ever to enter the church again. Later, Little Soul came with us to St. Hilary, where her religious observance was limited to producing kittens by some means or other on the great Feasts of the Church.

In 1912 my Vicar resigned and, as I was only the curate, there was nothing for us to do but to leave this attractive place. The Bishop, when applied to, wrote kindly but unhelpfully, suggesting that good men were needed in the North, which was evidently intended to convey in as polite a way as possible that my kind of goodness was not wanted in the West.

We were in despair, when quite unexpectedly one morning came an offer of the living of St. Hilary. Beyond the fact that it had a lovely name and lay somewhere in the West of Cornwall, we knew nothing about this St. Hilary. But what did it matter where the place was or what it was like? Anything was better than the North. A hastily written telegram - 'Tremayne Butler, Esq., Downes, Crediton. Gratefully accept your offer St. Hilary Walke' - was to settle our future for the next twenty years. Having sent the telegram we started out the same morning to discover this place which was to be our future home.

It was high tide as we rowed up the harbour and made fast the boat at a derelict shipyard adjoining Fowey station, where we bought two return tickets for Marazion. Years before, when I was at St. Ives, in passing through to Penzance by train I had been attracted by the name of this station as it stood out in bold letters, MARAZION, and regretted that so few words in our language possess this decorative letter 'Z'. The porter who claimed the half of our tickets advised us to go to Marazion town and inquire the way; so we walked in the rain along the wind-swept road bordering the sea to the town, where we hired a pony and jingle to take us to St. Hilary. The going was slow, for the road was uphill and the pony was old; but before we had gone far we saw a spire among the trees. One of the peculiarities of St. Hilary is that from wherever you see this spire it seems a long way off, with never a road that leads there. Its far-away hiddenness best characterises this church among the trees. It is now known to millions of people as the church of the broadcast of *Bethlehem*, the Nativity Play, yet it retains a secrecy that makes its discovery an event to be remembered.

Beyond the village of Goldsithney we came upon an avenue which led in the direction of the spire. The word avenue suggests a stately procession, but this avenue was of

Cornish wind-swept trees of ash and elm, bent to the wind like old men carrying bundles of sticks. On that November day, shrouded in misty rain with no end in sight, the avenue looked too secret for strangers to enter and we turned away up the hill until we found a road that led us to the church.

My first impressions were of the loveliness of the tower and spire and the peace of the raised churchyard which lay above the pathway, where rested the bodies of many thousands of the men and women of St. Hilary. This was the pathway over which they had been carried to their christenings, on which they had walked proudly to their weddings and along which they had been borne to their graves. They had sat and laughed and talked on the stone seats that lined the way; and here was I, a stranger to St. Hilary, accepting by telegram the charge of the parish which they had known and loved.

There were two Celtic crosses set in the stonework bordering the path and a Latin cross from a Priest's tomb, but what interested me most was a stone by the gateway, with an inscription below some Runic device, which was evidently pre-Christian. It is known as the Noti Noti stone, and although archaeologists are uncertain as to its exact meaning, there are grounds for believing that it commemorates 'The man who was much loved'. Who could wish for a more lovely epitaph - to be known only as the man who was much loved?

In the days that were to follow when I went in and out of the gateway many times a day I rarely passed that stone without a thought of the unknown who lived at St. Hilary and was much loved before the Christian faith was brought to Cornwall.

An old man at the farm by the church, who was holding our pony, told me how one Good Friday morning seventy-five years ago snow lay on the roof and round the churchyard, and when the sexton opened the door a fire, which had been smouldering through the night, burst forth, and by noon there was nothing left of the church but its tower and spire. Last century was probably the worst period of English church architecture in history; but by following the lines of the old foundations and utilising the mullions of the windows and much of the old stone-work, those responsible for its rebuilding achieved a certain dignity in all but the porch. This porch, an example of meaningless decoration, was nearly the cause of the death of Annie Walke, who, running into the church one dark winter's night, struck her head against one of its projecting spikes and was found later unconscious on the pathway. Since then I have employed a stonemason to cut away its offending projections.

Within, the church was full of pious distractions: a Holy, Holy, Holy on red baize decked an altar too small for the proportions of the building; the walls were disfigured by stencil texts; the Lady Chapel was blocked by an organ and the chapel on the opposite aisle crowded with pews. It had no beauty except for its slender pillars, and lantern with four windows in the roof at the entrance to the chancel; and yet there was a quiet friendliness and feeling of holiness about the building that redeemed it.

The Catholic Church has always taught that the world apprehended by our senses is capable of bringing us into relationship with another world. In addition to her seven sacraments she consecrates places and things for spiritual uses. On Holy Saturday she blesses the new fire, the water and the Paschal candle. The Rubric says:

At a convenient time fire is struck from a flint outside the church and coals are lighted from it... meanwhile there are no lights in the church, so that they may be lighted from the blessed fire.

There are few prayers more beautiful than that for blessing the Paschal candle, of which the following is a translation:

We therefore pray Thee, O Lord, that this candle, which is hallowed in Thy name, may avail and fail not to scatter the darkness of this night;

may it be received as a sweet savour and be mingled with the lights of Heaven, may the morning star find its flame alight; that morning star that knows no setting, which came back from Hell and shed its kindly light upon mankind.

It is not therefore surprising that certain places have a special significance as places which attract or repel us. The story of the haunted house is too persistent to be altogether disregarded. I do not know what historical evidence there is for connecting Tintagel with the Grail legend, but I am convinced that something of spiritual import happened there. The moors of Cornwall, 'whose paths are worn by Angels' feet', contain many saintly spots where the spirit of prayer still lingers. The chapel of St. Levan, overlooking the sea, the cell of some unknown hermit among the fir trees at Sancreed, the baptistery at Madron are places where to sit in quiet is to be conscious of a world strangely unlike and yet like the world we know.

Here in this church, with many things to offend, was a peace which told of centuries of prayer. Five hundred years ago it had been consecrated as a home of the Blessed Sacrament, and in the years that have passed many prayers and sighs have gone up to Heaven from within its walls.

Some years after this first visit to St. Hilary, Walter De la Mare, the poet, who sings so exquisitely of the enchanted country of childhood, came to spend a week-end with me. We had both been staying at Sennen and on the way over to St. Hilary he told me that he thought Cornwall was a haunted land and that he would never venture to stay there again. After supper, when we were walking in the garden, he returned to the subject and said that the fear that had haunted him in Cornwall was absent from this place and that within its trees was a magic circle of peace. In the twenty years of which I am writing, how many have found something of this peace within the walls of the church which we entered for the first time on that November day!

As we were leaving the church, a little man who had

been tidying books and had probably heard something of our conversation, came and spoke to us and told us that his name was Smitham and that he was church-warden. He knew who we were and insisted on taking us to look over the vicarage house. I have no recollection of anything about the house except that it seemed absurdly large for two little people like ourselves and that there was a tower which looked like a French mill.

Saying good-bye to Mr. Smitham, who incidentally was an undertaker and told us in parting that he had been churchwarden to two vicars and had buried them both and hoped to do the same for me, we started out to find the village but discovered that there was no village, only the church-town, scattered farms and cottages. What we did find, half a mile away, was some trim villas such as Cornishmen love to build when they come home from abroad or retire from business. The mist had blotted out the hills of Godolphin and Tregonning; there was nothing to be seen but fields of decaying broccoli stalks, not a dog or a child in sight, only these fields and those villa residences. If the telegram had not been sent in the morning in all probability we should never have known more of St. Hilary than we discovered that November afternoon. But telegrams are final in their brevity and this particular one provided no way of escape.

We could never acknowledge that we had accepted the place without knowing what it was like and that, now we had seen it, we could not go there because the country looked dreary and the villas in Relubbus Lane pretentious.

Annie Walke and I knew so surely what we each were feeling at leaving Polruan for this empty countryside that there was no need to say anything. The only comment I remember making was: 'We need not stay here if we find it as depressing as it looks'. It was growing dark and the mist had turned into a drizzly rain as we drove down to the village of Perranuthnoe, where the sea, from the low crumbling cliffs, was as unwelcoming as the fields through which we had walked in the afternoon.

As we stood and looked down on the desolate beach at Perranuthnoe we knew nothing of the coast to the eastward with the Great Cudden reaching out into the sea, where for centuries ravens have built their nests, nor of the coves that lay beyond, where the last of the smugglers made his home and landed his cargoes.

That is the danger of first impressions; some detail or aspect is seen or felt so vividly as to be mistaken for the whole. We had walked through sodden fields and looked at a dull coast and thought we had seen St. Hilary.

When we left the train that evening and climbed down the embankment we found our boat safely afloat. The tide had ebbed and flowed while we had travelled a hundred miles, and seen St. Hilary. Yet looking back on the afternoon, for all that we had discovered about the character of this place, we might as well have sat in the boat and watched the tide flow out and back again. As we rowed across the river to the Bodinnick side we passed under tall ships with riding lights to Point Pill. Ahead lay Polruan, with layer upon layer of lights from windows where the houses mount the hill and where, down at the water's edge, one light burned very brightly from the window of our cottage.

How little we thought that the smell of wood smoke, which always greets us as we come down the avenue at St. Hilary at night, would in the days that were to come speak of home as surely and tenderly as the light in the window at Polruan.

2 COMING TO ST. HILARY

It was on a dull morning in February, with the wind, which would bring rain later, coming in from the sea, that we left Polruan. The weather was a great consideration, as our furniture was to be loaded into a barge, which was to be towed to the landing-place near the station, transferred to the railway, and finally drawn to St. Hilary in a wagon lent by the farmer who rented the glebe. There had been a change in the arrangements that morning: it had been decided previously that it would be safer to load the barge at the quay where there was enough water to float the boat at all states of the tide; but early that morning Arthur Hicks - Captain he was usually called, not that he had ever been to sea, but out of respect for his commanding appearance - arrived to say that it would be more convenient to load the barge from the steps at the end of our garden. A most disastrous decision, as we were to discover later. Removal of furniture, even if it was only to the next street, was always of interest to the people of Polruan. But this was no ordinary removal from one street to another. We were leaving Polruan altogether; consequently all our friends were there to assist in loading the barge.

We had taken refuge in an upstairs room, where we sat on boxes packed with china, ate sandwiches and watched the turmoil that was going on in the garden below. People were rushing about carrying things, and not finding anywhere to put them, disappeared with them into the house. Four men were struggling with the piano when one slipped on the steps and fell into the water and had to be rescued and given brandy. A crowd of children from the coastguard station arrived with a toy wheelbarrow and were singing hymns while they carted small ornaments round the garden in their wheelbarrow. Arthur Hicks, who always contrived to give an air of romance to anything he was engaged in, was too busy shouting instructions to notice that the tide was ebbing and the barge was on the ground. The work of loading now became increasingly difficult, for as the tide ebbed the barge settled in the mud with a list, so that the rest of our furniture had to be carried across a narrow plank. But what gave me greater concern was the discovery that the barge was leaking and that much of our furniture must be already soaked with seawater. Arthur Hicks, who had procured this leaky barge and persisted in loading her at the steps where she had gone on the ground, remained undaunted at what had happened, assuring us that if we would leave things to him we would be well satisfied. There was nothing else to be done.

Without a word of farewell except to the children, who followed us to the quay, we unmoored our boat and rowed to the station. It is more than twenty years since I tied up that boat at the shipyard near the station, and yesterday I received a letter from Ernie Slade, the boat-builder at Polruan, in whose charge I had left her, asking if I would sell this same boat which since that day had been laid up in his yard. It would be sacrilege to sell this old boat, and yet to leave her forever in a loft with her planks dry and her seams open away from the water for which she was built, is a poor return for the services she has rendered. I comfort myself with the thought that some time I will go back to Polruan and take her down from the loft and sail with her to Lantic Bay, where I have spent so many happy days; but whether that day will ever come I do not know. Sailing in a small boat is one of the joys of youth rather than age.

That night we stayed in Penzance at the house of Norman Garstin, whose wife had invited us to make our home with them while we were settling in at St. Hilary. It was not until much later, during the war, that I got to know Norman Garstin in any true sense; but even on the slight acquaintance of this first visit, I knew him to be a man with an intense reverence for truth, and an eagerness to discover the motives and aspirations that directed human activities.

Often after we had talked on some subject connected with religion he would end by saying, 'I don't know, my boy, I don't know'; it would be said with a solemnity and sadness that conveyed his failure to understand what to me was the deepest concern of human existence. The morning after our arrival at Penzance, Annie Walke developed a violent cold, so that I had to bicycle over to St. Hilary and face the arrival of the furniture alone.

Have you ever taken possession of a house from which the furniture of the late owners has been removed a short time before? Everywhere there are signs of someone who has gone away; the house does not belong to you and resents your presence, your footsteps have a hollow sound as you wander from room to room, speaking in a whisper from fear of the echoes that your voice will raise. This was the kind of house in which I spent a whole afternoon waiting for the arrival of our furniture. I had as a companion Susie, the old cook, who was now in our service, but who, like the house, did not belong to us and was constantly reminding me of the glories of the vicarage in the old master's time.

Susie was a tyrant and, as we discovered later, terrorised any young girl we got in to help by saying at bed-time, 'You had better be quick or you will meet Him on the stairs,' followed by a detailed description of an old man with a red beard whose ghost haunted that part of the house.

I feel she must have exercised her power of inspiring terror on me that evening, for as it grew dark and the house more and more alien and desolate, I longed for the arrival of the wagons so that I might escape, and yet dreaded their coming, when our poor furniture, soaked with rain and sea-water, should be inspected by this unfriendly woman. Some of the furniture that was arriving I had known from childhood, and the sense of loyalty to these memories made me want to explain to Susie that many of these old things were much more beautiful than grand modern furniture; but I was too proud or too shy, I do not know which, and so Susie and I waited for hours, mostly in silence.

It is strange how an unimportant event like waiting for the arrival of a load of furniture should have made so lasting an impression; but those hours in that empty house with Susie as a companion persist as a memory of desolation where many other things have been forgotten. When at last the two wagons with the furniture arrived it was dark; and as we had no light beyond the stable lantern, nothing could be done that night; everything was carried into the big dining-room; tables and chairs, beds, crockery, household linen and kitchen utensils were all crowded into this one room. The man in charge of the wagons had gone, Susie had somehow disappeared, and I was left with a guttering candle to lock up.

The next few days were occupied in interviewing churchwardens and arranging the house in preparation for the visit of the Lord Bishop of the Diocese, who had announced his intention of coming to St. Hilary to institute me as vicar the following week.

As it was the first occasion on which we had ever entertained a Bishop, we made a great effort to provide a supper which, while fulfilling the obligations of Lent, should have an air of friendliness and festivity. The supper we planned was to begin with oysters and Moselle - the 'Doktor' that Annie Walke and I had once drunk at Berncastel, when we were on our honeymoon, and which I had discovered at Poole's the wine merchant in Penzance. This was to be followed by lobster mayonnaise and trifle. We had provided for a large number of guests, as on these occasions the clergy of the Deanery are accustomed to attend in great numbers to welcome the new vicar. But when the time came the only clergy who arrived for the ceremony were Father Rogers, the Vicar of Penzance, his two curates and Father Wason, whom I had known many years ago in London and who was now Vicar of Cury and Gunwalloe in the Meneage district, where he had obtained great notoriety by what were considered extreme practices. So great was his fame that the interest of the congregation in myself as the new vicar was overshadowed by his presence. As I walked up the aisle behind him I could hear whispered remarks, 'There's old Wason over to Cury. He's a proper old Roman Catholic they do say - Can 'e see 'm, my dear? The one wearing a hat like a tea cosy'; although why a biretta should be described as a tea cosy, I do not know.

There are few men living round whom so many legends have grown up as round Father Wason. Many of these stories have little foundation; but the fact that they exist and are believed give him distinction in an age when so few achieve a personality to which it would be possible to attach any legend. I can picture him as 'The White Knight' in *Through the Looking-Glass*, for ever falling off his horse with the setting sun illuminating his white face, or better still as a Confessor of Gnomes, bending down and listening with interest to the little sins of those small people, or even as a certain medieval saint who caused great inconvenience to his Bishop by refusing to be parted from a crucifix and image of Our Lady which it was his custom to carry in either hand when he walked abroad. I can picture him in any or all of these guises, so unpractical is he and so aloof from ordinary affairs. But for me his charm lies in a tenderness that expressed itself in a telegram when he first heard of my illness:

Saying Mass for your intention tomorrow 10.30 a.m.
followed by another telegram the next morning:

Too late overslept - To-morrow without fail,
and the arrival by post of a relic of St. Teresa of the Child Jesus, his most treasured possession.

After knowing him for many years I find his whimsical nature too difficult to describe, except by saying that his scale of values is different from ours and often disconcerting to his friends. I remember a luncheon party he once gave at Cury to which we and Dod and Ernest Procter were invited. We arrived tired after a long bicycle ride from St. Hilary, and found a notice pinned to the door, 'No one to enter.' After a time of waiting Father Wason came from the garden with his cassock tucked up round his waist and his arms full of iris blossoms. He made no attempt to welcome us but hurried by, murmuring as he passed, 'Colour scheme of the table all wrong. Must get it right for Dod Procter.' After a further time of waiting and knocking on the door, an upstairs window was thrown open and Father Wason shouted down, 'Table all wrong without a black centre. Am looking for my tall hat.' After a further delay the door was opened and we were greeted by Father Wason, as if we had at that moment arrived, and were led to the dining room where in the centre of the table was the tall hat filled with flowers. There was no hint of eccentricity in the tall hat as a table decoration, its shape and glossy blackness supplied a note that would otherwise have been lacking, so that one began to wonder why people had never thought of using tall hats as table centres before, although possibly it was not the tall hat that pleased us so much as the subtle compliment that had been paid us.

He had come over now to take part in my induction and to help to entertain the clergymen whom we expected but who never came.

The service began with the usual legal formalities, and when they were completed I was conducted round the church and given the key of the main door, which I locked and unlocked; having accomplished this I was led to the belfry and told to 'ring myself in'. This ringing of the bell is to announce to the parishioners that a new vicar has been installed, as the smoke from the chimneys of the Vatican proclaims to the world that the conclave is over and that a new vicar of Christ has been elected.

I was aware of a tradition that the number of years a parson remains in a parish is determined by the number of times he tolls the bell. But having no experience of bellringing I inadvertently seized on the rope of the tenor, the heaviest bell in the peal, and the one most difficult to control; with considerable effort I started the bell and could feel it swinging high above me, but in place of the decent tolling which should have announced the new vicar there was silence, followed by a wild clanging and further silence as the clapper failed to strike the bell.

The Bishop fidgeted and looked at the church wardens as if to inquire if anything could be done; but the churchwardens leant on their staffs with bowed heads, as if engaged in some secret devotion. I was aware of what was going on but was in no mood to give way until I had mastered the bell and rung a sufficient number of strokes to provide myself with a long period of residence at St. Hilary.

I lost count of the number of times the bell had rung, and began to count afresh, and had got to the number twenty when I was exhausted and let the rope go. It is a curious coincidence, if I did ring the bell twenty times, that after twenty years I should have had this breakdown and be ordered away from St. Hilary for a year; but I am not without hope that I shall return to fulfil the number of years that I failed to count.

After the bellringing I returned to my stall in the chancel and the Bishop proceeded to the pulpit to preach what should have been a sermon commending my ministry to the people; what he did preach was a thinly veiled warning against my extreme practices. My efforts in the belfry had no doubt confirmed him in the opinion that I was unsuitable for his diocese.

Up to now Father Wason, who was sitting in the stalls, had taken no part and shown no interest in the proceedings, contenting himself with saying the rosary, over which he had apparently fallen asleep. He had spread a handkerchief over his face and might have been dead, so unconscious did he appear of all that was going on, when suddenly he rose to his feet and was on his way to the pulpit (whether to remove the Bishop or remonstrate with him will never be known) when I caught him by his surplice and dragged him back to his stall. Waving the handkerchief with which his face had been covered, he said in a voice sufficiently loud for all to hear, 'You ought not to allow these things, Ber, to be said in your church.' In the vestry later I made my apologies to the Bishop for the interruption of his discourse. After listening courteously the Bishop smiled and said, 'Mr. Wason, I think,' as if that were a sufficient explanation.

There still remained the supper, over which I anticipated no difficulty. A Bishop at supper presented no problems; sitting next to his hostess he would engage in polite conversation about Cornwall and its people while I attended to the other guests.

Having very few chairs and expecting a large number to sit down we had carried in oak benches from the church and set them on either side of the trestle table which reached from end to end of our dining-room, in readiness for the guests who never arrived.

Whether the depression that overshadowed the party from the moment the Bishop said grace and we sat down was due to the number of empty places or to the Bishop refusing wine and not liking oysters, I do not know. After the oysters had been hastily and rather shamefacedly disposed of by the other guests while the Bishop crumbled his bread, there occurred one of those unfortunate breakdowns that might ruin any party at which a Bishop was a guest.

Bessie, our maid, who had come with us from Polruan, was seized with shyness at the thought of waiting on such distinguished company and refused to enter the room. I rang the bell for her to remove the oyster shells, but no one came. I rang again, and after a time Annie Walke went to the kitchen but returned without Bessie. If only there had been chairs instead of high-backed benches, or if one or two of the visitors had been content to do the waiting at table and the removal of dishes, or even if Wason had not continued to glower across the table at the Bishop, the meal might have been a comparative success. But everyone got up at once, and as there was no way out, climbed over the benches and then climbed back again, so that frequently the only persons left at the table were Annie Walke and the Bishop.

I am of the opinion, however, that the party was a success after all as far as the principal guest was concerned, for the Bishop, a very shy and sensitive man, was evidently touched by our unsuccessful efforts to entertain him. For although he did not wait for the coffee, which was served later, and hurried away to catch his train, he waved a kindly hand from the cab we had hired to take him to the station.

3 THE FIRST YEAR

In Cornwall, where local tradition is probably more alive than in other counties, a man crosses a road or a stream which divides his parish from the next village and he is in a strange country, among people with a different tradition from his own. I knew an old man at Gunwalloe who would take you to a spot where, by stretching his legs very wide and reaching out with his arm, he could touch three parishes. Stretched out in this position he would look up and pointing with his finger say, 'That's Cury; they are queer, they Cury people, terrible people for carrying on at a funeral, and here's Mawgan,' stamping with one foot, 'I reckon they'm of no account down to Mawgan; and here we be in Gunwalloe,' as he stood upright. He was a Gunwalloe man. It was his village, and so evidently superior to Cury or Mawgan that it needed no recommendation.

Soon after my arrival at St. Hilary a man came to see me whom I knew as a rabbit-catcher in the winter and a farm labourer in the summer, a man whom I should have judged to be incapable of any emotion. But as he stood in the doorway, uncertain as to whether he would come in or go away, his eyes had the look of a man who was caught in a trap, much the same look as he himself must have seen many times in the eyes of rabbits he had snared.

'Come in,' I said; 'come in and sit down.' But there he stood fingering his hat. 'Are you in any trouble?' I went on.

'Trouble, Parson?' he said. 'That is what I've come to see you about. Do you know my woman? What do 'e think she has done? Without a word to me she has put in notice to leave, and taken a house down to Perran.'

'Whereabouts in Perran is this cottage?' I asked.
'If you want to know, Parson,' he answered, 'it's on the Downs.'

'Well, that is only a few hundred yards from where you are living now,' I answered.

'You'm like the woman, Parson,' he replied. 'You don't understand. Might as well be a few hundred miles for all I do care. 'Tis in Perran Parish,' he went on, 'and I shall be no longer a St. Hilary man and when I die they'll put me down to Perran Churchyard and there I shall be.'

To lie forever outside the parish, down in the churchyard at Perran, and never to be recognised as belonging to St. Hilary, was for him the greatest calamity that could happen to a man.

In the churchyard among the thousands of the dead, on that first day that I entered the parish, I had an intuition that however many years I might remain here I should be a stranger at St. Hilary, an intruder, knowing little of its history and having no part in its tradition. I felt that it was the dead who counted at St. Hilary, and knew of no way in which I could propitiate them. Since that day I have often sat in the cottage of an old blind woman and listened to her as she related family histories and told of great doings, when at funerals you might have walked on heads wearing black hats for a half a mile, in the time of Parson Pascoe who was vicar nearly a hundred years ago. Nothing had escaped her: stored up were the memories of her father and grandfather and the histories of the grandparents and great-grandparents of the present generation. These histories were not only of persons but of places, small fields and cottages, how these last were built and on what terms and conditions the fields were enclosed.

As I listened I have wondered whether I might not to future generations become part of this continuous life, one of the stones marking a boundary, a queer character who lived for a time at the vicarage and drove round the countryside with a donkey and shay, or whether the years that I have spent at St. Hilary are the beginning of a new epoch, a return to an older and more Catholic tradition.

There still remain, incorporated into the life of the

people, faint memories of their Catholic past. There is Corpus Christi Fair at Penzance, to which people flock from all the neighbouring villages; there is the Feast of the patron saint, known at St. Hilary as Feast Monday, and best of all Roguery Tuesday, a delightful substitute for carnival, when the young men of St. Hilary go about unhinging gates and engaging in other rogueries. But these celebrations have little religious significance; they remain, like the placenames, a witness to a past that has long been forgotten.

For the last hundred and fifty years Nonconformity has been responsible for fashioning the lives and the character of the people of Cornwall. In the fourteenth and fifteenth centuries they built chapels and shrines in honour of the saints; there are ruins of them everywhere in Cornwall. In the eighteenth and nineteenth centuries they were equally busy building meeting-houses; there are no less than four in St. Hilary and not a public house in the parish.

It is difficult to gauge the influence of the Church of England on the village life of today. With Cornishmen, the Parson up to vicarage is their parson, as the Church is their church, although they may be rigid Nonconformists and never enter it except for funerals and Harvest Thanksgiving. The Parson and the Church, and to some extent the life at the vicarage, must conform to the standards and traditions of the village if they are to be acceptable to the people. 'What we belong to do,' a judgement from which there is no appeal, is applied with unrelenting rigidity.

How we must have disappointed the people at St. Hilary when we arrived there in 1913, and how ruthlessly we must have offended against the vicarage tradition. The first intimation of village gossip about ourselves came through John Laity, the tenant of the Glebe Farm, who rode up one morning to tell me that there was a good deal of talk going on, and that people were saying that we had no money to pay our bills. I shall always remember how, bending down from his horse so that his face was level with mine, he whispered, 'They are a pack of damned mischief-makers, and if you want the loan of a hundred pounds you can draw on my account at the bank.'

In those days Berryman's bus ran between St. Hilary and Penzance. On Thursday, market-day, there were three buses driven by John Charles, Ernie and Uncle Harry. Uncle Harry drove the best horses, and his was the fast bus that only carried passengers and never stopped to deliver parcels. The other buses would take two hours to do the five miles, with John Charles jamming on the brake and jumping down from the box every few minutes to deliver parcels and exchange greetings and gossip with their owners.

These buses were always crowded.

'If you can get in, my dear,' John Charles would say, 'I can shut the door. I wouldn't say but what there is room for another if Mrs. Trevorrow will oblige and sit on Mr. Tregembo's knee.' Going home from Penzance on market-days, inside that dimly lit bus, was an opportunity never missed: hours before the bus was due to start women with their marketing would sit there and talk.

'A parcel of talk' went on in that bus:- 'I wouldn't mention no names!' No names were ever mentioned. 'But they're saying in Mr. Berryman's bus that the Parson's wife ain't no better than she ought to be. If she go to church, she's afeard to sit up in front where people can look at her. You do never knaw where she'll put herself. Like as not she'll stand up there at the back with the boys, same as if she were a bad woman. They've scat the stable to pieces; tore up the ceiling and put it down as a floor, and made a great window in the roof and calls it a studio. I'd like to know what do go on in there. They've made a whisht place of it, sure enough. 'Tis no better in the house neither; Parson got up one morning in a raging temper and tore out a lovely great mantelpiece. As for the goings on up at the church, they do pass understanding. To see Nicky Peters bowing and burning the incense is as good as a pantomime. You go and have a look at him, my dear, but take care you don't fall down dead with laughing.'

Talk of this kind filled the bus for many market-days; each week bringing something new about the goings on of the parson and his wife.

I had been brought up in the Catholic tradition, my grandfather and father being among the first of the Tractarians to adopt a Catholic form of worship, and was convinced that the Catholic movement in the Church of England, which began in the rediscovery of the Church as a divine institution, could have no other end but a corporate union with the Apostolic See of Rome. Outside that unity there could be no assurance of the preservation of the faith and morals of the Christian revelation. I was also persuaded that the religious instinct of the Cornish people would never find satisfaction apart from the teaching and worship of the Catholic Faith; as the last of the English people to forsake the old religion they would be the first to return to the old ways.

The religious revolution of the sixteenth century had robbed them of their ancient faith, broken down their images, scattered their relics and left them as a people destitute of religion. The new Prayer Book, which was intended to take the place of the Missal and their book of prayers, was in an unknown tongue. They could 'tell' their Pater Noster, Ave Maria and Credo and were familiar with the Latin of the Mass, but, seeing their native tongue was Cornish, the sonorous language of Cranmer's prayers had no meaning for them. In the petition for the restoration of the Faith they pleaded for 'the return of the simple service of the Mass' on the grounds that the new service of Morning Prayer was like a Christmas Play.

When John Wesley came to visit this county nearly two hundred years later, he found the people wild and uncouth, given to drunkenness and fighting, but with a hunger for God. On his first visit he was stoned and driven out of their villages; but he came again and again until he won them for God, and Cornwall was once more, if not a land of saints, a land where the people were in deadly earnest in their search for God. The moorland chapels bear witness how widespread was this religious revival in Cornwall, and many family journals are records of its reality. But by its very nature it was incapable of permanence; like a moorland fire it must burn itself out by its intensity. Nonconformity in Cornwall no longer produced the elements which were responsible for the fervour of its early days; social activity and pulpit oratory had taken the place of conversion and personal experience of the love of Jesus. The preachers themselves, versed in modern psychology, had learnt to distrust many of the old methods of conversion; class meetings and revivals had given way to Wesley guilds and tea drinkings. As a religious factor Nonconformity no longer supplied the needs of a naturally religious people, nor could it be claimed that the Church of England had taken its place.

Here, as in many other parishes throughout England, the Oxford Movement had resulted in a quickening of the life of the Church; but, as in many other parishes, Morning Prayer remained installed as the chief act of Sunday worship. Now Morning Prayer, however devoutly rendered, is not the type of service to kindle the faith or stir the emotions of a Celtic people who have known Catholicism and have passed through the fire of revivalism. The band of the Salvation Army and the ritual of the Mass demand attention, but Morning Prayer, lacking the violence of the one and the mystery of the other, makes no appeal either to the emotions or to the intelligence.

I attended this service a few months ago in a village church, for the first time since I was a boy. A bell was ringing when I entered the church, where there was a congregation of half a dozen farm labourers, who sat at the back, a few women and a number of children. When the bell ceased the sound of a harmonium announced the entrance of the clergyman. The congregation stood and waited until he reached his stall, when they sat down. 'Dearly beloved,' the clergyman began, and the congregation again stood and waited. Throughout the lessons, psalms and canticles they maintained this attitude of waiting. The only moment of which I was conscious of any emotion except among the children, who were constantly arranging their dresses and spreading out their handkerchiefs, was when the clergyman gave out 'Hymn two hundred and eighty-eight' and read the opening lines:

A *few more years shall roll,*
A *few more seasons come.*

There was a sound of turning over of pages and a shuffling of feet as they stood to sing of life's struggles, its partings and tears. When the hymn was ended and the clergyman went to the pulpit, they relapsed into a state of patient waiting for the service to end.

There was nothing here to kindle the faith that gave to Cornwall so many saints or to light again the fire that burnt so fiercely in the day of John Wesley. Only the worship of the Mass, where time and space have ceased to be the supreme realities, and where bread and wine have become the Body, Soul and Divinity of our Lord and Saviour, to be adored and to be offered by man as the all-prevailing sacrifice for the sins of the world, only the Mass could ever hope to win back man to the reality of God's love.

For weeks before my induction I had been in the parish seeing people in their homes and in the fields, attending the services on Sunday to give instruction on the Catholic Faith and endeavouring to prepare the minds of all who would listen for the changes I contemplated making in the services.

All had been made ready for the solemn offering of the Mass. Nicholas Peters had learnt to swing the censer, and a little boy (Percy Curnow, whose parents lived in the Churchtown) to make the responses, when on that first Sunday morning after my induction the people of St. Hlilary flocked to the church and found, in the place of a clergyman reading 'Dearly beloved', a strange figure in vestments at the altar with a little boy who knelt at his side. Many were watching for the first time the drama of the Mass. They were there as spectators who watch a play with a symbolism and language unknown to them. Man cries for redemption, 'Kyrie eleison, Christe eleison, Kyrie eleison.' God answers man's despairing cry in the opening words of the *Gloria in excelsis* proclaiming the advent of the promised Saviour, but still they do not understand.

'Whatever is he doing up there now?' they say. 'Can 'e make it out at all?' The summit of the drama is reached when, the whole company of heaven having been summoned to man's aid, the words of consecration are spoken and the bread and the wine become the Body and Blood of Jesus who offered Himself on the Cross at Calvary. They are aware of the silence, broken by the ringing of a bell. 'Did 'e hear the bell? What is that for, my dear?' they whisper. The bell rings again at the *Domine non sum dignus*. There are a few who kneel in wonder at what is being accomplished; it is for them a moment of prayer such as they have never experienced before. But for many who crowd the church the great drama of the Mass remains without meaning.

Never in the memory of any in St. Hilary had the church been so crowded as on those first Sundays; 'it were like as if every Sunday were Harvest Thanksgiving'. The whole village came, people from neighbouring villages, all came to see 'the goings on up to St. Hilary'. So far had the Catholic Faith been lost to them, that what their ancestors had termed 'the simple service of the Mass' was now 'like to them as a Christmas Play'. They crowded the church Sunday by Sunday to watch the games of Parson and Nicky Peters and the bit of a boy, who were all the time bowing down and crossing themselves up at the altar. They came again at night to listen to the preacher. 'A proper preacher,' they said. 'He do sweat like a bull and no mistake. Suit us all right, he would, if he'd give up his old Mass, as he do call it.' There was no stoning as in the days of John Wesley, but the motive that led them to reject the Catholic religion was much the same. They did not want anything different from what 'they belonged to have' any more than they had wanted the strange preacher who visited this parish a hundred and fifty years ago. When the service was ended they stood about in the churchyard, and, however friendly they might have been during the week in their homes or in the fields, none would speak: all faces would be turned away until I had passed, when there would be laughter and some one would shout, 'There goes the old Roman Catholic.'

During these difficult months and throughout the years that followed I was fortunate in never having a quarrel with any of the St. Hilary people.

Whatever they may have thought about my 'goings on' and however many wild and unreasonable words they may have spoken, we always retained, if not respect, some kind of liking for one another, which grew with many, as the years passed, into a deep affection.

'The parson isn't a bad old sort. We don't dislike he, but we don't altogether hold with his goings on,' would, I think, fairly reflect their attitude towards myself in those first years.

4 FURTHER MEMORIES

I have been listening from the sanatorium at Tehidy to a broadcast from St. Hilary, a revival of my own play *The Western Land*. First came the announcement from London: '*The Western Land* - a dramatic dialogue between a farmer, fisherman, flower-grower and miner - by Bernard Walke, produced at St. Hilary by Filson Young' - then a wait which seemed interminable, as I sat up in bed eager for the first sounds from St. Hilary.

I pictured every detail in that room of mine at home, where the four men would be sitting round the table near the window.

At last came the voice of Filson Young: 'We are sorry that Father Walke is not here with us, but I am sure he is listening; so before we begin we will let him hear his rooks, who seem to be asking a number of questions without getting any satisfactory answer.' Again a pause; and then a sudden burst of cawing - caw, caw, caw - deep caws, high petulant caws, rich fruity caws of young rooks clamouring for supper, the rustle of their wings among the branches, the voice of Mrs. Jenkins, a noisy neighbour, calling her children to bed, and above them all the song of two thrushes, while at intervals I could hear the notes of a Jenny wren.

I was not prepared for the effect these sounds were going to have on me in those first few moments of listening. I saw the garden as it was at that time of the evening, the walk under the beech trees, the two thrushes, rivals in song, one in the magnolia by the kitchen and the other on the wall above the shrine of Our Lady. I saw them as I had seen them on many such evenings in spring, to awaken to the realisation that I was not at St. Hilary but sitting up in bed in a sanatorium miles away.

When I had adjusted the earphones again, Hocking of Penberthy Farm, whose kitchen I had sat in scores of evenings, was speaking. Then came the voices of Robert Carnell and John Rogers, both of whom I had held in my arms at the font, while there continued as a background to the voices the cawing of the rooks and the song of the thrushes. All the voices I heard were familiar, even the Jenny wren had nested last year beneath the window, but none was so familiar or had so many and varied associations as the rooks.

When we came to St. Hilary there was not a single nest in any of the tall trees; but very early in the spring of 1913 I heard rooks cawing. There in the tallest of the trees in the avenues were two rooks building their nest. One morning, after a gale of wind, the nest in the elm tree had gone, and all that was left of their labours was a scrubby heap of twigs and grass. Annie Walke and I feared that they would be disheartened and go elsewhere; but they started to build again that morning and were successful in bringing up a brood, or whatever is the right term for a nestful of rooks. It is the descendants of these rooks whose cawing I have heard tonight.

How many hours have I spent listening to them as they have talked and argued and fought up there in the trees. How I have enjoyed watching them on windy days when there have been more than a hundred birds in the air at one time, some coming down on the wind, others beating their way up in spiral flights, crossing and re-crossing, filled with the mad spirit that possesses children on windy days. When I was tired of watching the rooks there were always the jackdaws, who were here when we came, and were probably here and in possession of the spire five hundred years ago. Insolent fellows these jackdaws; I have often watched them, after they have accomplished some piece of mischief, look round with their wicked little grey eyes as if enjoying the joke. But the most insolent behaviour I ever witnessed was one evening of a spring in which they had taken to digging up my early potatoes. Hearing them chattering in the trees, I got up from dinner and rebuked them for their theft. They were silent while I was speaking, until one fellow more daring than the rest gave an ironical chawk-chawk which was taken up by the whole company. One of the new potatoes was dropped on my head and they all flew away screaming with delight.

Our garden today is a garden of birds more than of flowers. A brown owl brings up a family every year in the same hollow tree, with a woodpecker's nest a few feet above them; there are always a pair of goldfinches and several pairs of bullfinches nesting in the orchard, and thrushes and swaggering blackbirds in every bush. No sight so delights me as a pair of goldfinches feeding daintily on thistledown or flying so swiftly from apple tree to apple tree that there is no time to see all their beauty or to be weary of watching them.

Thomas Pascoe, Vicar of St. Hilary a hundred years ago, must have been a great lover of trees, for it was he who planted the avenue that enchanted us on the day of our first coming to St. Hilary and the avenue of beech trees in the garden where, on the Feast of the Assumption, we build an altar in honour of Our Lady.

There are many celebrated gardens in Cornwall, gardens of rare flowering trees, but none have the charm of the old rectory gardens where for centuries succeeding families have contributed to their making. There are registers that tell of the coming and going of the parsons, but the gardens hold the most interesting record of their lives. Here, in the old apple trees their children have climbed, the sunken gardens and paths they have made, lawns they have laid and grottoes they have built from shells gathered from many beaches, you may learn the kind of men they were whose names fill the registers.

These gardens have no order or plan as in the gardens of great houses with a continuous tradition. As each family have taken possession they have started, as we did, to remake the garden. One vicar has built walls and provided for fruit trees. Another laid a bowling-green which later became a tennis court. Some have planned a formal garden, others have planted trees and allowed the formal garden to grow into a wilderness. Time has dealt with these individual efforts and given to many of the old rectory and vicarage gardens a rare charm. They remain a record of many lives and many sad farewells, as family after family have left their old home and the garden they have helped to make.

My most successful speech at our Ruri-decanal Chapter was on the subject of rectory gardens. We meet once a quarter, presided over by the Rural Dean, to discuss a paper written by one of the clergy and to consider matters of importance to the deanery. On this particular morning the agenda contained a proposal from the Church Assembly that all vicarage and rectory gardens should be entrusted to the care of the Parish Church Council. Now as men we had suffered many humiliations under the tyranny of the Church Assembly; but that our gardens should be taken from us and placed under the charge of officious churchworkers, was a thing that no self-respecting rector or vicar could tolerate.

When I arrived and looked round the room I saw that no one from the deanery was absent. There was the Vicar of Penzance, whom all the children knew as Daddy Rogers; Trymer Bennett, the Rector of St. Levan, who would boast he was so old that no man living knew his age and would on occasions refer to himself as 'a deathshead on a mop-stick'; Stona from The moorland parish of Sancreed, who had once 'put the weight for Oxford'; and Thomas Taylor, the quiet scholar from St. Just. All these were assembled, and many others, for Penwith is a large deanery and, as I have said, none of the clergy was absent. Boscawen, the Rector of Ludgvan, a celebrated horticulturist, was in the chair and, after having read the resolution, said that he would leave it to the brethren to express their opinions on such a proposal.

I saw several of the clergy exchanging glances as to who should be the first to speak as I rose to my feet.

'Mr. Rural Dean,' I said.

The Rural Dean held up his hand and the clergy sitting in front turned round to view the speaker. The Rural Dean, still holding up his hand to enjoin silence, then said, 'Will Mr. Walke come to the table so that the brethren may hear him the better?'

With this encouragement I walked to the table and began to speak, my subject being the expulsion of our first parents Adam and Eve from the Garden of Eden for partaking of the fruit of the tree of knowledge. I am no gardener, but I successfully introduced the names of several rare trees grown in Cornish gardens that were presumably in the garden of Eden.

'Now,' I said, 'we of the clergy have sinned in many ways and on many occasions, but we have never committed the sin of which our first parents were guilty. So it is our duty to resist the attempt of the Church Assembly to deprive us of our gardens, and to bash this monstrous proposal on the head.' Any implied criticism of the learning of the clergy was overlooked in the joy of discovering a phrase which so adequately expressed our feelings. Boscawen rose and said with passion, 'Walke has told us what we must do,' and then turning to me inquired, 'What was it you said we must do, Walke?'

'I think I said, 'Bash it on the head,' Mr. Rural Dean,' I answered.

'Yes,' said Boscawen. 'Bash it on the head - that is the thing to do - bash it on the head.'

Other Chapters must have also 'bashed it on the head', for we heard no more from the Church Assembly of this sacrilegious proposal.

We found an excellent garden at St. Hilary. But it was not our garden; it was a gardener's garden with circular and diamond-shaped beds, filled in the summer with lobelias, calceolarias and other bedding-out plants. We were ruthless that first spring in our determination to make the garden our own, and to reduce to some kind of pattern, what to our eyes appeared a meaningless collection of geometrical-shaped beds. It was a very difficult task as the house and walls encircling the front of the garden were built at an angle which it seemed impossible to reconcile with the garden beyond. Possibly our best contribution has been the planting of many rare flowering trees given to us by Compton Mackenzie when he left England for the Island of Capri.

I had known Compton Mackenzie and Faith when they were living at Cury Vicarage, before he had published any work beyond a volume of poems. They were now living at 'Rivière', a great gloomy house surrounded by tall elms at Phillack, where Mackenzie was writing Carnival and growing shrubs and daffodils in the great walled garden.

We were constantly at Rivière in that first year. I spent many mornings in the spring of 1913 sitting in the garden with a butterfly net to watch over the flowering of some daffodil and save it from the yellow butterfly which would be looking for a very rare bloom in which to lay its eggs. On windy days in the autumn we flew kites on the sand-dunes overlooking St. Ives, and after dinner, if we were staying the night, as we often did, we would all go to a room, high up and overlooking Hayle Estuary, called The Lady's Bower, where Faith would play the piano while Monty wrote *Carnival* and I lay on the floor and built cathedrals and castles from an inexhaustible supply of toy building-bricks that Mackenzie had obtained from Germany, and of which he was very proud. I would sit on and build while Mackenzie wrote, long after Annie Walke and Faith had gone to bed, sometimes until two in the morning, when Mackenzie would read me the chapter he had written.

When I take down *Carnival* from my bookshelf, my thoughts go back to that friendly room at Rivière, the floor strewn with bricks, and Mackenzie lying on the broad couch which is now in my room at St. Hilary, reading aloud for the first time the story of Jenny Pearl.

Annie Walke and I were invited to a dinner given by Faith and Monty to celebrate the publication of *Carnival*. We rode over on bicycles early in the afternoon, and after tea Mackenzie and I visited the cellars (reported to have a secret passage to the sea), and selected several bottles of champagne and two bottles of the port that his father had laid down some years previously. We did not wait for dinner to drink to Jenny Pearl, but opened a bottle of champagne in the hall, and Martin Secker, the publisher, proposed the toast of success to *Carnival*. While we were drinking, Faith suggested that Father Wason ought to have been invited and a telegram was sent, signed by all of us, commanding his presence. The answer that came back was, 'Have gone to bed to think out the best way to get to you. Sandys Wason.'

He arrived eventually in a cab from Gwinear Road Station, very tired and very cross that we had not waited dinner for him.

'You ought to try and think, Monty,' he said. 'I told you that I had gone to bed. It was hardly necessary to say that I might be late.'

'That's all very well, Wason,' said Monty, 'but what we want you to explain is why you went to bed if you intended coming here to dinner.'

'When I have had some wine - and you had better open another bottle of champagne,' he continued, 'I will explain to you how much easier it is to think out the kind of problem I was faced with when you are in bed.'

The nature of the problem we never discovered. One day Wason will refer to that evening and explain the difficulties that confronted him. I suspect that he had no timetable of trains or buses at Cury.

We pledged ourselves that night to meet and celebrate the publication of each successive novel that Mackenzie was to write, but I can only remember being present at one other of these celebrations, that for the first volume of *Sinister Street*, which was published when we were staying with them in Capri.

Another friend of ours at this time was a little girl,

Mary Anne. Her mother, an American whom we knew at Fowey, had asked us to take charge of her while she was abroad; so Mary Anne brought her governess to live with us and for a year was our constant companion. It was a sad parting when the day came for us to leave her. We were going to Capri for three months to stay with the Mackenzies, leaving Mary Anne at St. Hilary to await the coming of her mother who had rented our house. When we drove down the avenue in the barouche-landau that in those days took us to the station, Mary Anne ran behind refusing to say good-bye; at the end of the avenue she turned and without a word or a wave of the hand raced back towards the house.

We heard later from her governess that, after being lost for hours, she was found asleep with a tear-stained face under her bed. Mary Anne has now a little girl of her own, but if she ever reads these pages she will remember the sadness of that parting.

We had already begun to attract the queer people with whom it has been our lot to be associated during the whole of these twenty years. Some have arrived on the strength of being spoken to in the train, a habit that I have tried to avoid - but without success - others have been sent by friends; but for the most part they are people who have drifted in as the birds drift westward in a hard winter, or have landed here by mistake, as did the American lady whom I found standing on the doorstep, and who refused to be sent away.

This is her story. Coming in from church one evening, I saw a fashionably dressed woman ringing at our bell, who met me with -

'I reckon you are the priest of this church.' I nodded an agreement, and she went on: 'Say, I have found something in your church that greatly interests me.'

'Is that the Roman milestone?' I replied politely.

'It is a milestone,' she answered, 'that records man's relationship to the infinite.'

This rather took my breath away, but I tried to look

intelligent and said, 'Oh, yes.'

'I am staying the night here,' she continued, 'that you may help me in my search.'

I then suggested a cottage where she might find lodgings, and offered to take her there, but in answer she said, 'I am staying right here if there is a spare room in the house.'

I could not deny that we had an empty room, and, while I was framing a reason why she should not stay the night with us, she slipped into her car, slammed the door, started up the engine and, circling round what a lady at St. Ives calls 'our sweep', was off to fetch her grip.

I had to break it to Annie Walke when she came in that I had met a lady who was coming back at 8 p.m. with a grip to stay the night. 'Why did you let her?' says Annie Walke.

'I wasn't asked,' I answered. 'She just said that she was coming.'

Punctually at 8 she arrived and we had dinner. Later in the evening, after one of those intimate conversations, which only seem possible with complete strangers, I was bold enough to inquire how she had had the courage to force her presence on us in the way she had. Never have I felt more embarrassed than when she got up hastily, saying, 'I was led to understand that this was a religious house. If I have made a mistake, I must go at once.'

Annie Walke and I were successful in persuading her that, although it was not a religious house, we were delighted to have her with us, and prevailed on her to stay with us for some days.

Another of the people who drifted into our lives was a tall youth, at one time an art student with Stanhope Forbes, who had come to live in the district, and was ostensibly writing a novel with which he would appear of a morning for what he called 'a crit'. This youth arrived one afternoon with his girl-wife to read the concluding chapter of his book. To understand the tragedy that was to follow, you must realise that this afternoon was to have been a great occasion for his wife, who had never before been present at a reading of the novel.

The lamp was lit and we were all sitting round the fire, the author, his wife, Father Wason and I. Father Wason, who on other occasions will listen most sympathetically to any attempts at literature, however feeble, was that evening pedantically critical, lighted cigarette after cigarette and threw them into the grate, muttering, 'Dreadful - dreadful,' and laughed cruelly at what the author had intended to be a moving passage describing the farewell of two lovers.

Never was there a more unhappy moment than when this poor girl - she had scarcely grown into a woman - burst into tears and fled out of the room. Father Wason and I got up hurriedly and followed her, but she had left the house. Her husband, who stood with us peering into the darkness, called her name several times, but there was no answer, and after a vague apology for what had happened he too left.

When we returned to my room the manuscript was lying on the floor where it had fallen; there it lay as accusing as the body of a murdered infant. All the evening we discussed how we could make some atonement for what had happened, but although we sat up late we found no way; our laughter had killed her hopes and for murder there is no restitution. We thought that loyalty to her husband was the cause of the outburst, but we were mistaken. She had been loyal in a way that only a woman is capable of being; but it was something deeper than loyalty we had offended, as we were to learn the next morning when her husband arrived and confessed that what he had read was the work of his wife, who had surrendered her authorship that he might be considered 'a man of letters'.

How she had laboured to write those pages in the cold of her bedroom all through the winter; and how often she had been cheered by fictitious reports of my appreciation! Now on this night she was going to listen to the praise that would follow the reading of her last chapter.

This was twenty years ago; yet even now it is difficult to think of that evening without a sense of shame for having unknowingly caused so much pain.

We had a maid with us at this time called Bessie Hicks, the daughter of the man who was responsible for loading our furniture on to the barge when we were leaving Polruan. Bessie was expansive; her character, her figure and her laugh were all on a large scale. While we lived at Polruan she slept at her home near the quay, and would flaunt her way down the Fore Street every afternoon 'to clean herself'. This journey from the top of the hill to the quay was taken leisurely with stops at every open doorway to hear the news with which she would entertain us on her return. When we told her that we had accepted St. Hilary she laughed scornfully.

'What are you going to do with yourselves in a vicarage,' she said, 'if I am not there to see to you?' So Bessie Hicks came with us and never failed to cheer and amuse us and, incidentally, many of our friends, with whom she was a great favourite.

She was now going to be married to a dapper little man who was serving in the Naval Reserve. 'He's not much,' she used to say, 'but what are men, anyway? They are poor creatures when you come to think of it, and my Russell is better than most of them.' We were very sad at the thought of losing our Bessie. 'But there,' as she said, 'seeing that Russell will never be contented until I marry him, it is best to please him. As she intimated that she was going to be married from St. Hilary, we promised her a very grand wedding with the church decorated and little girls to scatter rose-petals along the way.

On the morning of the wedding the church was crowded. Four little girls were standing at the door clasping their baskets of rose-petals, the boys were ready with the canopy to shelter the bridal couple, and the bridegroom, with his hands deep in his trousers pockets, was waiting at the entrance to the chancel. We were all expectant for the coming of the bride. She, laced tightly in a white muslin dress and holding a bunch of red roses, was sitting on the vicarage stairs arguing with Annie Walke as to whether she should go to the church.

'What do I want to go off with a man for?' she said. 'There's no sense in my going away with Russell and leaving you two to yourselves. How are you going to get on without me, do you think?' Sitting on the stairs in her bridal dress, while we all waited in the church, she arrived at a compromise. 'I'll get married,' she said, 'and return to you in a fortnight.'

It was a grand wedding and Bessie looked very pretty in her muslin dress. 'She might have been her ladyship by the style of her,' I heard a woman say, 'and as for the Parson, Roman Catholic or no, he's a pretty little fellow for a job of that kind. If it had to be again, I wouldn't mind him doing the same for me.' The reception that was held in the drawing room, where all the presents were set out, was not so successful. Bessie was in no mood to tolerate a facetious remark of the bridegroom on the absence of a bassinet from the wedding presents.

'You rude man,' she said, 'how dare you talk to me in that way! Married or no, I shan't speak to you for a week.' When the time came for going away no persuasion could induce Bessie to take her place in the carriage by the side of the bridegroom. She climbed to the box seat and sat proudly with the driver, while Russell was forced to sit alone in the landau. After a fortnight, when her husband went to sea, she returned to us. 'I never went back on my word,' she told us. 'For a week I did not so much as open my mouth. It would have never done for he to think that he could talk to me in that way, with his sauce about bassinets and all. He'd know better another time.'

That was many years ago. Bessie now has a home in Polruan and six sons. 'I was always fond of the men,' she said, when I once asked her why she had all boys. So fond of them is she that, according to the last news I heard she has adopted a baby boy to add to her family.

5 THE YEAR 1914

Twenty years ago Feast Monday, the first Monday after the fourteenth of January, was a general holiday for the parish. The children did not go to school, and the farm labourers, except for meating the cattle, did not go to work. There was a rivalry in those days between St. Hilary and Goldsithney such as exists in Catholic countries among local saints.

'They've got a fair down to Goldsithney - for their feast,' I have heard a St. Hilary man say. 'A pretty lot of good that is to 'em. Better they have fine weather, like it belongs to be at St. Hilary. I don't reckon a saint of much account if 'tis always wet on his feast.'

The tradition of a Patron Saint remained, but the keeping of the Feast amounted to little more than a strange preacher in the pulpit on Sunday, when the church was crowded, and an entertainment, or concert, as it was called, in the Board School on the Monday evening. 'Must have a strange preacher, Parson, or Perran people will have the laugh of St. Hilary,' is what the churchwarden told me. I procured the strange preacher, for it is a compliment to be asked to preach at the Feast. But the concert was more difficult. I obtained a programme of the concert of the year before and invited all the performers of that year, but no one was willing to take part. To sing at the concert, I discovered, would be considered an avowal that you approved of 'the goings on of Parson', and at that time there were not many who were prepared to take so definite a side.

After Christmas I was constantly being asked, 'Ain't there going to be no concert this year, Parson?' 'There has been a concert for Feast since the days of Parson Pascoe; it will be a shame on the Parish if there ain't one this year.'

In all probability there would have been no concert that year, and we might never have gone to Capri, had not

Annie Walke met Gladys Hynes, who had been a student with her at the London School of Art and was now working at Newlyn. Gladys Hynes had a sister, and this sister, who wrote plays, when she heard of our difficulty, offered to produce one of her plays at St. Hilary and provide the cast. I was doubtful at the time if the play would meet with the approval of the people of St. Hilary. A play is different from an entertainment or concert. A concert is all singing or playing on the piano, and an entertainment is, as we all know, an entertainment. It was something between a concert and entertainment, I was told, 'that you belong to have for Feast'. But as no one was prepared to sing at this concert, I accepted the offer of Poppy Hynes to produce her play.

The morning after the bills of the play were posted, Nicholas Peters, the sexton, came to see me. 'What is this play that you've got for Feast?' he said. 'It's a pity that you have gone and done a thing like that Parson. They'm all talking down to Relubbus that Feast is not going to be same as it belongs. It's a pity,' he went on. 'We've enough trouble with 'en as it is.'

It was a pity, but it was too late now to make any change. On the morning of the Feast, after the sung Mass, I went to the dreary school buildings, with their high windows from which a child can barely see a patch of sky. I had gone to superintend the stage arrangements and, finding no one in the building but the old cleaner, attempted to lift the piano off the stage. I remember only a sudden pain followed by the sensation of leaving the world in a pleasant manner, my first experience of fainting, and later on returning to my senses, and being lifted up by the charwoman, who proceeded to brush the dust off my cassock. She seemed more troubled about the cassock than myself, but, 'There,' she said, 'a little dust won't hurt 'en, for it's what we're all made of.' When she had finished brushing she patted me kindly and said, 'Shall I put 'e home, my dear, or do 'e think you can manage?' I thought that I could manage and stumbled down the lane, sitting by the hedge every now and again.

There was still the play; an entertainment never to be looked forward to had now become a nightmare. How was I to meet all the disapproving faces that I knew would be there? How could I pretend that I was enjoying myself and thank the players for 'this pleasant evening', when I hated everything connected with the entertainment and longed for the peace of my own room?

My memory of what actually happened that night is confined to the sensation of a strange pain in my chest that seized me whenever I moved, my arrival at the door of the schoolroom, where a crowd of village youths were trying to press into a room already overfull, and the last scene of the play, in which the heroine, a Russian Nihilist, having murdered a policeman, escaped out of the window of the schoolroom. The ledge of this window was crowded with the youths who had been turned away from the door, so that the heroine, Gladys Hynes, in her flight scrambled through this group of youths and fell into the arms of a further crowd of young men who stood below. I was sitting in the front row, where I heard people saying, "Tis shameful. Wonder 'tis allowed. 'Tis all of a piece with the games that do go on up to church. Nothing but play-acting I do say.' Whether it was the murder of the policeman or the sight of Gladys Hynes in the arms of the young men on the window-ledge that was shameful I did not know. 'Anyway, it's not a concert. That's certain, and the Parson ought to be ashamed of himself,' was the opinion of the people sitting in the front row. Other parts of the audience were of a different opinion and thought it delightful, especially this last scene when the policeman, who was stabbed by the girl, lay dead on the stage, while she escaped out of the window. The boys at the back of the room and the youths on the window-ledge, some of whom had climbed in on to the stage, stamped and shouted until the scene was replayed, and Gladys Hynes fell again into the arms of the youths.

'They'm properly upset,' Nicholas Peters told me next morning. 'Better you stuck to the concert. Though I wouldn't say that you'd have pleased them if you'd had a concert. They'm a teasy old lot, is what I do think of 'em.'

The next few weeks were the beginning of a new experience. The doctor whom we called in discovered that I had strained the muscles of my heart, which was greatly enlarged, and ordered complete rest, to lie in bed, and not even to lift a hand.

How many men and women I had visited in the same condition and thought at the time that to live without effort, with nothing expected of you, must be a happy experience. But I was to discover that of all the weariness of life there is nothing so burdensome as remaining still. How Simon Stylites remained for the last thirty years of his life on a pillar, seventy-two feet high and four feet across at the top, how he remained there and achieved sanctity, is beyond my understanding. Bodily inaction had for me at any rate nothing to offer. Often, when I have posed as a model for Annie Walke, I have found all capacity for thought slipping from me. I have tried saying the rosary and repeating lines of poetry, but however much I struggled I was in the end conscious of nothing but a weary emptiness. It was to this immobility that I was condemned for weeks, while Annie Walke read me D*avid Copperfield*, the one adventure to which I looked forward. David and Peggotty, Dora and Agnes were the only people I knew or wanted to know during those weeks. I was so lost in the lives of these people that I never suspected how tired Annie Walke was, not of reading, but of Dickens, until one evening, when she got up and threw the book out of the window.

As soon as I was well enough to move we went to Capri as guests of the Compton Mackenzies, staying a night in Paris and Marseilles. That morning in Marseilles, when I came out of my bedroom on to a balcony flooded with sunshine, and saw high on the hill the white figure of Our Lady overlooking the harbour, brought with it a sense of escape from a sickroom that I have never experienced on any other occasion.

Those months spent in Capri are so much of an interlude that they can have no great part in a book which is concerned with our life at St. Hilary. I look back on them with intense pleasure as days of freedom from the cares that had overwhelmed us in that first year.

Before I was strong enough to walk I rode a donkey, with Rosina, its owner, running behind and making strange noises to encourage the creature to go faster. I rode all over the island on this donkey from the Piccola Marina to the mountain top above Anacapri, that Monty had bought from a number of contadini, who were part owners, after bargaining and drinking wine with them the whole of one Sunday morning.

When Monty, who was at the time writing the second volume of *Sinister Street*, wanted to work, he and Faith would return to their cottage in Anacapri, while Annie Walke and I remained at the villa in the Via Tiberio and entertained the guests who were constantly arriving. On one occasion Mackenzie invited a man on the staff of *Punch* to spend some days with them, and went away and left him for us to entertain.

'Take care of him,' said Monty on leaving. 'He has always given me good notices in *Punch*. I have written and told him,' he continued, 'that a man with a red tie will meet him.'

I protested that I did not like red ties and that I did not possess a red tie.

'You will find one in my drawer,' he shouted as he drove away to Anacapri.

For two mornings I wore this tie, while I waited on the Piazza for the arrival of the boat from Naples, but, as no one anything like a man on the staff of *Punch* arrived, I abandoned the tie. On the third morning I saw him get out of a carozza; no one could mistake him as he stood in the centre of a gesticulating crowd. After watching for a time his struggles to explain where he wanted to go, I went up to him and introduced myself. He pointed at me reproachfully with his umbrella, saying, 'You ought to be wearing a red tie.' This same umbrella caused a sensation that morning at Morgano's Café; for, sipping a Vermouth and soda on the terrace above the street in the full blaze of the sun, he opened the umbrella and lit a cigarette, happy at having escaped from the noisy touts in the square. There the little man sat, when suddenly and for one brief second his head was encircled with a halo of fire and next moment he was gazing with mild concern at a skeleton frame.

'What a surprising place this Capri is,' he said. 'Nothing like that has ever happened to me before.' He afterwards complained that he had been shown nothing of the island and had never been taken anywhere except to Morgano's.

Easter passed and the Feast of St. Costanza, when the saint's image was carried round streets that were golden with broom flowers strewn from the windows as he went by, and we were still at Capri, spending our days bathing at the Piccola Marina, and driving up at night to dine with Faith and Monty in Anacapri.

After dinner we would walk down the mountain road in the moonlight, and on occasions drink a bottle of sweet champagne, poured into a bowl of wild strawberries, at the cafe in the piazza.

We returned early in June on a P and O steamer from Naples. On the second morning after sailing I was awakened by the roar of an engine and looking out of the porthole I saw a seaplane for the first time. We were at Toulon in the midst of the French Fleet assembled for manoeuvres.

As we steamed through the line of French battleships that morning in June 1914, each vessel dipped the tricolour in recognition of our salute, and on coming abreast of the flagship the band on board played the National Anthem. Though I had no premonition of what was coming, I remember the passing of that French fleet as one of the few occasions in my life when I have been conscious of the form of patriotism which finds expression in such songs as *Rule Britannia*.

A few days later, landing at Plymouth in the early morning and passing in the train through the green country of little fields and farm places, listening to the familiar talk of the men and women who got in and out of the carriage at country stations, I recognised another patriotism - a love for the earth of the country in which you were born, its moorlands, its villages and farm places, a recognition of the strange sweetness of being among the people of your own race.

It was a joy to be back at St. Hilary. It was high summer, and the rooks had built more nests in the elm trees. There was no shadow of the coming war; the murder at Sarajevo had not yet been accomplished. Never did a summer open more happily for us than in June 1914. I was feeling strong and able to enjoy life, spending the days visiting the people, bathing at Prussia Cove and laying out the garden.

It was not before that fateful Sunday in August that it broke upon me that England would be involved in the war which was now inevitable. It was very hot that Sunday night and the church was crowded with men and women, many of whom I had never seen there before. The same thing was happening all over Europe - in England, France and Russia, Germany and Austria, cathedrals and churches were crowded. Some were there, as animals will herd together in the face of a common danger, to find assurance in the midst of a crowd; others came to seek for God and to discover an escape from the destruction they felt to be overtaking them.

When I stood in the pulpit, looking down on the people whose faces were now so familiar to me, I had the sensation of being in the centre of a cataclysm which was approaching as inevitably as a thunderstorm against the wind. It was contrary to reason, yet no ingenuity of man could prevent it. The noblest motives would be exploited and the most generous natures would offer themselves willingly to this monster that was about to destroy them.

I felt strangely alone standing there in the pulpit before all these people, with nothing to say, with no word of comfort or assurance to offer them. I was certain only that I could have no part in what was coming. Up to that moment I had never visualised the possibility of so great a catastrophe, much less the part that I might be called on to play.

Once, as a youth, I had arrived at a decision in much the same way. It was after a run with the New Forest Stag Hounds, when a stag, accompanied by a young hind, whom we had hunted from Bramshaw Telegraph, through Amber Wood and across Bratley Plain, soiled in some deep water where it was impossible for the huntsman to throw a noose over his antlers preparatory to cutting his throat. The field, most of whom had dismounted, stood looking on while hounds bayed round the water-side and some of the more venturesome swam out to the stag and were gored by his antlers. The master, Captain Lovell, seeing that it was impossible to kill the stag, gave orders for the hounds to be whipped off. After the field had ridden away it was very quiet, and, as I lay in the heather watching the stag with the hind close up to his flanks, I could hear a sucking sound as he bent his head to drink. After a time I ceased to be interested in the stag and was conscious only, as people often are when they are very young, of being intensely sad. The horse at my side started, and on looking round I saw the stag, with the hind following, come out of the water and trot slowly to a hill not far from where I lay. There they stood, and as I looked at them I became alive to the beauty of everything round me and thought of the stupidity of man who would destroy its fairness in his lust to hunt and kill.

I had probably been making up my mind as I lay there, but I was not conscious of coming to any decision about hunting until the stag threw back his head and brayed defiance. The call of that stag with the hind at his side was as final as if it had been the trumpet of the Angel Gabriel.

On another occasion, many years later, I was fishing the Trevayl stream near Zennor and had hooked a fair-sized trout. It was a fast piece of water and I was having difficulty in landing him; suddenly I became aware of the struggle that was going on between myself and the fish whose fight for life was delighting me. I landed that fish, unhooked him, and threw him back into the stream with a resolution that it should be the last time I would handle a fishing-rod.

'Wear it as long as thou canst,' was the answer that George Fox made to an inquirer who sought to know whether a Christian man might wear a sword at Court. I had acted on the advice of George Fox on these occasions which I have recounted. I was acting on it now.

'Wear it as long as thou canst.' I could wear it no longer. As I stood looking down on the people on that Sunday night in August 1914, I saw no way of reconciliation between the way of the Gospel that I had been called to preach and the war that was approaching. I was not, as far as I know, carried away by my emotions; I was empty of all feeling but an awareness that this rejection of war as an altogether evil thing, was at one with whatever intelligence I possessed.

I had no intimation that night of what was before me, the shame that never left me of being separated from and regarded as an enemy of that great company who offered themselves so freely in those first days of the war, the suspicion and the isolation that was to follow. I was only conscious that night of my inability to offer any consolation to the men and women who had been committed to my care.

After the first shock of the declaration of war had passed, the life of the village went on with little change. A few Territorials were called up for home service and quartered at Falmouth. Jim Curnow went away for the day and came home to say that he had joined the army.

'It is what you would expect,' his mother said. 'Jim was always one for going out with a gun.'

Jim was the first to go and the last of the men of St. Hilary to be demobilised. He served on every front and ended the war in charge of a convoy of mules in Salonica. 'Mules are nasty old things if you don't treat them right,' is all that Jim has ever been heard to say about the war.

We knew nothing of what was happening in France while our soldiers were making their great retreat from Mons. It was 'a strategic retreat', we were told, and waited, expecting any day to hear of a British victory which would bring the war to a close before the harvest was ended. The harvest had to be brought in, and men can give little thought to war when they are in charge of a reaper and binder, building a rick or pitching sheaves on to a wagon. Every night I rode a bicycle into Penzance to buy an evening paper that was published in Plymouth; and every night as I passed through Goldsithney on my way home, men would come out of the 'Trevelyan Arms' and the 'Crown' and shout after me, 'What is the news to-night, Parson?'

6 ON DEATH

A man died in the cubicle next to mine last night, a youth of about eighteen named Tommy Triggs, a great favourite with the men in this block of buildings. I had seen him on the way back from my bath a few hours before, sitting up in bed reading a comic paper. He had a haemorrhage some days ago and was forbidden to talk, so I said good night and left him. After being asleep for some hours I was awakened by a violent ringing of the bell for the night nurse, and the sound of a choking cough which, half asleep as I was, I knew must mean that Tommy had another haemorrhage. I listened again and heard two nurses run by and, as they opened the door, the voice of one saying, 'Call Matron.' Before I had time to get up and go to him there came the sound of a terrible cough, and then a silence, followed by the nurse speaking. 'Go and see the time,' I heard her say; and then I knew that Tommy had gone. For the next hour I heard, through the thin partition, sounds of the nurses about their last offices; and then the door was shut and there was silence. I said some prayers for the peace of his soul, and must have slept and did not wake until the dawn was showing over Carn Brae. It was morning and a thrush was singing when the door was opened and I heard the trundling of wheels on the gravel pathway as the body of Tommy Triggs was placed on a hand-bier and wheeled away.

As each of the men passed the door of the cubicle on his way to breakfast, I heard the same words spoken. 'Tommy has gone. Iss, Tommy has gone, poor lad.' Passing that empty cubicle later with its stripped bed, empty now of the shell which had once held the gay spirit whom we called Tommy Triggs, I felt how right were the words of these men and how inadequate were any other words to describe the happenings of that night.

I thought, too, of how many from St. Hilary had set

forth on the same journey as Tommy Triggs during the twenty years that I had been parish priest. Looking back on those years, I would put the number at no less than three hundred. A great company to have committed to the earth. Some so young that their life was numbered by days or even hours. How poignant are those burials where the little body, a sad memento of a short hour of passion, is carried unmourned to the grave under the arm of the sexton and committed to the earth without love or honour. Others so old that their going was little more than the falling of a leaf in November. Death has strange ways. I have stood at death-beds at St. Ives waiting for the tide to turn, knowing that at the moment when the water begins to go out of the harbour the soul will more easily depart from the body.

It is the same with the season of the year. Death rarely comes immediately before Christmas. It must wait until the time of rejoicing is over; but that season must not be far away, as death will not tarry overlong. The registers at St. Hilary show more deaths in November than in any other month of the year; it is a seasonable time for death. I have stood at the head of a grave on one of those quiet days in November when, with the leaves falling lightly and a robin singing, the heap of clay by the graveside has appeared less unfriendly to the body it is to hide from the sight of men. Here in the country there is a dignity in the last ceremonies of death which is denied to those who live in great towns. I think of Jimmy Curtis, a farm labourer, who worked at Perran cutting and packing broccoli in the winter and picking flowers and planting potatoes in the spring. He was a little man with white hair and a red face, who spoke with an impediment that made it difficult to follow his conversation. Years before I had prepared him for his first communion. The classes were at night when he would call on his way to 'The Crown', where he often spent his evenings. They usually lasted an hour, with Jimmy leaning forward on his stick and nodding his head to all that I had to say, but never speaking a word until he got up to go, when he would say,

'When am I going to have this 'ere Communion?'

I would answer, 'When you have learned a little more, Jimmy.'

'What more is there for me to learn?' he would say. 'I do know everything. You go into the box and confess your sins and then you do have Communion.'

The time came when he did have Communion after he had been into the box. He never spoke of confession by any other name. 'It's time I went into the box, Father,' he used to say.

He was churchwarden for a number of years and, as he went round 'to take up the collection' every Sunday, it was his custom to make a bow to all who contributed. This little man loved ceremony, as did his mother, who always kissed my hand when I visited her, and in turn I would kiss hers on leaving. I was not with Jimmy when he died, for it was on a Sunday morning that he passed, at a time when I was saying Mass. When Mass was ended I saddled my pony Aladdin and was riding down to see him, not knowing of his death; all the way down Relubbus Lane, neighbours came out of the cottages and called, 'He has gone, Parson. Jimmy has gone.' Many stopped me to say how Jimmy was loved. 'It won't be like Sunday, Parson, without Jimmy going up and down. He would always shout out and say, 'Come to Mass with me, my dear, it's proper up there. I'll look after 'ee and see that you do have a book." This was the talk that I heard on my way to his cottage. His relatives were Nonconformists and, under the pressure of the Kensit agitation that was going on, his brother came to me demanding what he called a Church of England funeral; but his wife was not to be coerced by a Nonconformist brother-in-law. 'Jimmy,' she said, 'belongs to me. He don't belong to no one else, he belongs to me, and I will have done with him what I think proper. Jimmy were a Catholic and he's going to be buried as a Catholic.'

So on a November night Jimmy was carried over the hill up which he had hurried to work every morning for fifty years. The dead are generally brought to church at St. Hilary in a hearse hired from Penzance, but there was no need for a hearse for Jimmy, there were so many anxious to share the work of carrying him to church. All the parish was there to meet him when he came to the church that night.

There he lay under the light of great yellow candles, visited by all his friends who came to say a prayer for the repose of his soul. All his life had been given to the honourable service of caring for cattle and work on the land. Now in death his body was honoured as it lay in state under the candles until the morning, when the Holy Sacrifice was offered on his behalf and the last absolutions pronounced for the forgiveness of his sins.

There is a story of the poet Donne who, when he felt death approaching, composed himself in a fitting manner. He gave orders that his room should be darkened and the coverlet of his bed straightened while he himself with closed eyes and folded hands awaited the intruder; and although death tarried for days he would not be disturbed lest it should take him unawares. There was something of the pride of life in such a death, with little of the surrender of St. Francis, or the 'leave me with my poor flies' of St. John de Vianney, but the poet and the saint in different ways expressed the same desire for a seemliness in death which is difficult to achieve in the fiercely unnatural life of great cities.

Death is certainly more seemly in the country, but whether it is easier to die there I cannot say. I only know that I have witnessed many times here at St. Hilary so complete a surrender to the will of God as to give an eternal value to that which, without such an acceptance, is merely a physical phenomenon. There was Tommy Carthew, a farm labourer whom I visited almost daily during the last months of his life when he was slowly dying of cancer in his face. His condition was so terrifying that few of his old friends had sufficient courage to face the sight of the figure that lay on the couch in the best parlour of his cottage. He had few visitors, and those who came to see him were mostly women who knew little of what was happening on the farm. My visits gave him pleasure, as I was able to talk to him of how the lambs were looking at Trevabyn and what fields they were ploughing for spring corn. But after a time his interest in the work on the farm began to lessen and our talk centred on the absorbing mystery of suffering. He wanted to master it in some way, to tame it as he had tamed the colt whose photograph he treasured by his bedside and which no one had been able to handle but himself. I taught him as best I could of how God had entered this arena of suffering and what He had accomplished in His passion and through His death on the cross and how he, Tommy, might avail himself of His suffering. When I read to him of how a grain of wheat must fall into the ground and die if it were to become fruitful, it was as if I was asking him to do something about the farm; a hard thing, true enough, but a job that had to be done. He had worked since he was nine years old and knew that the way of life on a farm was hard. There were no more questionings; he must concentrate on making a good job of it. He would call the children in at night to pray that 'Daddy might be able to do what God wanted him to do'.

I set up a crucifix at the foot of his bed and taught him about mental prayer, and how by looking at the figure on the cross he might unite himself with the suffering of Jesus so that his sufferings might become fruitful. It was during the time that we at St. Hilary were being subjected to bitter and sustained attacks by Protestants, and I invited him to offer his pains on our behalf and on behalf of those who were responsible for causing the disturbance. This gave him a fresh incentive to prayer. As long as he had been able to get about he was on the farm at Trevabyn, driving in the cattle, sharpening and setting the reaper and binder, working at anything that he was capable of undertaking; but there came a time when he could no longer stagger up to the farm place, nor could the men at work with him bear the sight of the wounds in his face which no bandages could hide. This, I think, was the darkest period of his suffering, when he felt himself to be an outcast no longer able to take any part in the work of the farm. Now, with the thought of offering his pain and isolation on our behalf, he was restored to his life of service. So anxious was he to exercise to the full this new power which had come to him that I had difficulty in persuading him to take enough morphia to keep his pains within bounds.

Sitting with him in that darkened room, I would at times be overcome with a sense of the terrible intimacy that existed between the figure on the cross and the body distorted with pain lying on the bed - an intimacy which reduced to nothingness all our human activities. Pointing to the crucifix, he said to me, 'I feel Him working powerfully in me. He must have His way before His work is done.' The end came very slowly, but he never weakened. His last words were a message to me. 'Tell Father . . .' He said it several times, but his wife never caught what the message was that he wished to convey to me.

'Nothing of any interest to record,' was how I filled in a form of inquiry as to the progress of his disease that I received from the Follow-up Department of the Radium Institute, where he had once been a patient. 'Nothing of interest', yet if I were able to record the nature of the intimacy that I believe existed between him and the figure on the cross, or the exact meaning of the words 'He must have His way before His work is done' - what light might not be thrown on the whole mystery of suffering!

This cannot be told, and can only be known by those who have looked as Tommy Carthew looked on that figure on the cross. What may be told is his life of service which made such an acceptance possible; how from a boy he had got up in winter before it was light to go out and meat the cattle, and worked in the fields in all weathers; how often, when he was tired, he had spent the night in a stable with a sick horse, and how at all times and in all weathers he had put the land and his work on the farm before his personal comfort. This was the school in which he had learned to serve so great a Master.

Lest you should be overburdened by the thought of death, I will end this chapter by recounting how Tom Osborne would not die, although night after night all who stood by and watched said that he would be a corpse before morning.

The Osbornes lived at Balawenath, the farm by the church. They were our nearest neighbours, so that hardly a day passed without my seeing one or other of the family. Often I would go across with no other object than to talk. If Tom were alone he would call up the stairs, 'Sarah, come down at once, you're wanted in the kitchen,' and down would come Mrs. Osborne, always perfectly dressed but never failing to rebuke Tom for not telling her that I was in the kitchen. Never have I known a woman for whom life in any form had so great a delight. She would stand in the granary, watching the men empty out sacks of seed-corn on to the floor, in an ecstasy at the sight of so much grain. Anything with life, a new litter of puppies (and there were always puppies at Balawenath), young calves feeding out of a bucket, little ducks waddling their way for the first time to the ponds - how these things would delight her!

In the spring the kitchen would be full of tubs of daffodils and anemones waiting to be bunched and sent away to market. 'I can't bear to part with them,' she would say; and Tom would answer, 'My gracious me, Sarah, I would be ashamed to waste my time talking such foolishness.' And then he would laugh, and we would all laugh, knowing how slight an occasion was required for Tom to waste time, and how often dinner was kept waiting and the work on the farm held up for Tom, who had met a friend at the 'Coach and Horses' or the 'Crown'. Cissy, the second daughter, was the only one who ever attempted to discipline Tom. 'Now, father,' she would say, 'they are waiting for you to start cutting the hay,' or, 'The cattle are wanting their meat,' and Tom would laugh again and say to me, 'It's too bad, Mr.

Walke, the way they treat father.'

Such was the Osborne household when their little girl Dorothy came over one Saturday evening in November to say that Father had come home very poorly and gone to bed and would we lend mother a thermometer. She returned to say that Daddy had a temperature of 102, so would we ring up the doctor.

It was an attack of pleurisy which was followed next day by pneumonia. He lay in bed making a mountain of bedclothes, while he rolled angrily from side to side demanding his shirt and trousers so that he might get up and see about the broccoli which needed cutting. On the following day the doctor suggested another opinion - and a nurse also was sent for, whom Tom called an 'ugly old devil' and ordered out of the house. Downstairs everything was in suspense and confusion; flowers were left half packed, piles of unwashed crockery littered the table. All the energy of the household was directed to listening for sounds in the room above and waiting for the pronouncement of the doctor, who now came two and three times a day. Albert Jenkins, the youth who worked on the farm, would meat the cattle and feed the pigs, and for the rest of the day, and often till past midnight, would come in and stand in the kitchen waiting to hear how 'Captain' was.

As the days went by, Tom grew worse and each night the struggle with death became more and more intense. He was living now on frequent applications of oxygen and alternate injections of strychnine and camphor, but these stimulants must in time cease to be effective. Life had fled from him; he was no longer interested in the doings of the family or what was happening on the farm. As he lay there, propped up with pillows, his body looked like the hulk of a great ship that had been battered by the waves and thrown up on to the sands.

On the morning after the storm which partially destroyed the avenue and brought down over a hundred trees on the glebe, I spent some time with him sitting by the bed holding one of his great hands. The hand would at times give a nervous twitch and Tom would look at me and give a nod with his head - very courteous it was - as if to say, 'Thank you for sitting with me.'

At one time I thought he had gone, but he opened his eyes and beckoned me with them to come close, as if he wished to speak with me. I stood up and bent over to listen, and this is what he said:

'Mr. Walke, my dear, I have something to say,' there was a pause whilst his chest heaved up and down. 'My dear, I can beat it. Tell Sarah I can beat it if they will keep me awake. They must watch me like a fox or I will slip away in my sleep. Tell 'em to keep me awake.' Then he lay back exhausted with the effort.

The room was very quiet. Outside I could hear the children coming down the lane from school, but inside the room there was no sound but his heavy breathing, and I wondered if he was going to sleep and I ought to wake him. While I was still considering, I saw a sight which set my heart beating; for there, sitting on the rail of the bed, was a robin which must at that moment have flown through the open space where the window had been taken out to enable Tom to breathe more freely. I am not superstitious, but the presence of a robin in a sick-room is so certain a sign of death in these parts that I feared what would happen if Tom opened his eyes and saw that robin sitting there. I was getting up to drive the bird away, when the hands on the counterpane moved, searching for the rope which in the earlier days of his illness had been placed there so that he might raise himself from the bed, but which for some time he had been too weak to use. He had found the rope and was raising himself from the pillows. His eyes were wide open, staring at the bird sitting on the rail. For one moment Tom and the bird faced each other, and then Tom gave a great cough and said, 'Get out, you b -, you've come to the wrong house.' Sinking back on his pillows he whispered to me, 'I said a bad word, Mr. Walke, but we can't have they fellows in the house.' The bird had gone, and when I looked again I thought a change had come over his face. His eyes were closed, but there was a smile round the corners of his mouth which I had not seen there for days. I sat very silently for a time and then crept out of the room, to find Mrs. Osborne standing at the head of the stairs.

'What made him cry out like that?' she whispered.

'You heard him?' I said. 'He was driving a robin out of the room.'

'A robin!' she said, and put out her hands as if to drive the bird away; 'that is a terrible sign, for it means death.'

'Not for Tom,' I answered. 'It will take more than a robin to kill Tom.'

When the doctor came that night he found his temperature down and his breathing easier. He had 'taken a turn', the doctor said. In a few days he was shouting for Sarah to bring him his clothes and giving orders for the slaughtering of some fifteen pigs.

7 FRIENDS AT LAMORNA

Ah, Sunflower, weary of time,
Who countest the steps of the Sun.

How susceptible we are to the sound of words. These two lines have haunted me for the past week. They came to me first when I was reading an old diary for 1915 with a view to writing this chapter. Many of the spaces contained no entry, but in the spring of that year I found the following - 'Met Dod and Ernest Procter. Met A.J. Munnings at the Red House. Met Laura and Harold Knight,' and frequently, 'A. and I went to Lamorna.' There was nothing in these entries to cause me distress, for they are records of some of our happiest days in Cornwall; but under the influence of these two lines I became intolerably sad. It was not the thought of the passing of years that depressed me; it was time itself that had become too much for me. Whatever I was doing I found myself saying - 'Ah, Sunflower, weary of time.' It added to my depression that I could not complete the couplet. I had no books, and did not even know for certain that they would be found among the poems of William Blake. In desperation I wrote to two friends, in case one should fail, and begged them to discover the poem. Because of its loveliness and to save my readers my own experience I will give you their answer:

SUNFLOWER
BY
WILLIAM BLAKE

Ah, Sunflower, weary of time,
Who countest the steps of the Sun;
Seeking after that sweet golden clime
Where the traveller's journey is done

Where the youth pined away with desire,
And the pale virgin shrouded in snow,
Arise from their graves, and aspire
Where my sunflower wishes to go.

Nineteen hundred and fifteen, as I was saying, was the year in which we first met the Procters.

Ernest Procter claims to be a Quaker and actually is a birth member of 'The Society of Friends', for I have seen family treasures and records going back to the days of George Fox. His ancestry is of men and women who, apart from their quiet meeting-houses, found little expression for man's desire to create and possess beautiful things. Ernest has both these qualities which failed to find expression in his ancestry. What a discoverer he is of beautiful things, and how he loves to possess them! He came to see me this summer at the sanatorium and in the car was a leaden cherub clasping a dolphin, which he lifted out and placed on the grass where we lay the whole of the afternoon, watching the sunlight play on the face and light up the smile of the little cherub.

I have seen many lovely things that I might never have noticed without him as a companion. It is his feeling and love for architecture that makes him essentially a decorator of spaces rather than a painter of framed pictures. Two altar-pieces at St. Hilary, of which I will write in a later chapter, are examples of his work.

I have lately received a letter from Dod Procter. It was in answer to one of mine and has no reference to our first meeting, nor does it contain news of any importance. My reason for including it in these memories is that it throws considerable light on the character of her work.

'DEAR BER, -
'I was so pleased to get your letter. I liked it being difficult to read because it made it last all through breakfast in bed. I am struggling to paint a nude with sun-spots all over her;

when the sun is out I nearly burst with heat and when it keeps going in I nearly burst with rage; it is the most trying job and the most difficult thing I have ever done. I hope it is coming off but I am not sure yet. I have got a cat. I didn't want it but it came with a broken leg half mended and it has a charming wistful little face; about three months old. It is now at the Vet's for a few days while he does what he can for its leg.'

There is an art of reading as well as of writing letters; how few possess this quality and can read a letter (written in a handwriting which reduces most of my friends to desperation) with such delicate attention or bestow such tender consideration on a cat, who will never be allowed to know how little she was wanted when she arrived with her broken leg.

It is this quality of delicate understanding that gives distinction to her work; this together with the passion she displays in recounting her efforts to paint a nude in sunlight.

After our first meeting we were constantly with Dod and Ernest during the spring of 1915. I remember how on one occasion we all walked to Trevelloe Wood to have tea with a Pole named Peartree who was living at the Red House, a sinister-looking cottage in a clearing of the fir-wood. Our friendship with this quiet scholar was to be cut short by one of those minor tragedies for which the war was responsible. He was at this time carrying on a correspondence with some children, conspiring with them as to who could write the most fantastical letters. One of these letters, written by the children and addressed to him at Sheffield, a hamlet near where he lived, by some mischance of the post arrived at the town of Sheffield, in Yorkshire. It was opened and handed to the police, who discovering that Peartree was an alien attached a sinister meaning to it and visited the Red House to make inquiries. It was strange that so innocent a correspondence should cause the death of a man, yet so it was; the suspicious looks of neighbours, the constant sense of being watched and never free from prying eyes, made life intolerable for this sensitive scholar.

Cornwall has always had its watchers - watching is in the Cornishman's blood. It is all that is left for old men who have spent their lives at sea - to go out to the end of the pier or up on the cliffs where they can watch the sea and dream away their remaining years. There are others who are on the lookout for driftwood or wreckage to come ashore. Jimmy Limpots, a man whom I knew at St. Ives, was always searching for bodies; he and his two dogs would haunt the coast from Zennor to Carbis Bay, picking up a rabbit by the way, collecting Osmunda fern which he sold to visitors, prying into caves and between boulders in the search for a corpse for which he would receive the reward of a pound.

Jimmy Limpots took a delight in his gruesome occupation; he entered a cave and sniffed the air, as a setter enters a turnip-field. 'Nothing here,' he would say. There was never a bathing fatality or wreck along the coast but what, after waiting nine days for the body to rise, Jimmy would begin his search. In many villages there are watchers whose occupation is not so honourable as searching for corpses, and whose activity is not limited to the sea. Courting couples on Saturday and Sunday nights have a special interest for them; they watch by doorways and peer into uncurtained windows, if only to discover what the neighbours are going to have for supper.

The war gave an added zest to these watchings. And nothing was too impossible to be believed: the ringing of bells from the church tower was held by some to be a method of signalling to the Germans; to be seen often on the cliffs was taken as a proof of being engaged in supplying petrol to enemy submarines.

For two years I was suspected by neighbours of preparing for a landing on Marazion beach. On one occasion a man, who had driven us with his old horse 'George' and his barouche-landau since the first day we came to St. Hilary, turned round on his box-seat, while driving me down the avenue, and shaking his whip shouted at me, 'You call yourself a parson, but you are nothing but a German spy. Half your pay do come from the Pope and the other half from the Kaiser. You ought to hang from one of your tallest trees.' He was very angry that morning and, after having settled himself down, turned round again and added, 'That's what you will do one night.'

For some natures it is intolerable to live in an atmosphere of suspicion: it was so with Peartree, who ended his life one Sunday morning in October. Some friends, who were lunching with him that morning, arrived at the Red House and knocked at the door. There was no answer, so they sat in the autumn sunshine and talked and laughed at the ways of this fellow, who had invited them to lunch and was not out of bed to receive them; until in exasperation they forced the door with a heavy stone. Still there was no answer when they called from the foot of the stairs. 'Some one must go and wake him,' they said, and as they spoke of waking him a fear came to them that all was not well. They went up the stairs together and knocked very loudly on the bedroom door. Again there was no answer, and after pausing a few moments they opened the door and found Peartree asleep on the bed with an empty bottle of veronal on the table at his side.

On the afternoon on which we arrived at the Red House, he was giving tea on a granite boulder to these same children who in a few months were to be the innocent cause of his death; while not far away two horses, a grey mare and a bay, were being held by a groom. Leaning up against the bay horse was a man in a flannel shirt without a collar wiping paint-brushes with a rag; it was this man who attracted my attention. The poise of his body and the tilt of his head as he leant against the horse watching our arrival suggested an arrogant, almost insolent attitude towards the strangers who were approaching.

Here, I thought, was a man whom I should most

certainly dislike, when Ernest Procter, seeing us eyeing one another, introduced me and said, 'This is A.J. Munnings.' The man in the flannel shirt looked even more insolent and then, as if he had relented, threw back his head and smiled a queer smile, giving the impression that his face had been lit up from within. The term smile does not adequately convey my meaning, for there is something of a conscious effort in a smile. What I saw then, and have seen many times since, was the invasion of a face by a vivid personality. At other times his is the face of a man who has spent his life with horses, but, lit with that smile, it is the face of an ascetic saint.

How he will laugh if he ever reads this. 'What a fellow this Walke is with his saints,' he will say. 'Why does he write such...' and then will follow a string of words not usually associated with saints. I can't help it, Mr. Munnings, I may have quite as false an impression of yourself as I sometimes suspect you have of me: but I will keep mine, for, although unlikely, I have a feeling that in some strange way it is true.

That afternoon, after he had sent away his two horses, Patrick, the bay, and the grey mare whose granddaughter, another grey mare, I rode the last time I stayed with A.J. at his home in Dedham, we sat apart and talked of books. He approaches literature with the freshness with which he looks at a landscape, and will describe what he has read with the same vividness as a scene that he has witnessed.

We talked of that great novel M*adame* B*ovary* which he had just read, and of P*ickwick*, his favourite book While we sat there he told me the story of the Bagman's uncle, and told it in such a way that I have never forgotten the picture of the old mail-coaches huddled together in the yard, with their doors torn from their hinges and the rain dripping through the roofs; or the terrific noise of the fighting when the Bagman's uncle plunged his rapier through the villain's flowered waistcoat and pinned him to the woodwork; or how the Bagman's uncle woke in the morning and found that he was sitting shivering with cold on the box of an Edinburgh mail. Never before had I met a man who gave so liberally of his personality to a friend of an afternoon. Wherever he lives or whatever company he keeps, he remains, at heart, a countryman. His people have lived for generations on the land in that wide county of Norfolk, where the sunlight falls unbroken on great stretches of corn-land. He himself has never forsaken the land; he looks at it and loves it, its pasture and plough, its cattle and horses, its villages and old churches, as a countryman loves these things.

Now A.J. Munnings is as enthusiastic over his friends, as he is over a landscape or passage of literature. Having discovered the Walkes, he was eager to introduce them to his friends in Lamorna. 'Mrs. Sidgwick shall give a party, and you and Annie Walke shall be there,' he said. 'I will get them all to come and see you; and you will love every one of them; Harold and Laura Knight, wonderful people,' he continued; 'Lamorna Birch and the Hughes. You will like them, I tell you.'

Annie Walke had already met Laura Knight and several other painters from Lamorna at the Newlyn Show. She would be at home with these people, but it was difficult for me to plunge into this company of which I knew nothing.

I remember being told how Annie Walke's sister, Hilda Fearon, happening to call at the artists' colour shop in the King's Road, said to the lady behind the counter, 'Isn't it dreadful? My sister is going to marry a curate.' 'Well,' said the lady at the colour shop, 'that's not so bad. If a curate can put up with an artist, surely an artist ought to be able to put up with a curate.' These people at Lamorna, I thought, might put up with me, but I did not know that I wanted to be 'put up with' and was diffident about going. Munnings, however, was insistent, and so it came about that we rode on our bicycles one morning in the spring of 1915 for the first time to Lamorna.

Lamorna is at its best in the spring. For while round Buryan, a mile and a half away, there is no touch of gold on the gorse and not a daisy to be found in the fields, here in the valley the tops of the ash trees are tinged with green, primroses and daffodils are in bloom, and the blackthorn is opening its buds. Such a flowering of blackthorn, from the head of the valley to where the stream flows over boulders into the sea, is not to be found in any other spot in Cornwall. Munnings had told us to come to the inn kept by Jory, down at the cove, where he was then living. I do not know if that inn has a name, for I have always heard it spoken of as 'The Wink', a term originally used to describe a beerhouse without a spirit-licence. As with many houses of the kind in villages round the coast, men went there as much to talk as to drink. Whether the talk is of the land or the sea, of the planting of bulbs or the catching of lobsters (for the men of the cove earn their living by fishing and flower-growing), it has a quality and directness which is only found when men speak of the daily things of their life.

Joe Ladner, a great talker, was always at 'The Wink' of an evening; he was a heavy-moving man who would lumber to the place reserved for him in the corner of the kitchen, where Jory without a word would draw him a pint of beer. After drinking and wiping his mouth, he would look round the room with his little eyes full of merriment and say, 'Good evening, all.'

One evening in September I was in ' The Wink' with Harold Knight, when Joe Ladner came in, later than usual, and called for some hot beer. 'Lace it with a drop of rum, my dear,' he said, 'I've earned it to-night.'

'What mischief have you been up to?' said Jory, with a wink to the company.

'I wouldn't call it roguery at all, more like foolishness to my way of thinking,' Joe answered, speaking as a man who was debating the question in his own mind. 'We had some crab-pots down to the west'ard,' he went on. 'The boy said to me, 'Uncle, we had better haul they pots; though it is the end of the season, we don't want to lose 'em.' The weather wernt looking too good, but there it was, the boy had his way, though I didn't like it at all. It were foolishness, as I've said. If you'm looking for roguery, you'm mistaken. We went away on the top of a flood, but when we came to haul the pots there was a parcel of sea running. I had a thought at the time that better we were at home drinking a cup of tay than hauling pots with a gale of wind coming on. Time we'd got the pots aboard there were a heavy sea owing to the tide making against the wind. The boat was down by the head and wallowing in the water like an old sow in a muck-heap. We were in a nasty old place sure enough. I looked round to see where we were to, when straight ahead I see'd the Lord coming to us. He knowed the state we were in. I shouted to the boy, 'Did 'e see 'm, boy?' and he shouted back, 'Who's that, Uncle?' 'Why, the Lord,' I said. 'You be daft,' he said. If he had been a boy of mine I would have made a corpse of 'em for answering his uncle in that kind of way. But that's the manner of boys to-day, it's no good talking to 'em for they won't pay no heed to what you do say.'

Joe spoke very slowly, as if he were summing up and pronouncing judgment on the follies of the young generation. After a pause, in which he looked round the kitchen to see that we were all in agreement, he continued: 'On top of the next wave I had another look round. It were the Lord sure enough. He knowed the state we were in and were making to help us. - I thought to myself, 'That will learn the boy that there is some one who do care for his old uncle.' He came alongside and called to me, 'Shall I give 'ee a tow, Joe Ladner?' 'Oh, my Lord,' I said, 'you'm our salvation.' On that He throwed a rope aboard and towed us in to cove.'

It was only then that I understood that Joe Ladner had been telling how Lord St. Levan in his yacht, the St. Michael, had given him a tow. Nor was I the only one in the kitchen who was under the impression that Joe had been telling of an apparition; for during the tale a man whispered to me: 'I wouldn't have credited that Joe Ladner would have taken up with religion; but you can never tell how it will take a man.'

On the afternoon of our first arrival at 'The Wink', it was deserted, but for a mongrel dog who lay across the doorway and a man asleep in the kitchen. On the table by his side was a slate on which was written, 'Mr. Munnings says you are to go on to his studio.' Jory the innkeeper had provided that his afternoon slumber should not be disturbed by any inquirers; so we left him to sleep and found A.J. Munnings in his studio, where he showed us his work, including the sketch of a picture which I saw recently in the Norwich Gallery, 'The Pony that lived in a Gravel Pit'.

I do not fancy that I made any advance towards friendship with the people we met at Munnings' party that afternoon. I was shy at meeting so many strangers; and Laura and Harold Knight, whom we were especially invited to meet, were not, as I had suspected, anxious to make my acquaintance. They have told me how they did not know, nor did they want to know, 'a clergyman'. Unlike falling in love, friendship is often of slow growth, built up and cemented by different happenings and experiences; such has been my friendship with Laura and Harold.

One of my most constant dreams is that I am being pursued as a murderer, and after waking in fear I often try to plan what I would do and whom I could trust with my life if such a fate befell me. At these moments between waking and sleeping, I find myself standing outside number sixteen Langford Place ringing the bell three times, a signal that will bring Harold or Laura to open the door. I wait and listen for the sound of footsteps. Yes, they are coming. The door is opened by Laura and I see Harold standing at the head of the stairs.

'You must hide me somewhere, I am wanted for murder,' I say. Laura, throwing her arms round me, says, 'Oh, my dear, whatever made you do it?' and Harold calls from the stairs, 'Shut the door and don't worry about things like that, Laura.'

8 DONKEYS

This chapter is concerned with the donkeys I have kept and the many happy days I have spent on the road with them during these twenty years of which I am writing.

Donkeys are strange creatures. They are late-comers to England, not having been introduced until the reign of Queen Elizabeth, and still remain as alien to our civilization as the Chinaman whom you may meet in London round the docks. There must be some connexion in my mind between donkeys and Chinamen, for when I sat down to write about them my thoughts wandered to a conference I once attended, where a young Chinese student, during a discussion on the difference between the Eastern and Western nations, said to me, 'A people who have had experience lose ambition.'

I understood what he meant and I think the donkey would understand; for like the Chinaman he is free from those lesser ambitions which prompt the horse and the dog to succeed in the things which give pleasure to their master. A donkey will stop suddenly in the middle of a race when he has outstripped his competitors, for no other reason than that he seems to think the race is not worth while. The spectators will laugh and gibe, not understanding that the donkey has become aware of the futility of such efforts.

Children often have the same characteristics, much to the annoyance of their parents; this is perhaps the reason why children and donkeys have so complete an understanding of each other without a touch of condescension on either side. Possibly the donkey at some time or other experienced the fascination of the friendship with man to which the horse and dog have surrendered, but, realizing its dangers, he resisted with a fierce determination which we term stupidity. The cat pursues a different method but her end is the same. Yesterday a kitten came to visit me and spent the day, delighting me with her antics. In the evening she went away without saying farewell or expressing any regret at leaving me. A dog would have gone back and apologized to his master for his absence with an elaborate ritual of tail-wagging, after explaining to his new friends his regret at leaving them. But the kitten owed no allegiance to any one; she was free to come and go as she pleased.

There is a further resemblance between the cat and the donkey in that they both have a past; the cat was a creature sacred to the Gods; the donkey has shared in the humiliation and glory of the Son of God, and still bears on his back the marks of His cross. The concluding lines of G.K. Chesterton's poem, *The Donkey*, expresses to perfection the secret endurance of his nature.

> *The tattered outlaw of the earth,*
> *Of ancient crooked will*
> *Starve, scourge, deride me: I am dumb,*
> *I keep my secret still.*

> *Fools! For I also had my hour;*
> *One far fierce hour and sweet;*
> *There was a shout about my ears,*
> *And palms before my feet.*

Norman Garstin, shortly before his death, was collecting material for a book *The Horse and our Civilization*. Our civilization, he maintained, was built on the horse, and so closely connected were they that the flower of medieval civilization went by the name of 'chivalry'. In discussing the book with him I remember remarking, 'What if man had followed the donkey in place of the horse?' 'In that case,' he answered with a smile, 'we might have had a Christian civilization.'

The horse has gone, he has long been driven off the roads and is fast disappearing from the fields. As I look out of my window on to a cornfield, there is a motor-tractor at work, where a few years ago there would have been three great horses with a reaper and binder. Even in war, where the horse has been supreme, he is displaced by armies of tanks and motor-tractors. And with his going the civilization that he has sponsored is everywhere failing. I would maintain with Norman Garstin that the way of recovery lies in following the donkey.

Neither in literature nor in history has the donkey figured as other than an ambassador of peace and healing. It was on a swift donkey that the Shunamite woman rode in search of Elisha for the healing of her son; a donkey carried the Mother of the Saviour in the time of her need, bore the child to safety in the days of His infancy, and carried Him in triumph on His entry into Jerusalem.

Apart from Sancho Panza, who was armed with a cudgel, I have only once heard of a donkey as a bearer of arms. An old lady wrote, after a broadcast I had given on donkeys, to say that the crest of her family was an ass. This is the story she told me. The horse of an ancestor having been killed under him at the Battle of Hastings, his man-at-arms, espying a donkey in a field near by the battle, caught him and brought him to his master, who mounted him and returned to the battle. In gratitude for this timely aid, she said, her family had adopted a donkey as their crest.

Our first donkey, Billy, was given to us by Ruth Manning-Sanders, a lover of donkeys and the author of a long poem, *Zachy Trenoy*, in which a donkey is one of the principal characters. Billy was a little brown ass with the softest muzzle and the sweetest breath of any I have known. How sweet a donkey's breath is, whatever the time of year; it seems always to carry the scent of the gorse. Billy had a most affectionate nature, which he did his best to conceal under a jaunty manner. When patted he would stamp a foot and give a swish with his tail, as if to say, 'I have no time for these blandishments.'

Later in his life, when the Austrian boys, who had been staying with us, had gone away and he had no companions, after taking up with a herd of cows whom he found dull, he got together from distant commons a band of the most dissipated donkeys in the district, of all sizes and ages, from donkeys grey with age to foals a few days old. After wandering round the country-side opening gates, trampling down gardens and cabbage-patches, he would appear some morning in our garden at the head of this mob. He never allowed himself to be caught when he was with these companions of his. As soon as I appeared, away he would go down the avenue followed by the others. After some days he would tire of this way of life and return home very penitent. But there were days when he did not return, and a policeman would call to say that Billy was 'in the pound' and that there was five shillings to pay. I must have paid a number of fines before this company was broken up and Billy took to going with horses. He was very clever at opening gates, and would go raiding the fields, collecting horses as he had once collected donkeys. I have seen as many as ten great cart-horses, led by Billy, gambolling on our lawn of an early morning with their heads down and their heels in the air.

So far I have only told you the bad ways of donkeys, and nothing of the joys of owning them and of travelling the road with a donkey-shay, joys which have become very rare. An old man in Sennen, with whom I was discussing the change that has come over the world, said to me, ''Tis all changed. They old motors have done it,' and then as a final condemnation of the modern world he added, 'They have spoilt the road for a donkey.' The old man was right; no longer is it possible to walk slowly uphill with a hand on the end of the shay, or to ride gaily downhill dangling your legs between the shafts, watching his little feet moving so swiftly and surely that it is impossible to be anything but gay. A donkey is never impatient like a horse, who is always wanting to be somewhere else; he is willing to wait anywhere and for any length of time while you speak to a friend or look at the countryside.

Donkeys

W.H. Davies understood the supreme pleasure of standing and doing nothing when he wrote:

> What is this life if full of care,
> We have no time to stand and stare.
> No time to stand beneath the boughs
> And stare as long as sheep or cows.

It is good to stand and stare; but the stare of a cow or a sheep is a stupid stare compared to the stare of a donkey. He is the true contemplative, whose stare is not at passing things. I have watched the donkey in many countries of Europe; he is often brutally treated, but he never expresses astonishment; he is concerned with other things, with the thoughts that arise in his own mind, thoughts that are hidden from us.

Not the least of the pleasures in owning a donkey is the company you keep and the kind of people you speak with on the road. No one ever inquired who I was or why I was on the road with my old clothes and painted shay (a seat on two high wheels with a swinging board to rest the feet); I was a traveller as they were.

Walking by the side of the donkey up Market Jew Street in Penzance, on my way to Sennen one morning, I was joined by a queer-looking fellow carrying a black box on his shoulders, who suggested that I should go into partnership with him. I asked him what his trade was, and he said, pointing to his box, 'I am in the mystery line.' By this I understood him to mean the conjuring business, and answered, 'I am in the mystery line myself, for I am the Parish Priest of a place called St. Hilary.' 'Whatever line you're in you're a damned sight better liar than I am,' was all that he said as he left me to go into the 'Plume of Feathers'.

When I was a boy there was a saying in our village, 'Who stole the donkey?' The answer was, 'The man with the white hat'. Why a man with a white hat should be branded with this crime I never knew; but I have noticed since that donkey-owners generally do wear a white hat, and, if they are real donkey-men, a rather long coat, and walk very slowly as if they were not concerned with arriving anywhere.

Some of my happiest days have been spent with Billy. On occasions we would go to Sennen Cove, where we had a cottage - starting early in the morning - or to Lamorna, where we would spend the night. But most enjoyable of all were days spent on the road when the donkey would go where he pleased, and when I would walk slowly behind the cart and ride merrily down the hills with my feet dangling between the shafts, and not a thought of where we were going.

We had another donkey, Antony, whom I used to drive in a pair with Billy in the shafts. Annie Walke and I were driving to Lamorna one day, when passing Rose Vale, where there was a gipsy camp, I saw a beautiful young white donkey tethered. I called to a small boy who was the only person to be seen, and asked what he would take for his donkey.

'If you give me thirty shillings, Mister,' he shouted back, 'you shall have him.'

'All right,' I answered, 'take him over to St. Hilary.'

Returning that evening I was stopped on the hill above Goldsithney by a gipsy driving a great white mare in a high cart, with the little boy from whom I had bought the donkey at his side.

'I have brought the donkey over to your reverence,' he said, looking down at us from, his high cart.

'But I have no money with me to pay you,' I answered.

'I am not concerned about the money, your reverence. If you like the donkey as much as I do you will pay me some day. I like to deal with gentlemen,' he added. He looked a great gentleman himself as he bowed first to Annie Walke and then to me and drove away.

Some days later he arrived bringing his wife, whom he said that he would like us to know. They got down from their trap and came into the dining-room. After I had fetched Annie Walke and drawn a big jug of cider for us all, the tall gipsy proposed the toast 'The mistress of the house', and I drank the health of his handsome wife; and then, after fetching another jug of cider, we all drank to the white donkey. On my asking for ten shillings change from two pounds, in payment for the donkey, he brought out of his pocket a canvas bag and, untying the cord round the neck, emptied on the table a mass of golden sovereigns, rings, bangles, brooches and ear-rings, all of solid gold. He apologized for the display by saying that he wanted the lady to see some of 'the pretty things'.

There we sat drinking cider with these heaps of gold on the table before us, until his wife said, 'Now, Jim, you've had enough cider and the lady is tired of your talk. Put all these things away now and come along.' So they got up into their high cart and drove away.

The white donkey was as beautiful to look at as it is possible for a donkey to be, with Zebra markings on his legs and a great cross on his back. He could go 'when he was minded to, like a flying machine', as donkey-men are apt to boast. But he was always a little queer and developed the worst possible trick that a donkey can have; suddenly without any warning he would stop and slide on to his quarters with his hindlegs between his forelegs; the cart would tip forward and I would find myself sitting by the roadside. If I attempted to pull him up or remonstrate with him, he adopted a more abandoned attitude and stretched himself out on his side with his head on the ground as if he were dead. There was nothing to be done but to take him out of the cart, when he would get up, shake himself and, after being re-harnessed, go on until the fit took him to lie down again. He has 'gone to lie', as I have heard it called, six times between St. Hilary and Penzance.

Gipsies and donkey-men could suggest no way of curing him except to light a fire to scare him; but how could I carry kindling wood and light a fire by the roadside whenever the donkey thought fit to lie down? Finally an old Irish doctor told me the secret. A few drops of water, he said, poured down his ear would set up such an intolerable tickle that the worst donkey in Ireland would spring to his feet to shake his head. It sounded cruel, but I only had to do it once. For ever afterwards I carried a very small phial of water in my waistcoat pocket and would merely have to bring it out and show it to him, when he would be up and away before I could get into the cart. People who did not know the secret thought it was holy water that drove the devil out of the donkey.

He really was a stupid donkey. One morning he came into the house by the steps leading from the garden, and found himself in a passage with a flight of stairs to the hall; fearing to walk down the stairs and being unable to turn and go back the way he came, he sat down with his back against the lavatory door. There he sat and brayed, not once or twice but continuously, without intermission - disposing of the theory that a donkey can only bray with his tail in the air. The noise was deafening and most disconcerting, as we had some people for lunch and conversation was impossible, while the whole house vibrated with his braying; it was also most inconvenient that he should have chosen to sit with his back against the door of the lavatory. Annie Walke suggested we should lift him up and carry him out on to the steps; so we all left the table and pushed and pulled until we got him to the steps, where he toppled over into the garden. I gave him away later to a man in the village, who was fined shortly after for driving with him down Market Jew Street to the danger of the public.

Billy was now very lonely. The roads were fast becoming impossible for a donkey to stand on his feet; the children who had been his friends had gone away; the donkeys who were his companions had been sold; he disdained the society of the cows and would spend his days wandering round the meadows or gazing wistfully over the gate into the Avenue.

It was at this time, when he seemed to be no longer wanted, that the opportunity came for him to return to the life that he enjoyed. The vicar of Phillack, a small village on the sand-dunes beyond Hayle, was looking for a donkey for his children; so Billy went to Phillack, where he was very happy until his tragic death in the great gale three years later.

During those years he never forgot St. Hilary. As I sit here and write of how and when he came back to us, I can with difficulty believe that what I am writing and know to be true is not a figment of my own imagination, so closely does it impinge on a world to which we have, as yet, little access.

The first Christmas Eve after he left us, Laura our maid came excitedly into my room as I was preparing to go across to the church for the Midnight Mass saying, 'Please, Billy has come to spend Christmas.' I rushed out to greet him, and found him standing in the courtyard where he had always come on Christmas night for a feed of corn. He stayed with us until after the midday Mass, returning to Phillack that afternoon as unobserved as he had come. It was still more strange that another Christmas should find him there again. What intelligence had he to figure out the calendar and discover the twenty-fifth day in the month of December? How did he know which of the years was Leap Year, adding one day more? What thinking in that little brain led him to find the answer to that difficult sum? I do not know, it is too difficult a problem for me to solve.

There was one other occasion on which he came, and that perhaps was stranger than all. It was a night, early in November, when I had taken down a collection of photographs of days spent in Sennen Cove. The pictures I had been looking at had awakened many pleasant memories of days with the donkey and the children who were then with us, and feeling very tender towards Billy, I said to Annie Walke, who was sitting near the fire, 'I must go over to Phillack one day soon and see Billy.'

That night I was awakened by the braying of a donkey beneath my window. So loud was it that I got out of bed and stumbled to the window, and there in the moonlight was Billy. I called to him, 'I see you there, Billy' -

and crept back to bed. When I awoke in the morning I could not distinguish whether I had been dreaming or had actually got out in the night and spoken to Billy beneath the window. It was Billy, and I had spoken to him, for in the flower-bed beneath the window were the marks of his feet.

Whether the tender thought that I had towards him that evening had led him across the causeway at Hayle, along the lanes through St. Erth village, to bray beneath my window, or whether his setting out and coming was made known to me, I cannot tell. It is again too difficult a problem for me to solve. If these things are true, the world we live in is not the safe place we sometimes imagine it to be.

9 YEARS OF DISTRESS

We were far away at St. Hilary from all that was happening in France. There were no troop-trains or convoys of wounded passing through the county; so that, apart from the mustering at Goldsithney of horses from the farms in the district, the first contact with the war was the march of a detachment of the Cornish Regiment through the county to gain recruits. I saw them march by the avenue gate with an officer riding at their head, and remembered the combined regret and pride with which I watched them, and how I experienced afresh a sense of divided loyalty which has constantly haunted my life.

Whether my frequent failures to discover a direct course among the complications of life have been due to some inherent characteristic in my nature or are the result of my upbringing I do not know. My father was the vicar of a country parish and had no money to send three sons to a Public School. He was old-fashioned and of the opinion that there were only a few schools to which a gentleman could send his sons, and as he was unable to afford these he kept us at home, where, up to the age of twelve, we received a classical education.

But at this age life became so absorbing to three boys with the sports and games of the country-side open to them that, with my father's failing health, lessons were pushed more and more into the background. My father would leave us with so many pages of Virgil to construe while he rode round the parish visiting his parishioners, to find on his return that we had gone off for the day. Thus the greater part of my boyhood was spent in doing nothing in particular beyond playing games and engaging in the sports of the country.

I do not regret these days of idleness, nor do I consider the knowledge that I acquired at this time to have been valueless. The son of the parsonage, whose youth is spent in the country among its people, has many advantages. He knows no social distinctions; he is as much at home on the farm or in the cottage of the labourer as in the house of the squire, and inherits a tradition of culture as naturally as he finds himself a person of importance in the life of the village.

Such an upbringing as mine involves the loss of scholarship, which I regret; but on the other hand it ensures freedom from a tradition which often leaves an indelible mark upon the outlook and personality of those who share it. In my own case the result of such an upbringing has been that throughout my life I have repeatedly questioned many of the accepted formulas of society. If I had been endowed with a Public School education with its code of morals, or rather of good and bad form, I would without doubt have been saved many of those indecisions which have haunted my life.

Now, as I watched this company of men who marched by so gaily on the way to what we at home now know to be the most terrible test of courage and endurance man has suffered since the human race began, I was tormented by my thoughts. - What right had I to make a choice when the fate of the nation was at stake? Ought I not to be with them? What had I to offer in comparison to what these men had given so willingly ? - These and many other questions of the same nature troubled me as I watched the men of the Cornish Regiment march by. I could not join them and yet I longed to be of their company.

On my way home I overtook an old man from Relubbus who had lost his grandson in France, and while we walked up the hill together I spoke to him of the soldiers who had passed. The old man turned on me viciously, and brandishing his stick, shouted, 'He is a butcher, that officer on his horse. A butcher, who has taken away the prime bullocks to the slaughterhouse, and has come back to drive in the lean.'

The judgment of that embittered old man, who had lost his favourite grandson, expressed a crude but terribly revealing indictment of our Christian civilization, where in Germany human life had become so much 'cannon fodder', while here in England the terms 'War of Attrition' and 'Man-power' were in daily use.

The winter of 1916-17 was the hardest I have ever known in Cornwall. The fields were full of golden plover and other birds from the far North, who had come further and further south, searching for food, until they reached the sea. All night they would cry as they walked ceaselessly over the frozen fields. So full of sadness was this crying that I could not sleep and would lie awake at night listening and thinking of the men in Flanders and Northern France, whose state was even more piteous than theirs.

My attempts at feeding them were of little value, for they needed worms and grubs, while I had nothing but corn to offer them. Probably the boys who went out with sticks, beating the hedge sides and killing those who had crept there to die, acted more kindly towards them than I did in my efforts to save them.

We were constantly at Lamorna that autumn and winter, going by Berryman's bus to Penzance and walking the remaining five miles. During the autumn Laura Knight, in clambering over a fallen tree, had broken her leg and now lay propped up in bed in the sitting-room of their house. Munnings was also a constant visitor. He arrived, most evenings, after dinner, with a copy of Jorrocks under his arm. There was a knock at the door and A.J. would come in, throw his hat into a corner, sit down and say, 'Well, Laura, are we going to have any reading to-night?'

There may be some for whom this book has little charm, but none could fail to enjoy the adventures of the sporting Cockney grocer when read aloud by A.J. Munnings. Often he would break off in the middle of a passage and say, 'Listen to this, Laura,' or, 'What do you think of that?' and Laura, who had been awakened by the abrupt ending, would say, 'Wonderful, A.J.,' and sleep again. At other times he would put the book down and roar with laughter, ending with, 'What a story, my G...., what a story,' and Laura would murmur, 'Wonderful, A.J.'

There was to be a Christmas dinner that year at Lamorna to which Annie Walke and I were invited. Harold Knight undertook to buy the wine and Robert Hughes the turkeys; the same two were responsible for roasting the turkeys and boiling the Christmas puddings. It was a very happy company that sat down to dinner that Christmas night; the wine was excellent and the turkeys roasted and cooked to a turn; but it was not the wine or the food or even the company that made that dinner memorable. Under other conditions its memory might have faded as have other happy moments in my life.

Since my attitude towards the war had become known we had experienced a sense of loneliness, of being apart and different from the men and women round us. What we craved for and what made that dinner memorable was the assurance it gave that such pleasures as sitting at table with friends, drinking wine and listening to talk in which it was possible to join without giving offence or raising suspicion, had not been finally lost to us. That night there was no leaving the table and starting the evening afresh in the cold atmosphere of another room. After we had dined and the dishes had been removed, we sat on, with bottles of port passing round the table, pledging the health of each of the company. When we were arranging the table A.J. had said, 'I will have Annie Walke next to me, for she is a woman that won't mind what I say.' So Annie Walke sat on one side and I on the other next to Gert Harvey, who, after several healths had been drunk, turned to me and said, 'Drink Harold's health. Stand up and say, Mr. Knight, may I take wine with you?' Encouraged by A.J., who shouted, 'Go it, Walke,' I stood up and made a speech, which annoyed Harold Knight because I said he was like a bishop. Apart from this incident and the fact that A.J. had composed a song for this evening, 'In the puddles with Julia', a parody on Compton Mackenzie's novel *Guy and Pauline*, I can recall nothing but a feeling of contentment at being among friends.

Shortly after this Christmas a man called to see me. I should recognize him now by the way he sat rigidly upright with his hands on his knees, by his closely trimmed beard, heavy watch-chain and quiet manner, as a member of the Society of Friends. He told me that he had a 'concern' to visit Friends in the West of England and invited me to attend a meeting he had arranged to hold in Penzance. This was the first of the many quiet meetings of Friends I was to attend during the coming years; and very grateful I am for the kindness they have consistently shown to me.

It had been my custom to say daily, after Mass, the prayer for the ending of the war composed by the saintly Pius X, who when asked to bless the armies of Austria replied, 'I bless peace and not war.' I had also instituted the service of Benediction on Sunday evenings, as an act of reparation to the Sacred Heart for the wrongs of war, and as a means of uniting ourselves with our enemies in that Sacrament that knows no frontiers. But as yet I had not spoken publicly on the evil of war except in my sermons at St. Hilary.

About this time I was visited by two young friends who invited me to become a member of a peace society, The Fellowship of Reconciliation. There was so much in their outlook with which I was in agreement that I joined this Society in the spring of 1917 and found myself launched on a campaign of peace which went on continuously to the end of the war. Looking back over the scanty records that I kept of those years, I find that I was engaged almost daily in writing articles and letters to the press, and attending meetings in London, Liverpool and Bristol and in the towns and many of the villages of Cornwall.

The message that I had to deliver was the one I had been charged to preach on the day of my Ordination. I could not regard that commission as having come to an end because the world was at war. It was still a message of 'Peace and good will'; an affirmation that peace did not depend on the armies in the field; that there was no other way to peace for nations or individuals but the way of Jesus who had met and overcome the forces of evil on the cross, and offered to those, who could receive it, a share in His victory. If that message of peace was ever to be effective among the nations, there must be some to witness to this power at a time when men had ceased to believe in it. To keep silence now was to seal our lips for ever. The world would rightly distrust a message of peace that could not stand the test of war.

It is difficult to reconstruct my mental attitude under conditions that were so shattering to all thought. Who could think clearly or act wisely while this holocaust of young life went on daily? There were times of despair when it seemed to me as if the war had destroyed for ever all powers of reasoning among men. There were times of hope, for which there was as little justification, a hope that a word might be spoken, a word so revealing, that the nations would recognize the truth and lay down their arms.

In the literature of the Holy Grail, there is found mention of 'A Hidden Word'. When that Word is spoken a heavenly peace will descend upon the world, while men gaze at the cup which held the precious blood that flowed from the side of the Saviour. It was for this word I waited - it might be spoken anywhere, here in England, in France or Germany, by a statesman, peasant, priest or child, or even by myself. It was no concern of mine by whom it should be spoken, for it would be so convincing that men would not inquire whence it came. As they listened they would recognize the truth and become free from the tyranny of hate, misunderstanding and lying propaganda to which the nations had surrendered themselves. Such was my state of mind as I went about the country during these sad years.

The first of these meetings was in the old schoolroom beside the church, to which Laura and Harold Knight came, and also a Wesleyan Minister named

Luckman, who spoke of the claims of Christ as paramount, overruling all national loyalties. The room was crowded with a good-natured and rather ribald crowd; among them was a refugee Belgian priest, who constantly interrupted with, 'God is no fool. He knows more about Germans than you,' to which I agreed.

Another meeting which I specially remember, was in the Labour Hall in Penzance. On the way to this meeting we passed by the dock where a ship torpedoed by a German submarine had been brought alongside. At the moment of our passing, the mutilated body of a boy was being carried ashore through a crowd of women who were calling down curses, and shouting threats on the men who had broken the law of the sea in attacking merchant vessels and killing boys. I was shaken at the sight of the mutilated body of the boy and the cries of the women. Was there any answer to such acts as these but further retaliation? Before that evening was ended, I was to find an answer to this question and to see naked hatred that blinded men to truth and justice.

Outside the door of the building, where we were to hold our meeting, were two convivial soldiers, home from France on a week's leave. Their belts were unloosed and their forage caps at the back of their heads as they came up to me and inquired with drunken solemnity, 'What is this b.... meeting about?' When I told them it was a peace meeting, they replied, 'Don't you worry about peace. What we want is more b.... money.' I was to hear that phrase, 'We want more b... money,' many times that evening, for they followed me into the hall and were constantly interrupting the meeting with their demands for 'more b... money'. At times they favoured peace, at others they were inclined to the opinion that war on the whole was a good thing, but they never varied in their demand for more money.

A Quaker lady was speaking from the platform when I heard the tramp of men marching up the narrow street. I knew what that meant. A girl, who was present, had told me she had been at a dance given by the Naval Reserve, when an officer had warned her to keep clear of any meetings in the cause of peace, as they were determined to end such meetings and it would be well for her not to be there. I learned later that it was a friend of mine, an American woman, who had notified this officer of our meeting, and who was now sitting there to see what would happen; so unlike themselves had women become during these years of the war.

The doors were pushed open and the body of men, whose steps I had heard marching up the street, about a hundred and fifty of them, dressed in mufti with an officer at their head, crowded into the room. For over an hour I struggled with this howling mob, while the officer stood by demanding that I would pledge my word never to speak again on the subject of peace. Looking down on this crowded hall, it was difficult to think of those who had lately entered as the kindly men I knew them to be, so changed by hate were all their faces.

I had met angry crowds before, but never had I faced hate as I did that night, a black and sullen hate that was beyond reason or appeal. I could not go on talking, for they would not listen, and if they had listened nothing that I could say would have removed the cloud of misunderstanding that enveloped them. I realized that nothing short of disowning the object of our meeting would have any effect. To close the meeting would mean defeat, which I was not prepared to accept. Yet it would have to come to an end, and inevitably its ending would be a scene of violence, which I looked forward to with loathing. Anger is always revolting. I found it especially so that night, for these men in their hate had for the time ceased to be human. Finally the officer jumped on to the table and called on his men to sing 'God save the King', which was evidently the arranged signal for breaking up the meeting. The women, with the exception of Annie Walke and the Quaker lady, were hustled out of the hall by their friends, while men laid hold of chairs and smashed them against the piano, throwing the broken pieces through the windows into the street. The room was in half-darkness, littered with broken pieces of furniture, empty of all but ourselves and the howling mob who crowded and shouted round us.

'I think we will go,' I said to the Quaker lady.

'If you are going, I will come with you,' she answered, 'but I must find my umbrella.'

How could we find an umbrella in such a room? But the Quaker lady persisted that she could not leave without it. 'I have had it for years,' she said, 'and would not like to lose it in this way.' It was only after the umbrella was found lying broken on the floor that she consented to leave.

On our way out I was cut off from Annie Walke by some men who came up from behind and threw a curtain, that had been torn down, over my head. While I was struggling to free myself from the curtain that enveloped me I received a blow that laid me out. I remember coming to my senses and finding myself supported by one of our soldier friends, while I heard the other, who was standing with his coat off and sleeves rolled up, say, 'If that's your game, I'll take on the whole b... navy.' They were two against fifty or more, who still crowded the room, but they both wore 'wound stripes' and were the British Army, that was enough.

I have no recollection of what happened to the Quaker lady, but I remember seeing Annie Walke, who had fought her way back into the hall, and thinking how splendid she looked standing among the wreckage of that room, speaking to a crowd of men who seemed to be listening with the closest attention. I had no idea what she was saying; I was content to admire her courage and the calm with which she spoke. It seemed no effort to her at the time, but for months later she suffered from the nervous strain of that evening.

We both came out of the hall under the guard of my two soldiers into an excited crowd that no longer regarded me as a pacifist and an enemy, but as 'the poor little Parson from St. Hilary' whom rumour reported to have been killed and thrown into the harbour.

I was in no danger among this crowd, but the two soldiers never let go of my arm until they had placed us in a car - as it happened, the car of the woman who was responsible for the disturbance of our meeting. She was silent, and so were we, as we drove home to St. Hilary.

I went into Penzance the next day to try to discover my friends the soldiers, but they had gone; their leave had expired and they had left for France. The debt of gratitude remained unacknowledged for fifteen years, when one morning a man called on me, looking for work. Seeing that his face was familiar, I asked him where he came from, and he told me that at one time he had lived in Penzance and perhaps I had seen him there. So strange are human relationships that I suddenly saw him as I remembered him in that room, with shirt-sleeves rolled up, offering 'to take on the whole b… navy'.

Shortly after this peace meeting in Penzance, I met a man, George Hodgkin, a member of the Society of Friends, who died a few months later in Mesopotamia on his way to relieve the starving Armenians. Together we decided to go on foot about Cornwall, speaking to those whom we met on seeking peace within themselves and avoiding, in the phraseology of Friends, 'all occasions of war'. Cobblers, basket-makers and men of other trades, whose work gave them time for thought, were among our most attentive listeners.

It was George Hodgkin who suggested that I should get permission from the Home Office to visit the conscientious objectors at Princetown. I came to this place by the little railway from Plymouth, of which Princetown is the terminus. On the journey I thought of those who had travelled by that route in the company of two warders, and wondered what were their thoughts as they stepped out of the train at Princetown and were escorted up the hill to the prison.

Before it became what was termed a 'work centre' for conscientious objectors, this building, originally built to house French prisoners of war, was a prison for long-sentence men who had been convicted by twelve other men of a grave crime against Society. When the war ended and the last of the C.Os. were discharged, the building became once more a convict prison. Some of the men there now are murderers whose sentences have been commuted to penal servitude. Watching them pass with an armed guard on the way to work in the quarries, dressed in grey marked with broad arrows, with shaven heads and resentful looks, you recognize them as criminals, but meeting them in the ordinary ways of life you might look upon them as men like yourselves.

I saw, in the quarries where they had worked, small holes in the rock and boxes set on ledges, and was told that these were places where the convicts kept their pets, a mouse, bird, or in some cases a rat that they had tamed. Men condemned to life sentences will make desperate efforts to keep alive the desire to love and be loved, a quality which alone gives value to the human soul.

I am only aware of having known one murderer. His crime was strangling a woman; but there were extenuating circumstances, of which his youth was one, for his death sentence had been repealed and he was now free after serving twelve years. I had come to the station to meet him and, as I stood on the platform waiting for the train, I tried to picture the kind of man he was likely to be and whether I should know him for a murderer.

I had no difficulty in recognizing him, as he was the only person to leave the train, a slight, delicately made man with quick nervous movements, who dropped his bag on the platform to search for a cigarette.

When I came up and spoke to him, he offered me one of his cigarettes, which I took and lit while I considered what kind of a man this was whom I knew to be a murderer. His eyes were very blue, the eyes of a child who has awakened in the night with the memory of a terrible dream; the hand he offered me had long tapering fingers, very sensitive hands compared with my own, which are big and clumsy. It appeared to me, as I stood on the platform talking to him, that my nature and make-up were far more a murderer's than this man's, and yet, as I looked again at his hands, I knew that they had closed round the young and tender throat of a girl; that those gentle eyes had watched her struggles and seen them cease and had looked on her blackened lips and protruding eyes, the work of those sensitive hands.

During the short time in which I knew him, he was always anxious to tell me the history of his crime and what his life had been since that night when he crept out of the bedroom of the girl whom he had murdered, not daring to look back. I would have given much to have heard the story, and to have known his experience as he sat in the condemned cell with two warders forever watching him. That story has been told many times in literature, but to hear it from the lips of the man who had endured it offered a strange fascination. I would like to have known what he felt when he saw the judge adjusting his black cap, and still more of his thoughts as he sat day after day in the condemned cell, or when, at exercise, his fellow-prisoners hid themselves as they heard the warders call, 'All away. All away.' But he had not yet made his peace with God, and it would not be well to hear his story before he had told it to a priest in the confessional. On my saying to him at our first meeting, 'What you have now to do is to try and find God and your own soul,' he answered:

'No man would ever find God or his soul in the place that I have come from.'

I do not know whether it was at Dartmoor that he had served his sentence, but no words could more completely express what I experienced on my first visit to Princetown.

It is not the stone walls of the prison so much as the moor itself that is terrifying. The moors of Cornwall are storm-swept and lonely; there are cromlechs, stone circles and cave-dwellings; but on every hill and headland are ruined cells and chapels of early saints who lived in this wild land, and by their lives and their prayers sanctified its streams and moorlands. On Dartmoor there are places where men worshipped gods as savage and cruel as the rocks around them, but no shrines to the God who came as a little child.

I spent a week in this place with the Conscientious Objectors. Never have I been so cold as on those early mornings in February, when I would get up before it was light, and wait outside the prison for the gates to open at 6, that I might hear confessions and say Mass at a time when it was possible for the men to attend. I had brought vestments with me and all the things that are necessary for the devout offering of the Holy Sacrifice, and, being unable to obtain permission for the use of the Church of England chapel, I set up an altar in the meeting-house of the Wesleyans, where I said my Mass: this was attended each morning by a few young men who had been brought up in the Catholic Faith and a number of Quakers who sat silently at the back of the building.

The Mass I remember best was the one I said on the last morning, for the repose of the souls of those whose bodies had been carried out beneath that grim gateway and laid in the desolate corner in the churchyard where convicts are buried. Only once, I was told by a man who had lived many years at Princetown, had a mourner followed a convict to the grave. He alone of all those for whom I said Mass that morning had a friend, a loved one from the world of the living, to follow him to his grave; those others were carried out beneath that gateway by four fellow-convicts, men as nameless as himself. Strange thoughts must pass though the minds of the four men chosen for this sad office at hearing one whom they had known as a number like themselves referred to as 'our dear brother' here departed.

At the time of my visit, I addressed a meeting of the colony of six hundred men. Was there ever gathered together so strange a collection of individuals? - quiet Quakers who sat unmoved while men stood up and shouted round them, wild-looking men from the Clyde and Rhondda Valley whose hopes for the regeneration of society lay in a class war, strange melancholy men whose message was the immediate coming of the Messiah and the end of the world, men of all trades and professions, mathematicians, scholars, musicians, actors, miners and farm labourers, with nothing to unite them but a refusal to bear arms in the present war.

I was distressed and dismayed by the clash and conflict of theories and personalities with which I was confronted. Some brandished Bibles, accusing me of not knowing the Word of God as revealed in the Book of Daniel, others with red flags proclaimed me as a traitor for not accepting class war and the dictatorship of the proletariat.

I had come, expecting to find, in this assembly of youth, some hope for the future, but failed to discover among these men who talked ceaselessly, waving flags and Bibles, the kind of material out of which a new world might be constructed.

There were other men whom I did not know at the time, in Wandsworth, Winchester and other prisons, sitting in their cells with a quiet determination to evade no way of hardship that was open to them. It is such as they, who in their willingness to accept without reserve the claims of conscience, have helped and will continue to help men to attain the vision of a world from which war has been banished.

10 THE CHURCH

Thirty years ago on a visit to Rome, walking in the Forum in the midst of broken pillars and fallen masonry, I saw a little pagan altar. There were many others of the same kind, but this one stood alone; it was not much more than a block of stone with flutings, but that block by some miracle had obtained perfection. I intended at the time to return and obtain its exact proportions, but I left Rome shortly afterwards and those measurements were never taken. Possibly it was as well, for something would have been missing and its beauty never achieved again.

I had that altar in my mind when I went to the granite quarries above Newlyn, soon after coming to St. Hilary to select a slab of granite as a stone for the High Altar.

The Cornishman excels in handling stone and dealing with water. He understands their nature and how best they may serve his purpose. He has worked with water during centuries of tin-washing, and leads it where it can be of service as a mother takes a child by the hand. He treats stone with the same quiet understanding of its nature. There is no hurry or violence about the man who handles granite. The block of stone I saw at the quarries, weighing over two tons, arrived at the church one morning on a trolley. On hearing of its weight I suggested that it might be well to erect a derrick for lifting it into position, but the old man in charge said, 'We don't want any contrivance for a job this kind. We can shift it better ourselves.' Within an hour four men had lifted this great stone into position with no appliances except some blocks of wood and two ash poles.

It was no idle boast when, on seeing this stone on its bed of cement, I remarked, 'Nothing but dynamite will ever move that stone.' Stark and bare, enclosing the relics of S. Rosa of Lima, 'the fair flower of the new world', it withstood the ruling of the Consistory Court twenty years later.

In the sixteenth century every parish in England was visited by bands of men who, without reverence for religion or beauty, sought in their zeal to destroy all that was reminiscent of the Catholic Faith. Glass of unrivalled beauty was smashed into fragments, carvings were defaced, altars thrown down and images destroyed. There is no record of how at St. Hilary the work of spoliation took place then, whether the villagers themselves took part or whether it was the work of religious fanatics who roamed the country. Whoever was responsible, the spoliation was complete. Altars, images, carvings, relics and chalices were all stolen or destroyed. Nothing was left but bare walls. These were destroyed in the fire eighty years ago and only the lovely tower and spire remain of the church that was built by the monks from St. Michael's Mount.

Tradition has it that the tower and spire were designed by a Frenchman and executed by local workmen. It pleases me to think that it was so, that at the time of its building there happened to be an artist at the Mount, that the monks commissioned him to design the tower and spire, and that he in his turn was content to use the material and workmen nearest to hand. It pleases me, for I have followed the same method in restoring some of the beauty that was lost. Nothing has been bought at a church shop; the six altars were built by the local stone-mason; the painting and decorations are the work of artists who happened to be living in the neighbourhood at the time, some of whom have become famous.

The first of these decorations was a series of paintings on the front of the choir-stalls, descriptive of the lives of Cornish saints, the collective work of Ernest Procter, Dod Procter, Annie Walke, Harold Harvey, Norman Garstin, Harold Knight, Alethea Garstin and Gladys Hynes.

Some of these legends tell of the love of the saints for the creatures; how St. Endelienta, an anchorite, died of grief when her cow was killed by a local tyrant and how as she lay a-dying she prayed that her body might be drawn to its burial by six young calves, going whithersoever they would; how St. Piran took as his first disciples a badger, a bear and a fox; how St. Neot impounded the crows at the time of Mass, and St. Petroc saved the fawn from the hounds; and how St. Kevin, when the birds built their nest in his hands, remained in the attitude of prayer until the young birds were fledged. Others are concerned with miracles and conversions and narrate how St. Pol de Leon prayed and a row of pebbles grew into rocks and saved the fertile lands of Gulval from the sea; and how St. Fingar, after having killed a stag, knelt at a forest pool to wash his hands and, seeing himself reflected in the still water, dedicated his beauty to the service of God. These and other strange old stories are whimsical memories of men and women, who in those dim pagan days landed on our shores.

The two chapels on either side of the High Altar were crowded up with an organ on one side, and benches that were never used, on the other. After removing the organ and clearing away the benches I provided two chapels, one of Our Lady and the other of the Sacred Heart. The Altar-piece in the Chapel of Our Lady, the work of Ernest Procter, is a picture of the Visitation painted on a gold background and let into a stone reredos, cunningly built as if to represent the home of the Visitation. In the Chapel of the Sacred Heart the Altar-piece is a picture attributed by Roger Fry to Quentin Matsys, the Flemish painter of the fifteenth century; I know nothing of its history beyond that it was bought by my grandfather in Florence a hundred years ago. It is now set, surrounded by the Emblems of the Passion, in a stone reredos of granite representing, with battlements and towers, the City of God. Angels' faces, carved in stone, look out from the windows of a city so beautiful that the people of St. Hilary, when they see it, must long to enter.

There is another work by Ernest Procter in the church, a picture of the Deposition from the Cross, above the Altar of the Holy Souls. In later ages he will be remembered as the artist from Newlyn who helped to beautify the church, as a Frenchman from the Mount designed the spire.

In the two side aisles are altar-pieces representing St. Joan and St. Francis, painted by Annie Walke and Roger Fry respectively. I have had a love for the Blessed Maid since, many years ago, I read the records of her trial. To read those records of how, for weeks, she stood alone and kept at bay the most astute lawyers of her time, is to be confronted with something more than a country girl of a homely and ready wit. Jeanne d'Arc was a peasant girl who never lost the simplicity of her upbringing, but added to this she had a swift perception and spiritual insight into the issues involved that is astonishing in one so simple and unlettered. Her weakness in the presence of the fire, when her courage failed and she recanted, her loneliness and despair when she was led back to prison, followed by her determination to endure the flames, go to make up a character that is unsurpassed in its appeal to our affections.

It was thought at the time, by some who knew my attitude towards the war, that I was ill-advised to erect an altar to a saint who was hailed by France as the patron of her armies. If she were so regarded it was no concern of mine, for it was not for her military exploits but for her faith and her steadfast witness to the supremacy of the individual conscience that she was raised to the altars of the Church. She was asked to deny her visions and renounce her mission by an authority that she longed to obey, but against that authority stood her own conscience and for this she was willing to suffer martyrdom.

The painting above the Altar of St. Francis owes its existence to a lunch I had with Roger Fry at a restaurant in Bloomsbury. Roger Fry, whom I then met for the first time, talked brilliantly on art and its relation to religion, especially the Catholic religion, of which he expressed his intense dislike. Waiters stood round waiting for us to finish our lunch and go, but Roger Fry went on talking about the Catholic Faith. When we did rise from the table he placed a hand on my shoulder and said, 'I would like to paint a picture of St. Francis for your church.' And so the picture was painted and set above the altar of the saint.

Much within the church is modern, but not everything; the richness and variety of a medieval church, the result of the mingling of different ages and styles, would be lacking if that were so. There are two images; one an early French Gothic St. Anne, the other a flamboyant figure of St. Joseph, the work of a Spanish artist of the seventeenth century. This is the story of how they came to be in St. Hilary Church. When in London, I often visited a shop in St. John's Wood that sold antiques and works of art. The owner, Leon Richton, a Frenchman, loved his treasures and welcomed any one to his shop who appreciated them. Going there one day I saw this image of St. Joseph.

'Some good Spanish work that I bought in Paris,' Leon Richton said.

'What price are you asking for it?' I answered.

'I will sell it for a hundred guineas,' he replied.

A hundred guineas! There was no possibility of my raising such a sum, but I took to going to visit that image whenever I was in London. The old man recognized the reasons for my coming but nothing was ever said. He welcomed me and showed me his latest treasures but neither of us ever referred to the image. I would say goodbye, give a last look at St. Joseph, wondering if he would still be there when I came again, and go out of the shop without a word having been spoken of my visit. And so things went on until after the second broadcast of my Christmas Play, when I was able to set aside the fee paid me for production. I was in London again shortly after this and went to the shop in St. John's Wood.

'Now,' I said, 'what is the very lowest that you can afford to let me have St. Joseph for?'

'What have you got?' the old man answered.

I told him.

'You are not a very rich man, Mr. Walke,' he said

sadly, as if sorry for my poverty, 'but you want St. Joseph. I have seen you look at him whenever you have called to see me. I think you must have him although what you offer is scarcely what I paid for him. But still,' he continued, 'I would like him to be in a church again.'

This is how St. Joseph came to St. Hilary....

The purchase of St. Anne was accomplished more swiftly. Again I had some broadcasting fees to dispose of, and happening to be in London I went, in the company of Ernest Procter, to the shop where I had bought the image of St. Joseph. The old man, on being introduced to Ernest, told us how he had sold some pieces of Egyptian sculpture to Epstein.

'His Rima,' he said, 'I do not understand, but he is a clever man and pays good prices.'

While he was talking we were engaged in looking at a much-worn Gothic image of St. Anne. 'If you don't buy her, I shall,' Ernest whispered to me.

I had no doubt that she was destined for St. Hilary; and arranging a price I took her away with me in a taxi. They both now stand in the Chapel of 'The Sacred Heart'. I am very fond of these two figures; St. Anne is so calm that to look at her is to find peace, while St. Joseph is gay with all the gallantry of Spain, as he stands there proudly with the Holy Child in his arms.

Near the Altar of the Dead is an inscribed stone that reads (supplying the smaller letters), IMPeratore CAESare FLAVIO VALerio CONSTANTINO PIO CAESare NOBilissimo DiVI CONSTANTIi PII AUGusti FiLIO.

This proud stone was erected by Roman soldiers somewhere within the bounds of the parish between the years 304 and 306, in honour of 'The most noble and divine Caesar'. When the Roman legions were withdrawn a century later, the stone that must have made so great a stir among the people of St. Hilary was forgotten until the fourteenth century, when the builders of the church, discovering a handy stone, built it into the foundations. There it lay until the church was burnt down, when it was discovered again and set up in the same building, dedicated to the saint who was exiled, at the time of the Arian controversy, by the son of this most noble and pious Caesar.

Along the pathway to the south door are other links with the past, the Noti Noti stone, probably of the seventh century, two Celtic crosses and a thirteenth century priest's tomb. Within the church are a holy water stoup, at one time a font, a rose chalice, a doorway and some stonework of the fourteenth-century church.

Years ago, when Joan Manning-Sanders was a child of nine, she brought out for our inspection her drawings of events in the Old Testament, the whole of which she proposed to illustrate. She had begun when she was four years old with Adam and Eve sitting in the Garden of Eden and was now engaged on David dancing before the Ark.

It was the sense of design in this last picture that led Annie Walke to say, 'You must be a painter, Joan.'

'Oh, no! I am going to be a writer,' she answered. (Her mother and father are both writers.)

'If you will be a painter I will give you your first commission,' I added. 'You shall paint some pictures of the childhood of Jesus for St. Hilary. From that day she became a painter; the pictures she painted for the parclose screen of the Lady Chapel are the quintessence of childhood. Only a child could conceive the Annunciation as in the first picture of the series, where the Angel Gabriel bears the Holy Child to Our Lady in a bird's nest, while lambs and heraldic lions rejoice at His coming. The same spirit pervades them all. When the angel comes to the shepherds, on the night of the Nativity, the boy is asleep and only one old shepherd is awake to listen. In the flight into Egypt, the little ass trips merrily along, carrying Our Lady and the Child, while rabbits peer from their holes and St. Joseph strides manfully behind. Like the poems in Blake's *Songs of Innocence*, the world of these pictures is the world of a child, a flowered path with no suggestion of evil.

Once in Rome, at the Church of the Ara Caeli, where at Christmas the Holy Manger is exposed for veneration and whence the Christ child blesses the Eternal City, I watched children at play flying coloured balloons before an altar where Mass was being said. Talking to one of the priests later I remarked on the children. 'Where may they play if not in their Father's house?' was the answer the old priest gave me. Now at St. Hilary the doors of the church are always open, children run in and out; it is a place where children play as well as say their prayers.

Christmas is a great feast at St. Hilary and the Mass on Christmas night is the service that is most loved by its people. How I have enjoyed decorating the church for this festival! Sometimes I made avenues to the altars with fir trees emblazoned with gold and silver fir-cones and lit with many candles. Round the crib, a shed thatched with straw, I made a forest of fir trees towering above the roof that was to shelter the Holy Child.

Tom Rowe has always built the crib. Each year he comes to tell me that he has built it differently from last year. ''Tis a handsome one this year,' he says, 'on a new pattern'; although I myself can see no change. So associated is he with building the crib, that if a stranger were to ask, 'Who is Tom Rowe and what does he do for a living?' I believe that the answer would be, 'We do all know Tom Rowe down to Relubbus Lane. He's a carpenter by trade, but what he does I can't exactly say, except that he do build the crib at Christmas-time.'

When I grew tired of fir trees I used bay, of which the garden is full. With golden oranges hanging from every twig, lit with candles, the church is transformed into the garden of the Hesperides. But the most beautiful of all Christmas decorations are the ash trees. Each autumn I cut down a supply of wood for our winter store, and as the trees are felled I set apart the straight boughs, and at Christmas I plant them in tubs, as I do the fir and the bay. These bare trees, the tallest, reaching to the roof, I hang with gold and silver balls; on Christmas night the light of candles without number are reflected a thousand times from each shining ball. The lightness and the splendour of the bare trees laced with spangles and decked with the gold and silver balls make a fit setting for the wonder about to be accomplished at the Midnight Mass. This Mass has a peculiar quality of childish gaiety due to the hour and the season. However tired I may be after long hours spent in the confessional, by the time the bells start to ring, about half-past eleven, all weariness has left me in the expectation of singing Mass.

Bells are a great feature in village life in England. In other countries there are chiming bells and bells that are beaten with a hammer, but in England round and change ringing has become an art which tests the skill and endurance of the ringers. Before the days of cricket or football there were bands of ringers and ringing contests with neighbouring villages. The ringers were often a godless crowd. In many parishes, now familiar to me, it was the custom for a company of ringers to carry a bundle of straw and a barrel of beer to the ringing tower on Christmas Eve. Here they spent the night. Some would sleep, while others would ring; after a time those asleep would awake and drink and ring again. Often there were prolonged quarrels between the parson and the ringers, each claiming the control of the tower. Legally the custody of the tower is vested in the parson, but in some parishes custom was too strong and the ringers remained in possession.

Apart from quarrels which are inseparable from village life, when a ringer will 'jack it up', put on his coat and walk out of the belfry muttering that 'never again will he ring with that party', there has always been good comradeship in the belfry and the ringers are men for whom I have great affection.

On one winter's night during the war I was sitting reading over the fire, when some unreasoned instinct, which I have never been able to explain, led me to lay down my book and rush across to the belfry. I had no idea why I was going there. I only knew that I was wanted and that I must go quickly. Some girls were being instructed in ringing, but I was not aware of this at the time. Pushing open the belfry door I saw that a ringer had let go her rope when the bell was at the top of its swing, and that the rope had curled itself round the neck of the girl behind her. I saw her lifted off the ground, and sprang at the rope. I too was lifted off my feet by the swing of the bell, but I had slackened the rope round her neck, and at the same moment two ringers, who were standing by, clasped the girl and myself in their arms. As we lifted down what appeared to be a lifeless body we saw, by the light of the lantern, a black mark round her neck from ear to ear, where the rope had caught her. While she lay unconscious on the floor, I went through all the horrors of telling her mother and leaving St. Hilary, which this tragedy had made intolerable. However, after we had carried her to the house and given her restoratives, the girl recovered; but she still wears round her neck the mark of the bell-rope.

To return to Christmas. When, at half-past eleven on Christmas night, the ringers start the bells, the people, many of whom have come long distances, begin to arrive at the church; there they sit and listen to the bells or walk round the church and light candles before the crib, where, after Mass, the Baby is to be brought from the altar and laid in the straw. A few minutes after midnight, ringers stand by the bells waiting for the priest at the altar to intone the words 'Gloria in Excelsis Deo'. As the message of the Angel 'Peace to men of goodwill' comes from the altar, each bell in turn rings out above the voices of the choir and the sound of the organ. There is a wild discord as the bells, coming down, ring faster and faster, and then a silence; and the priest turns from the altar and says *Dominus Vobiscum*.

Such are the beginnings of Christmas at St. Hilary. On other feasts the church is as beautiful; Easter has swaying baskets of daffodils hanging from the roof and boughs of beech trees with tender leaves as a canopy above every shrine; on the Feast of Pentecost the church is red and gold with rhododendrons and boughs of the laburnum with its trailing blooms; for Corpus Christi, the floor is strewn with box and rose-petals and children throw flowers and wave tall lilies, as the Blessed Sacrament is carried by. I love each of these, but it is the Christmas Festival I associate most closely with St. Hilary.

11 MY MOTHER

At the beginning of 1918, the last year of the war, I received a telegram from Jessie Hartley, who had been engaged to be married to my brother Bill before he was killed in a motor accident. Jessie, who was now living with my mother in a cottage near our old home at Redlynch, had wired to say that she was very ill. My mother was a very wonderful woman. She was now eighty-three, and yet, a few weeks before when I was visiting her, she had walked with me several miles each afternoon visiting old friends in the village.

I had received a letter from her that morning, for it was her custom to write to me every day; and now, before I had finished reading her letter, this telegram had arrived saying 'Mother dangerously ill'. I started at once to see her and, after a long cross-country journey, arrived that evening at Downton, our old station, where I was met by Hopkins and his pony-cart. I had known Hopkins from my cradle. My earliest memories are associated with his white pony, his farm and the little house where the front door-step was always spotless; so white was this stone that as children, when we entered by that door, we were careful to stand on the red bricks at the side in order not to leave marks of our feet on the white stone. In the front room, to which we were invited on Sundays, there were painted ostrich eggs on the mantelpiece, a picture of 'Rent Day' and a coloured engraving of the Crucifixion with forked lightning playing round the three crosses and people flying in all directions, a picture that always intrigued us. But it was the kitchen with which we were most familiar. As boys we would often go there at night when we were thought to be in bed, and sit and drink cider and listen to the talk of Hopkins and the neighbours who happened to call. Mrs. Hopkins had three brothers, all bachelors, who lived across the road and made birch and heather brooms; 'Broom Squires' they called themselves. Mark, the eldest, whom I remember for his side-whiskers, went to church on Sunday mornings and did the housework for his two brothers who went to fairs and sold horses as well as brooms. Mrs. Hopkins did not approve of these two; they were wild, she said, and went too often to the 'Foresters' Arms'. But they delighted us with stories of the fairs they had attended, and we always enjoyed the evenings when they were present. Sometimes my father would call at the front door and inquire of Mrs. Hopkins, 'Are my boys here, Harriet?' and she, having seen us disappearing out of the back door, would answer, 'No, sir.'

Hopkins, who was a great favourite with us, was a tall man with crooked legs and very long arms, which he waved when he walked, and a habit of saying,'You are right, sir.' Any remark that we happened to make met with the same response, but said with such conviction that we never doubted his judgment. When we were small it was Hopkins who drove us with his white pony to children's parties. I remember how the bottom of the cart had a layer of straw to keep our feet warm and how on the way home we would often lie in this straw and go to sleep. One winter when the roads were ice-bound, he walked with us to several of these parties, carrying my youngest brother a good part of the way on his shoulders. When it was time to return home and other children were escorted by nursemaids, we were very proud at having Hopkins waiting for us in the kitchen.

Now after thirty years, when I got out of the train at Downton, he was waiting for me in the station yard with a white pony and cart.

'I see that you have another white pony, Hopkins,' I said.

'You are right, sir,' he answered.

It was another white pony that stood in the shafts but the illusion that I had gone back to the days of my childhood was complete when I recognized the twisted step and knew that it was the same cart in which we had ridden as children. After looking at the new pony we drove away together with the horse-rug that had always smelt of stable over our knees. When we came to the hill outside the station yard Hopkins said, 'Now you sit where you are' - a privilege of those arriving by train - while he got down and, with the whip and reins in his hands, walked by the side of the cart. Nothing was changed - Hopkins, the cart, the smell of the horse-rug, were the same as I remembered them as a child.

I had visited our old home several times since our leaving, but my return that night had a significance that was absent from any of the other visits. The telegram had told me that my mother was very ill, and although Hopkins and I talked of the people whom I had known as a boy, many of whom were dead, and all that had happened in the village since those days, not a word was said about my mother. Hopkins was silent and I did not like to inquire for fear of what I might hear. She was the last link with my boyhood and the knowledge that she was dangerously ill endowed the country-side with memories that I had long forgotten.

The one lamp, with a smoked glass on the off side of the cart, showed little of the road on which we were travelling. But I had no need of a lamp to see the country-side; the woods, the fields and orchards were all familiar and lit up within me recollections of the past - the discovery beneath the roots of a beech tree of the cold round ball of a sleeping dormouse that came to life in the warmth of an inner pocket, the joy of standing in running water and building a dam to divert the stream, the taste of certain apples, quarrendens they were called, that grew in one of the orchards we passed. It was as if all the small happenings of my childhood along that road were present with me. I was sitting by the side of Hopkins, who, in the darkness, had grown very large as I had known him as a child, the man who took us on his back, waved long arms and said, 'You're right, sir.' These and many other things came to me on that two-and-a-half-mile drive with the unexpectedness and bewilderment with which a child meets each new experience.

As we drove up the lane to the cottage where my mother lived, I could see Jessie standing in the open doorway waiting my coming. I called and asked her how my mother was.

'No worse,' she answered, 'but she is still unconscious and knows nothing of your coming.'

I went straight to her room, which was as I remembered it - crowded with photographs and small ornaments that she had kept for no other reason than that they had at one time belonged to myself or one of my brothers. Many of the things in that room were familiar to me from childhood, most of all a pair of china elephants which she had treasured since we had given them to her as children, little knowing that we had stolen them from a cheap-jack named Jimmy Long, who set up a stall in the village each Christmas. The room was lit by two candles that left my mother in shadow. That I might see her better I knelt by the bedside where my face was close to hers. She lay as I had often seen her, with her right hand beneath her face, a face so pale that, with her silver hair, of which she was very proud, it made little more than an outline on the white pillow. She lay so quiet that I would not break the silence by any attempt to make my presence known; Jessie had told me that she was unconscious and that I must not expect any recognition. I was content to kneel there and watch the face that lay on the pillow and the worn hand with the thin wedding-ring at rest upon the counterpane.

How long I remained there I do not know, for time ceases to be a reality at such moments. When I left I bent forward and kissed her. My lips scarcely touched her forehead; but that touch brought her back to consciousness and awakened all the love that she had for me. I heard her whisper my name as if to assure herself that I was really there, and then, raising herself on her pillow, she clasped me in her arms and kissed my face. Nothing was said as she held me close to herself, beyond the repeated calling of my name in every tone of endearment. Stirred by the familiar scenes of that drive along the road with Hopkins, I had gone back and lived again the days of my childhood; but my kiss had awakened in her deeper and more tender memories than mine. It seemed, as she held me in her arms, that all the love that she had for me was enclosed in that kiss. I was the eldest of my three brothers, and it was as if she had gone back to that day in June when she heard the cry of a baby and the nurse laid me in her arms - so great a welcome was there in the kiss she gave me as I knelt by her bed. It was also a kiss of farewell, for never again was she fully conscious of my presence.

Without any sign of emotion she patted my cheek and said, as I had often heard her say in the days of my childhood, 'Now go and have some supper and come and see me again.' When I left the room she was lying as when I entered, with her hand beneath her face on the pillow. I was often to see her again, and there were times when she would know me as one she had loved in the past, but never again was she to take me into her arms as she did that night. The brain that had thought and planned for us for so long had given way under the strain of this illness; and the desolation, more terrifying than death, of a spirit enclosed in a body that will no longer respond to its need, had overtaken her. I knew my mother that night as I was never to know her again.

12 BRETHREN OF THE COMMON TABLE

Travelling in Spain many years ago I was beset with beggars who pursued me with extended hands, asking alms for the love of Jesus. To be asked to give 'for the love of Jesus' is an appeal that it is impossible to disregard. I was told later by a man who had lived many years in Spain that the customary answer is, 'For the love of Jesus pray forgive me, brother.' I used the phrase shamefacedly a few times but always with complete success. On one of these occasions Charles Marriott and I came to the monastery of La Cartuja, near Burgos, where a number of beggars were lying under the shade of the monastery wall, waiting for the doors to open. On our approach one of them got up and made the accustomed appeal; on being met with the response, 'For the love of Jesus pray forgive me, brother,' he beckoned us to join his friends in the shade and informed us that there was no chance of any food until four o'clock.

In Spain, where begging is an honourable profession, men can ask for money and be refused in the love of Jesus. Among us, to ask for a loan or gift of money more often than not will result in the ending of a friendship. We all know the joy of sharing food or drink with our friends; but any form of giving which involves money, like the tip to the waiter, must be accomplished in secret, a deed of which both parties are ashamed and which conveys nothing beyond its value in cash. Who has not experienced the difficulty and shamefulness of such acts of giving? And yet money in itself is not evil. It should be possible to give money with the same grace as you give a bunch of flowers.

I was once walking with a little girl in a country lane when we met an Indian on the road, selling shawls and silk scarves. The little girl, who was fascinated by the sight of an Indian with a turban, caught me by the hand and insisted on our speaking to him. Rather hesitatingly I turned back and found him sitting by the roadside about to have his dinner. He made a gesture when he saw us coming as if he would open his pack, but having only sixpence in my pocket I shook my head and turned to go away; thinking, however, that I should not have disturbed him for nothing, I returned and asked him to accept my sixpence. Bowing very gravely, first to the little girl and then to me, he opened his pack and, spreading his scarves and shawls on the grass by his side, he replied, 'If the lady will accept some small gift from me.' For a moment I contemplated a refusal, but fortunately the little girl saved me from so discourteous an act by exclaiming, 'I would love to have one of your beautiful scarves.'

We selected one that appeared to be the least expensive, but it must have cost considerably more than my sixpence; and yet, by the look on his face as he presented it to the little girl, I do not think that he was a loser by the transaction.

Before I had left home on the visit to my mother which I described in the last chapter, my mind had been greatly occupied with this subject of giving, and whether it might not be possible to find a way in which men could escape from the secrecy and fear on which our social life was built. As pacifists we had rejected war as altogether evil and yet we were content to live in a society which was built largely on fear and distrust of our neighbour.

At the moment of His farewell, when the Son of God was to leave the friends that He had gathered round Him, He had set up a Common Table where men might meet, and in sharing His gifts of bread and wine, find Him present with them. For those who share in the gift of the 'Corpus Domini - the body of God', there must be a way, I thought, in which they could share more completely in the daily things of life.

I had the Spanish beggar in my mind and his 'Give me alms for the love of Jesus' when I invited a number of people to stay with us at St. Hilary, so that together we might try and discover how, whilst living under ordinary conditions of society, we might escape one of its worst evils.

Those who came in answer to my invitation were mostly strangers. There were priests, Presbyterians, Nonconformist ministers, workers from the Clyde, people from our own village, and a man who walked from London begging his way and sleeping in casual wards. This last had grown a beard on the way and appeared, wrapped in a plaid shawl into which he had inserted a vast pocket where he carried turnips, potatoes and any broken food that was given him. I was ringing the bell for Compline when this stranger entered the church. A queer figure I thought him. He told us, that night at supper, a story about his shawl; how on going through Winchester, after having been turned out of the Cathedral by the verger for eating his dinner there, he had entered a little Roman Catholic church where he had seen a picture of a horseman giving part of his cloak to a naked beggar. So interested was he in this picture that he rang the bell of the presbytery and asked to see the priest, who told him the story of St. Martin, how on the night that he had given the half of his cloak to a beggar his Saviour, wearing the half-cloak, had appeared to him and greeted him with the words, 'See what Martin has given me.' The Catholic priest gave our bearded friend a card with the picture of St. Martin, and a prayer for his patronage; which he in his turn promised to say every morning on his journey to St. Hilary.

That morning on the road between Winchester and Lyndhurst he was overtaken by two tramps who asked him for money; on being told that he had none, the woman, who was carrying a baby, offered him sixpence for his shawl to wrap the baby in. He had no wish to sell the shawl. Of his few possessions, it was the thing he most valued, since it was all he had to keep himself warm when he was compelled to sleep out of doors. But the woman insistent. 'Will you let the dear little baby die of cold?' she asked him, and raised the price from sixpence to a shilling. It appeared to him that the baby was more likely to die of suffocation than cold, but there was the picture he carried in his pocket and the prayer he had promised to say daily that he might follow the example of St. Martin. It looked very much as if he would have to part with that shawl. On the other hand, St. Martin's beggar was naked and this baby seemed well provided for. But what finally decided him was not whether he or the baby stood more in need, but the thought of his own particular St. Martin story ending with the words, 'See what George has sold me for a shilling.'

Some of those guests we lodged at a house which at one time was 'The Jolly Tinners' Inn, which I acquired later as a home for my London children. Each day was planned on the lines of a religious retreat, with times of prayer, household work and silence. After supper we met to formulate an outline for the contemplated order. We were a queer company with little in common beyond a feeling of dissatisfaction with our social system. A young Socialist, whom I can only remember as Ernest, had lately been reading some new philosophy based on Karl Marx which he was anxious to explain to us. During times of silence or in the midst of washing-up the breakfast things, he might be heard arguing with Bill Paton, a Presbyterian minister. 'I take it,' Bill would say in a crisp cultured voice with a slight Scottish accent, 'that there are three main systems of philosophy.'

'I take nothing of the kind,' Ernest would answer. 'Marx lays it down that our industrial system….'

It was not only Ernest's Marxianism and Bill Paton's systems of philosophy that caused trouble. There were others who were impatient and intolerant and one who left and found a home for a time with the monks at Buckfast. It seemed hopeless - we had not learnt even to tolerate each other and our different systems - until we decided to spend a whole day together in prayer before the Blessed Sacrament. So wonderful was the power of this silence that after a day spent in the church we met that evening as men and women who were more than friends, since we could now speak to each other with the certainty of being understood. The fear that prompts men to set up barriers and to hide themselves and their affairs from their fellows had gone.

I have a vivid recollection of that moment. I can recall where we were all sitting in the dining-room, and the look of exaltation on the faces of those round the table as we drew up a simple rule embodying our experience. To any one who was not there, what happened that evening must appear a matter of little importance, but it seemed to us that we had made a great discovery. We had learnt how in the love of Jesus a way could be found for men and women differing as completely as ourselves, to speak the truth to one another without fear or embarrassment.

We realized at the time that if we were to set up other Chapters, as we planned, there would be many who would find in so much simplicity an opportunity to exercise their talent for living on others. But would not complete disarmament provide sufficient protection? Even if it were not so, was it not in the acceptance of misunderstanding and evil treatment that St. Francis found an answer to his question. 'Wherein is perfect joy to be found?' Such was our state of mind when we separated that night after having made plans for the setting up of Chapters of 'The Brethren of the Common Table' wherever it was possible.

The failure of an adventure which started with such high hopes is a sad story. Chapters were started in London, not without benefit, I think, to those who shared in them. Some continued for a short time; others for longer; but none have survived. All that is left is a memory, which I still cherish, of that night at St. Hilary.

If I had been a person other than I am, or even if at this time I had not been immersed in so many troubles in connexion with the church and its services, together with the daily expectation of being arrested on account of my peace activities, I might have been successful in preserving this venture. As I write, after years of disappointment and failure in many affairs I have undertaken, the way of the 'Brethren of the Common Table' still seems to offer a solution for some of the difficulties of our modern society.

The Bishop was pressing me to abandon certain services and had held a public visitation in the church, a few months before, at which he had condemned many of the Catholic practices at St. Hilary. Father Wason had been deprived of his living by a Court which he rightly held to have no spiritual authority, and considering himself to be the lawful parish priest, was resisting all attempts to turn him out of his vicarage. The living had been declared vacant, but the Bishop was unwilling to proceed further since an action for contempt of Court would involve an indefinite term of imprisonment. But the farmers around Cury were of a different mind. His living had been declared vacant, and if the Bishop would not proceed against him for contempt of Court they would deal with him themselves. 'We'll have 'en out,' they said, 'like as we draw a badger.'

I had long been anxious as to what might happen to my old friend who, living in a world of his own creation, had transformed his quiet vicarage house into a castle, where he and his few followers were beleaguered in defence of the rights of the church. This continued throughout the summer, the garrison consisting of Father Wason, his cousin Geoffrey Biddulph, Ralph Nelson his gardener, Ralph's wife Emma and their little girl Stella.

Knowing the cunning and ferocity that Cornish people can show when their religious passions are aroused, I was daily expecting to hear of an attack on the Vicarage, but when it came it was none the less of a surprise to me. We were entertaining some people at lunch one day when Jan Gordon, a friend of Annie Walke's student days, who was sitting opposite the window, remarked, 'There seems to be a car-load of people coming to visit you.'

Looking out I saw Father Wason climbing out of the car. 'He came into the room dressed in his cassock and biretta, followed by his housekeeper Emma, who carried a roll of toilet-paper which she waved in the air as she shouted excitedly, 'The brutes have thrown us out and we have nowhere to go to but St. Hilary.' Why out of all the wreckage she should have chosen to save a roll of toilet-paper, I do not know.

Father Wason, with a face ashen white, walked slowly towards the mantelpiece and pointing to some candlesticks which had been placed there since his last visit, said, 'You must have yellow candles there, Ber.' When I said, 'Come and sit down, Wason, and tell us what has happened,' he answered, 'I have the Holy Oils and must go to the church and place them in the aumbry.' It was at this moment that I saw him first as the White Knight adjusting his helmet after he had fallen from his horse.

As he left, carrying the Holy Oils, the rest of the party entered the room. Stella, Ralph, the bull terrier, who had been sick in the taxi, and Geoffrey Bidduiph. Emma, still clinging to her toilet-paper and constantly being interrupted by Ralph, who stammers, told us how they were all seated at breakfast when Father Wason came into the kitchen saying, 'There is a knock at the door, probably a sick call' (he was always expecting a sick call that never came), and without waiting for either of them to get up from the table he went to open the door. While he was talking to the man he found standing there, a number of farmers who had been concealed in the garden rushed the door and forced an entry into the house.

There are people against whom, like children, it would seem impossible to use violence. Father Wason is one of these, for his aristocratic face like a Chinese carving in ivory provokes no passion. I think the men who invaded his house that morning must have closed their eyes, as men about to destroy something very old and rare.

'Stupid people,' Father Wason said when he returned from the church. 'Dreadful, dreadful to have disturbed your party. You had better go now to the kitchen, Emma,' he said. As he waved her out of the room he turned to Jan Gordon and with the air of a man of the world spoke about the excellence of the cellar at the Café Royal. He was pale and shaken, but like the White Knight he had scrambled on to his horse and was riding away on some fresh adventure.

Emma told us that the men intended carting the furniture which they had thrown out of Father Wason's house over to St. Hilary. 'The parson over there is one of the same sort,' they said. 'Let him have his furniture.' It was not until it was dark that I heard the wheels of the wagons and saw men with lanterns coming down the avenue. Each wagon, piled high with furniture, was drawn by two horses. So high and so badly were they loaded that tables and chairs were swept off by the boughs of the trees as they came along the avenue. Father Wason by now had settled down to play chess with one of our guests and refused to show any interest in anything outside the game.

'Don't be fussy,' he said. 'It is clergymanly to get fussy. Sit down. Sit down and watch the game. Most interesting.'

He would have been useless at handling furniture and was better playing chess, but in my state of irritation I went out of the room, very cross at seeing him sitting before a chess-board indifferent to what was going to happen to his belongings. It was now raining and tables and chairs, bedding and books, unwashed dishes and plates were being piled without order in our courtyard.

When I had visited Cury a few days before, I found the vicarage invaded with caterpillars from a field of cabbages alongside the house; caterpillars were everywhere, crawling over the dining-table, in the beds, dropping from the ceiling, invading every part of the house; and now they had arrived at St. Hilary. Many were dead and had left a stain where they had been, others were crawling among the bookcases, china and bed-linen.

You may remember how, at our coming to St. Hilary, we abandoned our furniture when the tide had ebbed and left the barge on the mud. But there was no going away from these things that had been unloaded at our door. We disliked the thought of introducing the plague of caterpillars into the house, whether dead or alive, but we had not the heart to leave all these poor bits of furniture out in the rain. With the help of the best disposed of the farmers, who were in charge of the wagons, we carried most of the furniture up three flights of stairs to an empty room in the tower until we could carry no more and crowded what we had left into the scullery. It was late that night before everything was housed and we began to prepare rooms and to make beds for the housekeeper, her husband and child, Father Wason and Geoffrey Biddulph. This party, with the exception of Father Wason, stayed with us for several months; the Nelson family had no home and Geoffrey had no work, so they all remained with us at St. Hilary. Father Wason's going was as sudden as his arrival. The next morning after Mass, he appeared in the hall with his suitcase. I tried to persuade him to stay but he paid no heed to my argument. 'Must be there to say Mass for those stupid people,' he said. 'Can't do anything else for them.' I said good-bye and saw him off at the door, but in a few minutes he was back again, still struggling to button his overcoat.

'Tell Annie,' he said, 'that the food was very good this time,' and so he returned to Cury, to say Mass in the cottage where he lodged, for 'those stupid people'.

All this happened fifteen years ago, but Father Wason has not forgotten and still devotes his Sunday Mass to these same 'stupid people'.

We had reached the end of those weary years of war that seemed as if they would never end. On the night of the Armistice I went out to be alone and to enjoy the peace that had at last come to the world. It was a still night and out there among the trees it was very quiet. I thought how strange the silence must be to the men in France. But what attracted me most was a new look in the country-side. What it was I did not at first understand, and then it came to me that there were lights down in the valley and over the hills where for years there had been blackness.

Each of these lights from Godolphin Hill to Zennor were from uncurtained windows where some little family was rejoicing, as I was, at the end of the war.

13 AFTER THE WAR

The epidemic that within a few months of the ending of the war had spread all over the world, and had claimed more victims than the war itself, visited St. Hilary early in November. On my way to stay for a few days at our cottage in Sennen Cove I had called at Trevabyn Farm to collect some eggs, and noticing that Mrs. Laity, the farmer's wife, was looking ill, I had suggested that she ought to be in bed.

'How can I be in the bed,' she answered 'with the threshing machine coming to-day and pasties and heavy cake to be baked for the men?'

That is the way of the land. The men have to be fed and the work has to be done however ill the women may be. On my return to St. Hilary on Saturday, after having been away three days, I was told that Mrs. Laity of Trevabyn was dead. Those who told me of her death spoke as if they were recounting something that could not be true. 'Mrs. Laity of Trevabyn gone dead! She were a young woman, with a parcel of children. Handsome she were and very well liked; 'tis a whisht thing if 'tis true.'

It was true, and before the end of the next week there were many lying at death's door. Each morning Nicholas Peters, who is postman as well as sexton, would come in and tell me of a death somewhere in the parish. 'Wherever you do go, from Resudgeon to Relubbus, there is no one to open the door to take in the letters,' he would say. 'They'm all up in their beds. What I'm going to do about digging their graves is more than I can say. They'm dying so fast I can't keep pace with 'em. It's a good job,' he would add, 'that you and I be left, Parson, or there wouldn't be any one to bury 'em.' There were six funerals in the first week of the epidemic, the highest number ever recorded in the register of two hundred and fifty years, except for the time of the smallpox, when fifteen were buried in one week from the hamlet of Relubbus. As I went about the parish visiting the sick, I remember recalling the story which had terrified me as a child, of the - Great Plague of London, when houses were marked with a cross and men went round the streets at night with a cart calling, 'Throw out your dead. Throw out your dead.'

On the following Sunday I missed a family who were usually at Mass, and in the afternoon I went to Gears, where they lived. After knocking for some time and getting no answer, I went into the kitchen, where I found a small boy in his shirt trying to kindle a fire. He told me that they were all 'sick in the bed', and that he had come down to 'fit them some tea'. Upstairs in the two small bedrooms were nine of the family who had lain there unattended since Saturday. 'Jimmie,' said his mother - his father had always called him 'the red-haired little beggar', although I could never distinguish the difference in colour between his hair and that of his brothers - ' Jimmie,' she said, 'went down to fit us a cup of tea, but he has been down there for an hour and I don't believe he has got the fire going yet.' Jimmy, who had followed me up the stairs, was now standing in the doorway - a shivering little figure in a shirt that did not reach to his knees.

It was late that night before we succeeded in getting the doctor and a nurse to attend to the father who was desperately ill. In the morning we removed all the children and put them to bed in a house that we had hastily got ready, the same 'Jolly Tinners' where we had housed the 'Brethren of the Common Table'. There were many families at St. Hilary at this time, who, like the family at Gears, were stricken with this plague with no one to tend them. St. Hilary was given over to fear. 'From pestilence and famine, Good Lord deliver us.'

I once witnessed the effect of the same fear on some children who fled from the approach of death. There were two boys in a family who kept goats on Perran Down, two very fair and beautiful children whom I had often met in the fir-wood playing with the goats. The youngest, a child of four, had been ailing for some days, complaining that his throat pained him and that he could not swallow. When I saw him his face was a dark purple and his fair hair damp with sweat as he lay on two chairs in the living-room of the cottage. The doctor had told the mother that he was suffering from croup and that there was no need for anxiety; but that night the child died after a struggle lasting for hours.

His brother and sisters would not be driven from the room and had watched his struggle throughout the night; when I came in the morning they were still crouching in the corner of the room, too weary to cry any more. The body of the dead child lay on the bed with the freshness of a flower lately picked, by his side lay the other child, aged six, who had also complained of being ill, and whose face on the pillow was darkened by the same struggle through which his brother had passed a few hours before. The father had put the horse in the cart and had driven away to fetch the doctor, while the mother sat watching the small figure on the bed and listening to the cries of the children who still resisted my attempts to take them from the room.

After hours of waiting the doctor arrived and gave the child an antitoxin injection for diphtheria. But it was too late; the poison of the disease had invaded the little body as it had that of his brother. The children knew; with the instinct of animals they sensed the coming of another death. They had remained for a night and day refusing to eat or to be driven from the room; but the dread of death overcame them, and, with cries like birds beaten out of a bush at night, they fled from the house into the darkness - anywhere to be free of that room and the presence of death.

The mother, who had taken the sick child from the bed and was now sitting with him in her arms, told me that the children had gone, and that she was afraid they might have fallen over the cliff or down an old mine shaft.

'Father jumped up and went after them,' she said, 'but they were running like hares with the dogs after them.

Father couldn't keep up and lost sight of 'em at Chiverton Gate. They've got the big boy with 'em,' she went on, ' but he were took with a fear same as the little ones, and there is no telling what may happen to 'em. Over cliff or down an old mine shaft as like as not,' she repeated, rocking to and fro with the sick child.

The children were found hours later by the hedge-side on the road to Marazion. They had fled without a thought of where they were going, driven by the fear of another night in that death-stricken room.

Apart from the danger of infection, home was no place for them that night, so I brought them to our house where Annie Walke put them to bed in the spare room. I went in often to look at them as they lay asleep with their arms encircling one another, as if they sought protection in each other from the horrors that had overtaken them.

I have known of several men who have run away and failed those they loved at their last moments, but only one woman, and that was at the death of her husband. Thinking that the end would come that night, she had asked a neighbour to sit up and keep her company. The two women sat together over the fire speaking in whispers, stopping to listen now and again to a sound of heavy breathing that broke the silence of the house. About two in the morning the change came and the man in the bed raised himself from the pillow and cried out, 'He's coming for me, Sarah. I'm going. I'm going. Take hold of me, Sarah.'

The startled women looked at him, and as the neighbour rose to go to his help his wife fled from the room, calling out, 'Keep away from him and let him go his own way. If he gets hold of you he'll take you with him. Keep away from him, I say, and let him go his own way.' It was her husband's last cry for help, a man she had lived with for thirty years, but she left him to die in the arms of a stranger. This is the only time I have ever known a woman fail at these last moments. I have attended many deaths, and many times have I watched the endurance and courage of women who have stood, like the Marys at the cross, witnessing scenes that would have tested the courage of the bravest of men.

By the middle of December the epidemic had passed its worst stage and I began to look forward to celebrating Christmas, the first Christmas that we had spent at St. Hilary free from the shadow of the war. There were still ugly cries of 'Hang the Kaiser', and 'Make the Germans pay', but these were raised by politicians eager to catch votes by an appeal to the lowest instincts of the people. They captured votes but did not long influence the mind of the people who were preparing to celebrate Christmas as a festival of peace and goodwill. The same spirit led companies of youths in Bavaria to go into the forests that Christmas night and stand round a fir-tree with many candles in memory of all comrades who had fallen in the war, pledging themselves to the service of peace.

The nature of Englishmen is too reticent for such a display of emotion, but the crowds who thronged the streets of Penzance, singing songs and carols on that Christmas Eve, were possessed by the same impulse as the youths in Bavaria.

Every one in St. Hilary 'belongs' to go to Penzance on Christmas Eve. It is a practice as old as going to the fair on the Feast of Corpus Christi; from Zennor to St. Ives by every bus and conveyance in the West of Cornwall, they flock in to Penzance, where they will walk up and down the lighted street, looking into shop windows, laughing, singing and talking to their friends. Between 10 and 11 p.m., when the shops close and the streets are growing dark, they crowd, with their parcels of provisions and the toys that they have bought for their children, into one or other of the already overcrowded buses. On this Christmas Eve there were many St. Hilary people returning from Penzance who had no mind to go back to their homes or stand in the square of Goldsithney and sing carols.

They wanted to prolong the gaiety of the night; if

not to walk up and down lighted streets and to gaze at gaily dressed shops, then to be where there were lights and music, and among others as happy as themselves. There was still the midnight Mass at the church; they could hear the bells sounding very sweetly from where they stood in the square. They did not 'belong' to go to church, but it was Christmas Eve. 'There will be some crowd of people, and pretty singing; may as well go there as anywhere else,' they thought. They came streaming down the avenue, merry-makers on the way to a midnight party. The church was crowded, so they stood in the tower and leant against the windows, as if there to watch a play rather than to offer their homage to the God who on this night was laid in a manger; but, before the blessing was given and they left to go home, these childish people had been captured by the Child whose festival they had been celebrating.

When the Mass was ended, fathers and mothers burdened with their Christmas shopping, young men with flushed faces, some shy and half-ashamed girls who glanced self-consciously at the young men, every one in the church, young and old, boys and girls, married and single, came that night to kneel at the crib and venerate the Child who lay on the straw between St. Joseph and Our Lady. When all had gone and the church was empty and very quiet I went to the crib and knelt to say 'my thanksgiving' to the Child who had welcomed these merry-makers on the night of His Nativity.

We had planned a Christmas dinner that year at St. Hilary with our friends from Newlyn and Lamorna to celebrate the peace which had at last come to the world. It was to be a Chaucer dinner, and all who came were to be dressed in clothes of that period. We never grow too old for dressing up; to become someone else by wearing their clothes is an illusion that never forsakes us.

I was staying some years ago in a Georgian house, and was shown the bedroom where the late owner had been born, and the four-poster bed with damask hangings on which he was laid after his death. He had been a hunting man, a M.F.H. up to the age of seventy-five, when one morning his old knees failed him in jumping a brook. He fell clear of the horse but landed on his head, and was picked up unconscious, carried home and laid in the bed which I saw in the room. He was a lonely man without relatives and was nursed in that darkened room by his manservant, almost as old as himself. After some weeks he appeared to recover his senses and spoke of his hounds and the horse he had been riding at the time of the accident, but when his servant drew back the shutters and the light streamed into the room, he cried and hid his face beneath the coverlet. This happened again and again whenever his man ventured to draw back the shutters; from now onward he lived in a candle-lit room from which all daylight had been excluded.

Mondays, Wednesdays and Fridays, hunting mornings, were days when he would be restless and unhappy constantly ringing the bell and sending messages to the stables or kennels. There was no calendar to tell the day of the month, no rising or setting of the sun to proclaim the beginning or ending of the day in that darkened room, but the old man in the bed never missed a Monday, Wednesday or Friday throughout that winter; these days continued to be days of distress with outbursts of temper at the slowness of his man in carrying out his orders.

Before the beginning of another hunting season his servant, with the understanding of a mother for her sick child, procured a rocking-horse larger than those usually found in children's nurseries, painted an iron grey, the colour of his master's favourite horse Anarchist. On the opening day of the cubbing season he entered the old man's room with the morning tea. 'A little late I fear to-day, sir,' he said. 'I have sent word to the stables that you will be riding Anarchist.'

Hurrying to and fro, he laid out his master's clothes, which had not been worn since the day of the accident. Trees were taken out from one of the pairs of boots that stood in a row against the wall, drawers were opened with a show of haste, clothes laid out to put on, and a pink coat taken down from a hanger in the great wardrobe. When all was ready the old servant approached the bed with, 'Now, sir.'

For a moment there was a look of bewilderment in the eyes of the old man; but the sight of the familiar clothes reassured him, and he surrendered himself to be lifted to the edge of the bed and to be dressed in breeches and top-boots, white cravat and pink coat. He had withered and grown thin since the day of his accident; the pink coat hung loosely from his shoulders, but the old man smiled as he sat in a chair looking at himself in the long glass of the wardrobe. He was wearing his steel cap and held his gloves and hunting crop in his hands, but there was still something lacking for which his eyes searched the room; it was his hunting horn he was looking for. 'Mustn't forget that, sir,' his servant remarked as the old man thrust the horn into the lapel of his coat.

When the head groom with a stable-boy appeared, wheeling in the iron-grey rocking-horse, the old man greeted him as he had on many hunting mornings in the stable-yard. 'Morning, Rogers. Everything all right in the stables?' Whether he consciously deceived himself into believing that this wooden horse was his hunter (as a little girl will be persuaded that the doll she nurses is her baby), or whether his brain could no longer distinguish between the rocking-horse and his hunter Anarchist, his old servant never knew. Without any look of surprise, he gathered the reins in his withered hands and, clutching the silver mane of the rocking-horse, allowed himself to be lifted on to the saddle; and as the groom and stable-boy touched their caps on leaving, he raised his hunting crop in acknowledgement, and settled in the saddle as if on the way to the meet of his hounds.

The old servant shut the door and waited outside, listening to the sounds that came from that shuttered and candle-lit room. After a time he heard his master's voice, thin but clear, as he spoke to his hounds, throwing them in to cover, 'Hector, Warrior, speak to him. Leu, Leu, Leu, in,' he cried and cracked his whip. There was silence for a time and then the servant heard his master call, 'Gone away,' and sound his horn, and then silence except for the beat of the rockers. The master must have made a cast, for he was speaking to his hounds and the horn sounded again. Listening there by the door he followed the hunt in that darkened room; hounds were racing now by the sound of the rockers going faster and faster. 'Master can't keep that pace going long,' he thought, and was about to enter the room when he heard the horn sound the 'kill' and the voice of his master faint and thin calling to the hounds to 'break him up'.

Throughout that winter the old man never missed a day's hunting. He would wake early and call for his man to dress him. The rocking-horse was wheeled in and he would ride away while his old servant waited outside the door listening for the horn to sound the 'kill' or 'gone to ground', when he would return and inquire, before lifting him on to the bed, of the day's sport. One morning in spring his master rode away as usual; his voice rang through the house as he called to his hounds and then there was silence, no sound of the horn or noise of the rockers. When his servant entered, the rocking-horse was still moving gently, but the old man was not in the saddle. He had fallen to the floor and was dead before his servant had lifted him on to the bed. It is a strange story and has little to do with our dinner, but it illustrates how largely our mental outlook is determined by the clothes we wear. To dress as a company of people met at an inn on the way to the shrine of St. Thomas of Canterbury had something of the same illusionary effect as the pink coat on the old man.

I watched our guests coming down the stairs on this Christmas night - Gladys Hynes, followed by Ruth Manning-Sanders, and behind her George, in a scarlet robe that I mistook for Father Christmas, Laura and Harold Knight, Dod Procter - all old friends; but tonight in these strange clothes they appeared to me as men and women of another age. Gladys Hynes in a wimple had discarded her ultra-modern outlook and become a fair dame who would reverence and be obedient to her lord; George Manning-Sanders, wrapped in his red robe (which I discovered to be that of Chaucer and not Father Christmas), was a teller of stories which might well have been told by the miller in the Tales. It was a company well suited to the room in which we were to dine, a room with white walls and high windows that at night are closed with black shutters reaching from the ceiling to the floor: an austere room on all occasions, and especially so on this evening when it held nothing but a bare trestle table and oak benches, the same that figured so disastrously at our supper party for the Bishop on our coming to St. Hilary. The floor was strewn with straw, over which was scattered sweet-smelling leaves of rosemary and bay; the only light was from a fire of flaming ash logs, and candles set in sconces round the walls and in a branched iron candlestick in the centre of the table. The straw lying ankle deep gave a rustling sound and the scent of fields at harvest-time.

Emma Curnow, our maid, had invited some of her friends from the village to spend Christmas with her in the kitchen, but when Christmas night came we thought it would be pleasanter if we all dined together. There was the difficulty of clothes, for dressed as they were in their Sunday best they would have destroyed the illusion of the party and possibly have felt shy and out of place. But with cross-lacings, jumpers and head-dresses made hastily out of bits of stuff; that difficulty was overcome. Mrs. Peters, Nicholas and Norman, May Crebo, Emma and Mabel Curnow joined the company whom I had watched coming down the stairs. There was still the difficulty of seating these unexpected guests at the table, but what did that matter? For who could wish for a more agreeable dining-place than with your back to the wall among piles of sweet-scented straw?

Nicholas Peters and the others of the party had never heard of Chaucer or the *Canterbury Tales*, but they were

Cornish people and the Cornish are true Celts in their love of dressing up and playing 'make-believe'. It was all part of a Christmas game that the Parson had got up - to sit in the straw and pick the bones of a turkey and to stand up and drink the health of the company. How well they played their part, and what a spirit of Christmas happiness was brought to the party when, after the table had been cleared, healths had been drunk and speeches made, they stood up and sang carols very sweetly to old Breton melodies!

14 CHILDREN FROM AUSTRIA

The two events of the greatest significance for us in the year immediately following the end of the war were the coming of Gerard Corner to live in our neighbourhood, a man with whom we were to establish a very rare friendship, and the arrival of the children from Austria. At the time of Austria's collapse, when the kroner fell to something like a million to the pound, a company of people were endeavouring to save some of the children from the starvation and misery which threatened to overwhelm them. We undertook to to have one of the boys to live with us, and to find homes in the village for three girls.

These children, after spending a month at an isolation camp, arrived at Truro, with several others, too late for a train to the West. On the following morning I went up to meet them and found five children on the platform of Truro Station in place of the four who we were expecting. A strange group they made, the girls in check dresses with little capes, and our boy Erwin Nedwid, in a sailor suit sufficiently different from an English sailor suit to be noticeable. Their shrill young voices speaking German attracted the attention of people waiting on the platform, some whom inquired of me whether they were really Germans and what they were doing in England; but from showing signs of unfriendliness, they smiled on them and bought them sweets from the refreshment stall.

I recognized how proudly the second boy, Marion Šafařik, a child of ten, carried himself as he stood aloof from the others while the woman who was in charge explained that a mistake had been made and no home provided for him. I longed to take this proud boy in my arms and tell him how glad we were to have him at St. Hilary, but I was sufficiently aware of the danger of impinging on a child's dignity to refrain. A year later, sitting round the fire and talking with the confidence that by then was established between us, the children confessed to a disappointment at this meeting with me at Truro Station. I had come away from St. Hilary immediately after saying Mass, and was wearing a threadbare and shabby cassock. 'You looked so funny and old,' they said. 'Not a bit like what you look now,' they added kindly, although I was wearing the same cassock.

When we arrived at St. Hilary in the car lent by John Laity, we were met at the end of the avenue by Annie Walke, who, wiser and aware of how much children are affected by clothes, had on her prettiest dress and so did something to remove the bad impression I had made. Behind her were some people from the Church-town who had come to have a look at 'the German children'. (It was a long time before the people of St. Hilary learnt to distinguish between German and Austrian.) Mrs. Jenkins was there with Harold and Albert and several of the younger children.

'Poor dears,' she said. 'Maybe they Germans ain't so bad as we've heard tell. Go forward, Albert, and speak to them.'

Albert and Harold came forward and, nodding their heads, said, 'Know how to play cricket do 'ee?' and the two Austrian boys bowed very gravely.

Among those at the gate was the woman who had engaged to take two of the little girls. There had been talk in the village about 'harbouring German children' and she had come to say that she and her mother had thought better of it. They weren't going to risk being murdered in their beds by Germans. These two little girls were only eight years old, but still, as she said, 'There was the old Kaiser. They hadn't ketched 'en yet, and there was no saying what games he might be up to.'

Annie Walke had prepared a room for one child, our boy Erwin, or Eddy as we called him later. She had bought a new coverlet for his bed, set a bunch of flowers on his dressing-table, put up pictures that she thought he would like and done everything that she could think of to welcome him. Now I had arrived with two boys, and here was this woman refusing to take the little girls. The children, guessing what had happened, took on a defiant attitude. The boys withdrew to the garden, where they sat on the stone seat with their heads close together, like two judges who had retired from court to consider their verdict, while the girls crowded into the room got ready for our boy, and sat on the bed. I wandered between these two groups, making gestures that we would have dinner soon and all would be well. For that night, four children slept at St. Hilary, two little girls in the room prepared for our boy, Eddy on a camp-bed in another room, while Marion was put to sleep on an ottoman in my dressing-room. It was a sad welcome for these children after all our plans to make their arrival a happy one.

On the following day the girls Olga and Justine went to Miss Ramsay, a maiden lady living in Goldsithney; as Margarita was already established with two nurses in the same village, we were left with the boys. They were good children, kissing our hands with a show of politeness but resisting any attempts at establishing a more friendly relationship. Only when Annie Walke and I would go in and kiss them good night after they were in bed, did they give any promise of the love and confidence that was to grow up between us. How this love grew until it became the most assured thing in our lives I do not know; neither do they, for we have often spoken of their first week and how strange it all was.

I find it difficult to write of these children who have now grown into men, Eddy married with a home in Vienna, Marion a doctor of law of Prague University, and Zdenko, whose coming I will relate, in business in Teheran. We have watched them from every stage of childhood to manhood. Each time they have returned to us we have wondered if everything would be the same, if a year in Paris, Prague, Vienna, or wherever they happened to be, would have so changed them that we should not know them when they came. Each night of their arrival we would debate whether to go and kiss them good night as was the custom when they were children. They were men when last they came, but they had not forgotten 'Good night'; they said, 'See you later,' as they got up to go to bed. They had not changed. When we went to visit them we found the same three children that we had known in the same three beds, waiting for the same intimate talk that had always accompanied this 'saying good night'.

I used to call Eddy 'Peer Gynt'; he was so detached and unrelated at times to the scenes and people around him. The first words he learnt of the English language, which he never failed to use on all occasions, were 'no matter'. Whatever happened, whether it rained or some one died, 'No matter,' said Eddy. I have watched him crossing a field, when, if he disturbed a cow lying down, he would bow an apology and politely ask the cow's pardon; at other times he would go from group to group of cows, lying down chewing the cud, and watch with delight the effort of each cow to raise herself from the ground.

It was not until the boys had been with us for some weeks that we discovered the existence of Marion's little brother Zdenko, who had been left behind at the isolation camp. 'He is very small and must have been overlooked' was the explanation that Marion managed to convey to us when we inquired how it had come about that we had not been told of him. We had already two boys instead of the one we had been prepared to entertain, and they were sufficient charge on our time; but who could leave a child in a camp among strangers?

It was arranged that Gerard Collier, who was returning from London about this time, should meet Zdenko at Paddington and bring him down. I found them both standing on our door-step a few days later, Gerard very tall and thin with a rucksack on his shoulders, and by his side a minute figure, also with a rucksack, who said, putting out a little hand, 'Please I have come' - a phrase that he had learnt so that he might greet us in English.

I have always loved the hands of very small children. Often, when I have held infants in my arms at the font and they have stretched out tiny hands towards me, I have taken them into my large ones and looked at them as one might look at a flower. I felt the same about the hand that Zdenko offered me at the door when he arrived and said, 'Please I have come'; it was so very small and confiding.

It was during this first summer when the children were with us that our friendship developed with the sweetest and gentlest of men, Gerard Collier. Gerard had been educated at Balliol, where he obtained a first in modern history and made many friends. Eton also had a share in the formation of his character, for it was there, he once told me, that as head of his house he was awakened to a sense of responsibility for the welfare of his fellows, the responsibility of one who feels himself deeply involved in the sins and failures of others.

Some years after his death I met two strangers in the church, who inquired of me if I could point out the grave of Gerard Collier. They were E.F. Benson and Percy Lubbock, the author of *Roman Memories*, both of whom had known him at Eton, Percy Lubbock as a contemporary and friend and E.F. Benson as his housemaster. These two men had made the journey to Cornwall together to visit the grave of one whom in different ways they had both known and loved. I remember how standing by his grave E.F. Benson turned to me and said, 'There lies the body of the boy who best understood what, as a master, I had to offer.' I have never known any man so conscious of the majesty of the law of God as Gerard, or with a greater reverence for His will. The guiding principle of his life was that there were no problems. The social, economic and international problems with which the world was distracted did not exist in the mind of God, nor need men remain in ignorance of His will. 'The mind of God is available,' he would say, extending his hands as if inviting all men and all nations to share with him in the knowledge of His will. He applied this principle equally to the confusion that existed in European politics, to the troubles in Ireland and to the domestic problems that might arise in his own household.

I do not know whether he had read the *Spiritual Exercises* of Ignatius Loyola, but his method was the same as that laid down for the choice of a vocation - a searching inquiry into the facts, with an all-prevailing desire to know and to do the will of God. Often in the midst of a violent discussion he would suggest very tentatively, for he was a shy man, that we might seek the presence of God. 'Let us try and discover His will,' he would say. At other times he silently withdrew from the conversation, when the quiet of his face was so arresting that it never failed to check our sometimes heated discussions.

There are two occasions of which I have a clear picture of him in my mind. He had been much concerned with the starvation prevailing in Russia, and the part that England had played in the blockade. Together with Will Arnold Foster we arranged a meeting at St. John's Hall, Penzance, at which a Quaker lady who had been working in the starvation area was to speak and to show lantern slides. We were uncertain how such a meeting would be received, for added to the growing fear of Bolshevism there still existed a feeling of resentment at what was termed the desertion of Russia from the cause of the Allies. I went into Penzance on the morning of the meeting, and as I got out of the bus in Market Jew Street I saw a crowd following a familiar figure with bowed head, carrying a sandwich-board on his shoulders - 'Come to St. John's Hall to-night and help to save Russia.' Wherever I went I met this figure, who turned very courteously so that the crowd that followed him might read the notice he carried. It was Gerard's act of reparation for our share in the starvation of a people.

The other occasion was in the Chapter House of Truro Cathedral. Bishop Warman had been speaking on 'Winning the world for Christ'. I saw Gerard, with a white face and clenched hands, walk from his seat at the back of the Chapter House to the throne where the Bishop was sitting. His attitude was so fierce and menacing, his action so unlike his usual courteous manner, that I came out of my seat and was about to follow him, when I heard him say, 'You must repent. You must repent of your share in the war before you can win the world for Christ.' There he stood for a moment, an accusing figure, and then turned and walked slowly back.

At the time of which I am writing, the years immediately following the war, a great catastrophe had overwhelmed Western Cornwall. From Truro to Land's End there are hundreds and hundreds of miles of dark ways cut in the rock by a race of men who for generations have been 'underground men'. Here is a county where men have been streaming, sinking shafts and driving adits 'since', as a miner would say, 'the days of Jesus Christ'. This ancient industry had failed. The mines were abandoned and in some cases already flooded; everywhere stamps were silent and whole families out of employment. We are accustomed to unemployment to-day and have made some kind of provision to meet it, but this happened at a time when most industries were flourishing. It was only West Cornwall that was affected with the blight of unemployment. In Redruth, Camborne, St. Just and Pendeen groups of sad-faced men were standing at street corners and round deserted mine shafts. The younger men had gone away to Africa and America, but these men had families and were too old to start life in a new country. They were without hope. Their industry had failed and their skill was no longer needed. It was then that Gerard and I took to visiting them, especially in the St. Just and Pendeen districts where the Levant mine runs out for a mile beneath the sea and where, in a storm, miners can hear great stones, or bullies as they are called, roaring and sucking overhead.

We were coming home one evening across the moor from Pendeen when it grew dark and, with a mist coming up from the sea, we lost whatever footpath there was and found ourselves entangled in furze brakes from which there seemed to be no way out. We struggled on, feeling our way at times with our hands, constantly in dread of falling down a deserted mine shaft. After struggling for hours in the darkness, climbing stone walls and battling with blackthorn and furze bushes, we struck the road at New Mill, where there is an inn kept by a family I know. The light from the window cast a red glow across the road.

As a boy I had always been attracted by inns where the light shone through red blinds; the memory of them still remains with me and conjures up a picture of warmth and good company. On the long drive from Salisbury to our old home at Redlynch there were two inns with red blinds on the road, the 'Stag' at Charlton and the 'Bull' at Downton, which, as we passed at night, invited travellers to pull up and enter their warm parlours. I was often very cold on these drives and I longed for my father to say, 'My boy, I think we will go into the 'Stag' (or the 'Bull') and get warm,' but I never remember him stopping at either, although we passed them many scores of times.

It was already late as we came into the kitchen of the New Mill Inn where a number of miners got up as we entered and invited us to take their places round the fire. There we sat until closing-time, drinking stout and listening to the talk of these men, who in their youth had worked underground in all parts of the world.

On the walk home, for we had still eight miles to go, we talked of the kindly fellowship that is to be found in wayside inns. It was the first time that Gerard had ever been into a public-house of this kind. He was a shy man, averse from anything that might appear to be an intrusion on the lives of others. 'I was waiting to be properly introduced,' he said, 'by one who was well acquainted with them.' I quoted him some lines from a poem by William Blake:

> *Dear Mother, dear Mother, the church is cold;*
> *But the alehouse is healthy, and pleasant, and warm.*

Besides, I can tell where I am used well;
Such usage in heaven will never do well.

But, if at the church they would give us some ale,
And a pleasant fire our souls to regale,
We'd sing and we'd pray all the livelong day,
Nor ever once wish from the church to stray.

Arthur Jenkins, a Member of the Society of Friends who lived at Redruth, frequently accompanied us on these expeditions. We were a strange trio going about the country, Gerard the scholar, the Quaker and myself. I had grown very fond of Arthur Jenkins during the War and had often stayed at Trewurgie, where he lived with his old mother and two sisters. The house was like Arthur; everything was quiet and comfortable; the furniture was solid and gave you the impression of having stood where it stood now at the time when Arthur's father, grandfather and perhaps great-grandfather had occupied the house. Nothing, I imagine, had been changed since the Jenkinses had first settled at Trewurgie a hundred and fifty years ago. When I stayed there I slept in a bed into which you climbed by means of three steps, a bed in which many Jenkinses 'had been born and not a few had lain dead', but none ever returned to disturb my sleep.

Arthur constantly came to Gerard and myself with what Friends term 'a concern'. His first 'concern' had to do with the miners and led to visits to St. Just and Pendeen and later to an effort to start the mining industry in Cornwall on a Christian basis. Then came the time when Ireland lay under the terror of the Black and Tans. 'We are a Celtic people,' he said, 'and owe the Christian faith to the Irish saints and missionaries who crossed over to Cornwall. Is Cornwall going to make no effort,' he would ask, 'to repay the debt at the time of Ireland's distress?'

We knew of no way of helping Ireland, but Arthur Jenkins, with the quiet persistence characteristic of Friends, urged that we could serve Ireland by inviting people to pray for her; and so under his tutelage we became engaged in holding meetings for prayer in different parts of Cornwall on behalf of this distressed country. Among others who welcomed these efforts at a reconciliation between the two countries was the Roman Catholic priest in Truro (himself an Irishman), who invited us to his church, where Quakers, Nonconformists, members of the Church of England and Catholics would meet for an hour in silence before the Blessed Sacrament, until Cardinal Bourne ordered that these meetings in a Catholic Church should cease. Later, Gerard and George Davis, a Welshman who, as another Celt, shared our sense of responsibility, went to Ireland. They obtained interviews with William Griffiths, Michael Collins and other Sinn Fein leaders, who entrusted him with a message to Mr. Lloyd George, that they would be willing to come to England and discuss the situation if they received an invitation. I believe that it is difficult to obtain an interview with the Prime Minister of the day, especially if the applicant has little to recommend him beyond his recent confinement in Wandsworth prison as a conscientious objector. But George Davis is a Welshman, a magician like Mr. Lloyd George, with the gift of winning people; he had also met Mr. and Mrs. Lloyd George one morning at Criccieth, and had been taken back by them to lunch.

On this occasion he sought Mrs. Lloyd George at No.10 Downing Street, who gave him tea, but held out little hope of his obtaining the interview that he sought with the Prime Minister.

Once past the policeman at the door and inside No.10 Downing Street, it was easy to wait, and so George Davis waited in an ante-room on the chance of catching the Prime Minister as he passed. There were others there on the same errand. Presently the door leading into the farther room was opened and Lloyd George, accompanied by two secretaries, walked by, avoiding the glances of those who were waiting. George Davis called out something to him in the Welsh tongue. Mr. Lloyd George is above everything else a Welshman, and no Welshman can resist the call of his own language. At the sound of the familiar words the Prime Minister hesitated, while George Davis approached him with a book in his hands - *Sacred Songs*. Pointing to the title page, on which was an inscription in the handwriting of a friend of Mr. Lloyd George's boyhood, he said, 'I want to give you this book that once belonged to your old friend, and I want you to listen for five minutes to a message that I have to deliver to you.'

'Make an appointment with my secretary,' said the Prime Minister, as he hastened away, glancing at the book that George Davis had left in his hands. The interview he sought was given a few days later and George Davis delivered his message. This was, as far as I know, the first step towards a reconciliation with Ireland.

The summer of 1921, of which I am writing, the second year during which the children from Austria were with us, was one of the great summers of the past twenty years.

Looking back over my childhood I seem to remember every summer as one of unbroken happiness and sunshine. There was always the sound of a flapping blind, drawn to keep out the sun, of bees swarming in the garden and a can being beaten to keep them at home, of a lawn-mower at work and the scent of newly-cut grass and of mignonette beneath the window. The days were spent in lying under a tree reading a book, at cricket matches, playing tennis and hay-making. There were thunderstorms, but never any wet days. The thunderstorms were always at night, when we climbed out on to the roof and watched the lightning, as we watched the great comet that came when I was a boy.

There are no such summers now. During these twenty years I can only recall three that can compare with those of my childhood. There was the summer of 1911, the year we were married, when little girls in Polruan bathed for the first time. At Polruan little girls paddled but never bathed; it was only boys who bathed. But one very hot day that year there were girls on the rocks on one side of the boys' bathing-place (it was considered immodest for girls to be on these rocks or anywhere near the boys' bathing-place). The boys resented their presence and kept calling to them from the water that they did not 'belong to' be there, and that they did not want to be watched by 'a passel of maidens'; but the girls sat on, and when I came there next day these little girls were in the water with the boys.

The sun that year was so fierce that it destroyed the convention that girls must not go into the water unless they fell in out of a boat or off the quay, as they constantly did. These little girls had no bathing dresses and went into the water clad in their chemises, but no one complained, for the summer weather had changed the view of the people of Polruan as to what was 'fitty' for little girls to do. It was so hot that our friends could think of no other wedding presents to give us than cut-glass tumblers, wine goblets and water jugs, a supply so large that some survive to this day.

I watched the beginning of another great summer, in 1933, from my bed in the sanatorium at Tehidy. When I arrived in the early spring of that year I could see a patch of snowdrops from where I lay under the veranda, and before they faded I watched daffodils come into bloom round the hut that was my home for three months.

In April, when the woods at Tehidy were preparing to break into a sea of bluebells, I left Cornwall, and for the next three months I was living in another hut, on a slope of the Mendips, overlooking a great country that stretched to the Vale of Avalon, a country golden with buttercups, where the wind was burdened with the scent of millions of flowers. When this summer was at its height, we went to live in a small village on the East Coast. There were no flowers here except tall hollyhocks and sunflowers, and few birds except swallows and martins, nothing but the sky, the sea and a wide country of fenland where, however hot the sun, the wind came with a fresh tang from the sea. Never have I spent a summer of such great ease and quiet happiness.

The other summer of continued sunshine, the summer of 1921 - the second year that the children from Austria were with us - was a summer in which never a day passed without something happening. Apart from the children, visitors were constantly arriving and the house was always full, but of the names of those visitors I can remember only one, and he can scarcely be claimed as a visitor since he slept in his own tent pitched on the lawn. This was Hope Johnson, who had written asking me to obtain a pedlar's licence for him as he proposed spending the summer walking round Cornwall, playing the flute and selling trinkets. He arrived one very hot afternoon with a tent and a pack containing cheap jewellery, needles, reels of cotton, bootlaces and other things that might obtain a ready sale. We had no bed to offer him, so, as I have said, he pitched his tent on the lawn preparatory to taking the road next day. But on making inquiries from the police he discovered that the pedlar's licence I had obtained for him at the cost of five shillings was only available after three months' residence in the county. A hawker's licence costing two pounds would have given him freedom to sell his goods at any time in any county in England, but not being prepared to pay this sum, and being unable to take to the road without a licence, he continued to live in his tent on the lawn, practising on the flute and telling stories at night to the children. At this time we had a sheep-dog called Driver, who took to crawling beneath the flap of the tent and curling up on the mattress. Hope Johnson would drop his flute and drag him out, but it was no use as Driver always returned. 'I would not mind if he had ordinary fleas, but they are elephants. They trample on me,' he said piteously. After about a week he could put up with them no longer and fled to Lamorna and pitched his tent outside the studio where Laura and Harold Knight were spending the summer.

Staying with the Knights at this time was W.H.

Davies, the poet and author of T*he Autobiography of a Super Tramp*. To a man who had spent his early life as a hobo, jumping trains in America, and who had lived for years in doss-houses and tramped the greater part of England, there could be no meaning in this talk of 'taking to the road'. 'What does he do it for?' he was constantly asking. At first he was inclined to the opinion that he was engaged in a plot in connexion with the police, whom W.H. suspected of any villainy. But as the days went by and Hope Johnson showed no signs of activity and no policeman called to make inquiries, he took to regarding him as mildly insane, a man with the illusion of being a tramp.

On one of the evenings I spent at Lamorna while Davies was there, after tethering the donkeys and having tea, Harold and I went out and collected wood from the furze brake near the studio to make a fire to sit round after dinner. Davies had been very scornful when we told him, at tea, of our intention. 'What is the use of making a fire?' he asked. 'You've got plenty of hot water in the kitchen. You're like this man here,' pointing to Hope Johnson, 'who thinks he's a pedlar.' It was the scorn of the professional tramp for people who light fires and take their meals out of doors for pleasure. However, when we had collected the wood and it was getting dark, he began to show an interest. 'This place here,' he said, 'with the donkeys tethered there and that man's tent, remind me of a camp where we had a fire that never went out for three weeks.' After telling a story about this camp and the trouble there was with a stranger who came each night and seated himself at the fire, he got up from where he was sitting and limped to the pile of wood. 'Look here, Knight,' he said, 'you had better leave this to me. I know more about lighting fires than you fellows.' Harold and I had gathered the wood and were not inclined to leave it to him; but Davies took it so much for granted that it was his fire that Harold and I said nothing.

'Now go and get me some good stones,' Davies said, 'and then you two can sit down.' As the wood we had gathered was mostly dried furze, he very soon had his fire going and sat tending it from a pile at his side, while Harold and I looked on and Laura made hasty sketches by the light of the flames that blazed up each time Davies threw on a fresh bundle of furze. After a time two little girls who lived in the house below came and joined us. 'Sit down' said Davies 'if you are going to stay.' The words were spoken in the tone of a man dealing with intruders. I thought of the unwelcome guest in the story Davies had told us and how he had got a nasty blow on the head for sitting round a fire where he was not wanted. These children had not heard the story; they were wilful little girls and only laughed and threw on more wood from the pile by his side. W.H. Davies was back again in the old days when no tramp, unless he was looking for trouble, would venture to touch another man's fire. He beat on the ground with his stick and shouted, 'Go away, you little devils, and don't touch my fire or I'll come after you.' But this did not daunt them. As the flames died down the youngest and most daring gave a shriek and jumped on the smouldering ashes. Now Davies is a poet, and judging from some of his poems I should imagine him to be fond of children; but it was a very angry tramp from whom the most daring child might well run away, who now got up on his feet and shouted, 'I'll lay my stick about you if you ever come to this camp again.'

At this time we had a cottage in Sennen Cove, or rather a share in one. We had owned the whole of it once, but at this time it was lived in during the winter by some fisher people who always went to the Scilly Isles in the summer for the mackerel fishing.

Though we occasionally drove with the donkeys the fifteen miles between St. Hilary and Sennen Cove, spending the day on the road, and stopping for lunch by the wayside, the donkeys disliked this journey, being unwilling to leave the rich pasture of the glebe for the rough living of the moors, and we often left them at St. Hilary and did the journey by the bus running from Penzance. Having no servant with us, a great deal of our time was spent 'doing for ourselves'. There was always coal to be picked up on the beach from a torpedoed steamer that had come ashore. There during the war each tide would bring in a supply, which, with the driftwood to be found among the rocks, would be sufficient for cooking and a fire at night in the parlour. One of the Austrian boys had to go every morning to a farm half a mile away on the top of the hill to buy butter and eggs, while I was responsible for the cooking and would leave the beach, after bathing, half an hour before the boys, to fry the fish for dinner. It was always fried mackerel for dinner (except for an occasional turbot, also fried) and an omelette each at night, but I don't remember that any one ever complained of the sameness.

At week-ends, Marion and I came back to St. Hilary, leaving Annie Walke with Eddy and Zdenko, who always boasted, on our return, of the cliffs they had climbed and the feasts they had eaten, and, on one occasion, of the cinema show they had visited in the village school.

Marion and I also enjoyed ourselves on these weekends. It was pleasant to walk round the garden together and to discover the flowers that had come into bloom while we had been away, to eat in the cool dining-room with a clean white cloth before us, to be waited on by Emma, who had prepared dinner, and to sit late and talk together. Never have I had a more delightful companion than Marion on these week-ends.

When we tired of Sennen we would all return to St. Hilary, where there were always fresh visitors arriving, cricket matches, and tennis tournaments on the court the boys had made. The whole of that summer was spent out of doors. We all ate and some of us slept beneath the canopy of beech trees in the garden and spent the days bathing and lazing on the cliffs. Day after day, week after week, we awoke to a blue sky and the assurance of another summer day; but for me the pre-eminence of that summer over any other summer of these twenty years was due to the presence of our three boys, Marion, Eddy and Zdenko.

15 THE CHRISTMAS PLAY

The Christmas Play at St. Hilary goes back so many years that I have almost forgotten its origin.

At the time I could find no play suitable to the place and the people who were to perform it. I wanted an act of worship rather than a performance, a return to the old miracle play which was performed either in the church or in some open space, such as the field known at St. Hilary as the Plain-an-guarry, 'the field of the play'.

Even in the modern theatre where the stage is separated from the auditorium, the audience is so important a factor that I believe the most skilful producer cannot estimate the whole possibilities of a play before the first night, when the indefinable relationship between actors and spectators will often produce a new situation. It was this combined action of players and spectators that I was looking for. The old Cornish miracle plays appeared to me to be too archaic and lacking in dramatic form for my purpose; and finding nothing among the more modern plays that corresponded to my conception, I determined that if there was to be one at St. Hilary it must be written by myself.

The plan with which I started was that there should be no stage and that the players should pass, as in a measured dance, from place to place round the church among the people. In addition I planned that the Christmas crib should take the place of a character impersonating Our Lady with the Holy Child, and that there should be a dance of children before the crib, as an expression of joy in the Nativity.

I had lately seen the Russian ballet and had been moved to tears at the tragedy of the dolls in Patroushka. I had the same experience at a performance in Penzance of Giorno's marionettes. Those diminutive figures, with their illusion of being of the stature of ordinary men and women, conveyed a sense of the strange sadness of our lives that I have rarely experienced in the theatre.

It would seem that life is so secret and elusive that it is only by detaching it from reality, as in the Russian ballet and in these marionettes, that we can hope to enclose its form and substance.

The most notable example of this remoteness from imitation is found in the ritual of the Mass. Nothing could be more unlike the scene of the Last Supper than a High Mass according to the Roman rite. And yet any other method than the one employed by the Church would have resulted, as it often has among Protestants, in little more than the reproduction of the outward order in which, for a moment of time, God willed to give the freest and fullest expression of Himself. It may be that much of our modern painting and literature has, in its pursuit of realism, been betrayed by the same purpose - seeking to express what lies behind the actual phenomena by a slavish imitation of the facts that conceal it.

I have often been weary of this play *Bethlehem* which has been produced so many times, and yet I never watch the grotesque figures of the shepherds with a fiddler at their head, followed by the children on their way to the dance before the crib, without experiencing a thrill of emotion. There is nothing in this crowd, in the music of the fiddler or the dances of the children, that is remotely related to the scene of the Nativity, and yet, as I watch them, I am more conscious of the joys of Christmas than I should be in witnessing the most realistic presentation.

I feel the same when the little girl arrives with the toy lamb in her arms. Children no longer care for woolly lambs as when I was a child. I searched the shops in Penzance to find one. 'We don't stock them,' was the answer I received. Teddy-bears were everywhere, but not a lamb to be found. At last I came upon a little toyshop kept by two old ladies in Market Jew Street. 'Yes,' said the elder of the two, who wore her hair in ringlets, 'I know what you want. Children used to be very fond of them when I was a girl, but we have not been asked for such a thing for years. Fancy now! Children like one of these things,' she went on, pointing to a yellow Teddy-bear with a pink ribbon round its neck, 'rather than a little white lamb.' 'I do believe,' said the younger woman, 'we still have one put away somewhere. If the gentleman doesn't mind waiting we might find it. Or perhaps you will call again?' she said. I determined to wait while the two old ladies busied themselves in turning out cupboards and peeping into boxes. At last, when all the cupboards had been emptied out, a lamb was found in a box on the top shelf, a woolly lamb with crooked legs and a bell round its neck. I have never looked on greater innocency. 'We won't charge you the full price,' they said, 'for no one wants them to-day.' I am glad that others loved the lamb as I did. Gert Harvey, a painter in Newlyn, came to me after the play. 'O Ber,' she said, 'where did you get that lamb? His crooked legs made me cry'.

The play has seen many changes since its first presentation, each year adding something; but the use of the whole church as a stage, and the dance of the children before the crib, still give to it any distinction that it may possess. Throughout the years it has retained its character as a religious play. All who take part make their confession and come to communion, pledging themselves to say daily during the weeks of rehearsal the Lord's Prayer, the Hail Mary and the prayer in the Prologue: 'Grant me, dear Lord, the power to act aright the beauties and the wonders of this blessed night, that all may see the tender mercy and the grace of Thy sweet coming to save our fallen race'.

Many of the players are the same as those in the first production. Tom Rowe and Nicholas Peters still play their original parts as shepherds. Tom has only two lines to say, yet after all these years he is apt to forget them. In answer to the inquiry of one of the other shepherds after the coming of the angel, 'What has brother Zack to say?' Tom starts boldly as a man who is certain of his lines would. 'I do say,' he begins and looks to me despairingly; at a smile of encouragement that assures him that he has not mistaken his speech here for his other lines, he goes on: 'Let us run as fast as our poor feet can go' - another pause before he adds, 'And kneel before God's Holy Child.' His hesitation when he offers his presents at the crib have an excellent effect: 'And I - a box of toys' - a long pause while he fumbles in his sack, thinking all the time of his next words - 'some lovely toys' - producing a Noah's ark, ending triumphantly - 'camels and elephants you'll find inside.'

Tom Rowe must have attended hundreds of rehearsals, but he never wearies. After each one it is always, 'When do you want me again, Father?' It is a small part and one that has often given me anxiety, but Tom with his simple smile and lovely voice, which is heard in the shepherds' song, is so complete a character in himself that he contributes more than his halting words.

Of Nicholas Peters it is difficult to write, for the affection he bears me. I do not know whether his eyes or his hands reveal his character the more completely. I have often looked at his hands whilst he has knelt in church. At these times his face has lain in shadow, while his extended hands are in the circle of light cast by a hanging lamp. Nothing can be seen clearly but these hands - very bony, like a drawing by Dürer. Watching them I understood something of the intensity of prayer which owes nothing to any intellectual concept; it is known by the Church as the prayer of simplicity, or of 'the loving look' - with Nicholas Peters it might be termed 'the prayer of the loving hands'.

Nicky, as he is called by his friends, is a very small man with the eyes of a bird. He goes about his work, delivering letters over a twelve-mile round of rough country, in so quiet a manner that he might be met many times on the road without being seen. I doubt if even the gulls and the ravens he passes along the cliffs on his way to some outlying farm are aware of his presence. On the few occasions on which I have seen him in a passion, his eyes have had the look that I once saw in the eyes of a very small bantam who was chasing my spaniel dog from her chickens; they were very angry eyes, so angry that the spaniel fled yelping up the lane before them.

At other times they have the watchfulness I have noticed in the eyes of a bird when she is sitting on her nest. He comes into my room almost every day on his way to dinner, to deliver the paper, and if I am writing or engaged in any way and take no notice of him he will say, 'Nothing wrong, is there, Father? You are not cross with me?' Reassured, he will make a very low bow and go away. Often he comes late at night, especially on Saturday nights, after he has been to Marazion for his weekly shave and has lit the fires in the church. I look up and find him standing at the back of my chair with a lantern in his hand. Our greeting never varies; it is always, 'Is that you, Peters?' 'Yes,' he will answer. 'Thought I would come in just to see you are all right. I'm going home now, Father.' This has gone on for years, and yet his look as he goes out of the room never fails to convey to me a rare and tender affection. It is because I know him so well that I have been able to write him parts to play in which he is completely himself. As one of the shepherds in the Christmas Play he says farewell to the Holy Family in the following words:

> Little Jesus, this is our rough way of showing
> how glad we are on this most blessed day.
> Good-bye now, kind Joseph, and Mary dear,
> Keep well. We shall meet again, have no fear.

It is the greeting of a man of another age than ours; an age when Our Lady and the saints were regarded with a tender familiarity which is lost to us; but Nicholas Peters belongs to that age. As he walks round the church in the play, with my old Spanish cloak on his shoulders, he might have stepped out of an Italian Primitive; and when he kneels down before the crib he prays as men prayed in the twelfth century, when they built the tower and spire of St. Hilary.

Albert Jenkins, who returned last year from Canada, is the third of my original shepherds in the plays. Albert is one of a family of six who live at home with their mother in the Churchtown. Each comes in and goes out, has dinner, and goes to bed when he pleases, while Mrs. Jenkins folds her great arms and laughs at anything they may do. 'What do you think of 'em, Parson?' she will say. 'I've well nigh beaten the life out of 'em; but it makes no difference. If you can do anything with 'em it's more than I can. Look at them,' and she will laugh again. They are as independent of one another as of their mother, but, if any one is so unfortunate as to offend a member of the family, the offender is faced with a solid family of Jenkinses. At one time Harold, the eldest, was working on Trevabyn farm as horseman, while Cecil, a younger brother, attended to the cows, and William, the youngest, who was still at school, was engaged on Saturdays and Sunday mornings to do odd jobs. The farmer, Mr. John Laity, had given orders one Sunday morning that a horse which Harold had been working was to be sent down to his other farm at Gears.

'If the grey horse do go to Gears, Captain, you can get another horseman,' was Harold's answer; when out came Cecil from the cowshed: 'If Harold goes, I'm leaving, too. So you can take your choice, Captain.' William, becoming aware of what was happening in the yard, slid down from the loft, a small figure with his hands in his trousers pockets, and joined his two brothers.

'What do you want up in the hayloft?' said John Laity, looking down at him.

'What do I want?' answered William. 'I want my wages, for I'm leaving; but I'm not going out of the farm-place before you've paid me my wages.' Sunday is not the day for paying wages; but they were paid that morning and the three walked proudly up the lane to the church, where they sat on the stone seat in their working clothes as a witness to the parish of their independence.

Albert was different from the others. He was tall and slight and when standing about the farm would lean against a gatepost or hayrick, as if incapable of standing without support. He once went to be a soldier, but wrote to his mother the first night: 'Can't stay here no longer, mother. You must get me home. Your loving son, Albert.' It was evident that Albert, with a face like a Fra Angelico angel, could never be a soldier, as they realized at the barracks, for I had no difficulty in obtaining his release on grounds of compassion.

'Don't know,' was his answer if any one inquired why he did not like the army. After a time he made up his mind to go to Canada. Neither his mother nor any one else knew his reasons, for to all questions as to why he wanted to go, how he was going to raise sufficient money for his fare, and what he was going to do when he got there, he again answered, 'Don't know.'

I have always been very fond of every member of this attractive family, who could be as loyal to their friends as to one another, but Albert was my favourite. He served at Mass, as a little boy, with the detachment with which he worked on the farm later. He was ready to do anything and to go anywhere, but always in the same dreamlike fashion. I think it was his way of walking that led me to select him for the part of a shepherd in the play. Willie Curnow, a miner with a deep melodious voice, speaks his lines far better, but no one walks with so much grace or leans against the crib with so great abandon as Albert.

This play at Christmas has become a tradition in the parish and has taken the place of the 'entertainment' that I so dreaded on my first coming to St. Hilary. 'Whether you be Church or Chapel you belong to go to the play up to St. Hilary.' Old people, who have not been beyond the end of the garden for years, will be brought, or hobble there on two sticks; young men will 'put their girls there' from neighbouring villages; mothers come with their babies and hold them up to see the procession go by, a procession of players that often has to force its way through the crowds that block the aisles. One night on my way through the crowded aisle to the altar for Benediction, I heard a woman say to a very fat friend by her side, 'Kneel down, my dear, for they are expecting of 'e to go down on your two knees for the service they'm going to have at the altar there.'

'Can't,' said the fat woman. She was right. There was no room for a thin woman to kneel, much less for the stoutest woman in the parish.

The first presentation is usually on Christmas afternoon, when the fading light of a winter's day strikes through the windows and gives further beauty to the candle-lit church. The tall ash trees glisten with their silver balls and 'The House of the Family' in the Chapel of the Sacred Heart is gay with many coloured cushions on which the children sleep before they are awakened by the shepherds.

On one presentation of the play, at which our Bishop, Walter Frere, was present, I had prepared a high throne from which he came to bless and sprinkle with holy water the players who knelt in a line across the church. Seated on the throne in cope and mitre with his pastoral staff he looked a very noble figure and so much part of the play that a stranger, who did not know him, said to me, 'Your players are all wonderful, but surely the man who played the part of the bishop is a great actor.'

On another night I saw a man enter the church whom I recognized as Bernard Shaw. He taunted me later for not providing that one of the kings should be black. 'There is always a black man,' he said, 'and people laugh when they see him as they often do at Ophelia.' He was greatly attracted by the dance before the crib and said, pointing to the children who were passing, 'Those children will remember this dance, and for them dancing will always be a holy thing.' By the way the children looked at him and the smile with which he greeted them I felt that he must be a lover of children and wondered why he had never written a book for them. What fantastic situations might he not have created to delight them?

I introduced him, while we were having tea after the play, to my old friend Norman Garstin, and witnessed the encounter between these two Irishmen. Norman Garstin opened the conversation in his most courteous manner: 'I am most delighted 'to meet you, Mr. Shaw, for we have several things in common.'

'And what may they be?' said Bernard Shaw, resting a hand on Norman's shoulder and looking quizzically into his face.

'I am an Irishman, Mr. Shaw,' Norman replied, stepping back with both hands clasping the lapels of his coat, 'and I too am an admirer of Bernard Shaw.'

It must be fifteen years ago since I first produced the play *Bethlehem*. In fifteen years there is much change in the life of a village. Many have died and not a few have been born. Of the players themselves, those who were children and danced in the play have grown to men and women, some with children of their own, but the play continues unchanged and has become part of the tradition of St. Hilary.

16 CORNISH MINERS

I have told in a previous chapter how, during the years immediately following the signing of peace, we were engaged in visiting the miners who were out of work in Camborne and in the district around Pendeen.

Up to this time I knew nothing of Cornish miners. Years ago I had been very intimate with the fishermen at St. Ives. 'Our little curate is a proper sailor,' they would say. 'Never knawed 'en sick or turn away from his meat.' That was a wonder, as the meat was usually boiled pork and cabbage which I had smelt all the morning cooking in the galley. I had also spent eight years among a seafaring population in Polruan and had on several occasions 'signed on' in tramp steamboats carrying china clay to the northern ports of Spain. I knew something about the lives of these men as well as of those who live on the land, but I had never worked among Cornish miners.

My first meeting with them had been on a night, over thirty years ago, when Charles Marriott and I, walking home across the moor from Penzance to St. Ives, came to a hamlet, not far from Ding Dong Mine, called Cripples' Ease. Among the collection of houses, which could scarcely be called a village, there was an inn, and, wanting a drink, we entered the kitchen where a number of silent men were seated around the fire. Beyond saying 'Good evening' when we entered, they never spoke a word while we were present. Sitting there in the dim light of a hanging lamp they seemed to belong to another world than ours. They were men who had spent the greater part of their lives in darkness, going to work in winter-time before it was light and not coming to the surface, or 'to grass', as miners say, before it was dark. They were strangers to the light of day, whose feet had trodden hundreds of miles of dark ways where a man can scarcely stand upright. Men whose lives from boyhood had been in constant danger from falling rock or a misfire in blasting. They had the appearance of having, through generations of working underground, lost touch with the world above.

I do not remember being in the company of miners from that night until the time Gerard and I took to visiting them. These men now called me 'Brother Walke'. 'Shall us have a bit of prayer before we start in to talk?' was the way they greeted me. Our talks were chiefly of the mine. 'She's been a mother and a father to we,' I have heard them say. They always spoke of the mine as 'she'. 'I've worked in she,' they would say, 'since I was a bit of a boy, as my father and grandfather did before me.' As I listened I understood how the dark underground chambers, where they worked by the light of the candles stuck in their hats, were as much part of their lives as the land or the sea is to other men.

Those meetings were a long time ago, a part of my life that is almost completely blotted out. I have forgotten the names of the men, but I have not forgotten the sound of their voices and the look on their faces as they stood up to offer prayer or discuss the future of their industry. Many of the gatherings took place at the Friends' Meeting-House in Redruth, a building with which I was familiar, having often attended there in the stormy days of the war. Like most Friends' Meeting-Houses it was secluded, hidden away among trees, a place to which people might go unobserved. Outside lay the bodies of many generations of Friends who had conducted their quiet worship within its walls and whose spirits seemed to contribute to its quietness.

This building, which had once sheltered those early Friends, was now filled with miners who sat in rows with expectant faces as if listening for sounds from another world. A man stands up to pray. 'There's no need to tell Thee, Lord, for thou dost know how we do feel with the mines shut down and full of water as they be.' As the prayer continues other voices join in 'Hallelujah! Praise the Lord! Let His glory shine. Amen. Amen.' They are mostly Methodists, but they are miners before they are Methodists. Their 'Amens' and 'Hallelujahs' are sharp and incisive and have the ring of the pick against the naked rock. Their prayers are often eloquent of the longing of the human heart for God, the cries of men who have spent their lives in darkness and whose souls long for light and splendour. Such worship was not unknown among the early Christians, slaves and outcasts, men of uncouth speech, who met in the catacombs to worship as God a man who died a felon's death on the cross.

When the prayer meeting was ended we sat in a circle. Each man in turn spoke his mind. There were some whose hopes lay in a Government subsidy. 'We'll all send a petition to the House of Commons,' they said. 'They're bound to help us when they do know the state we're in.' But the older men and those with most intelligence held to the belief that mining might one day be free of Company promoters. 'It's they black-coated gentry up in London what's ruined mining,' they said. 'They've starved the mines and put all the money on the top to make a show.' Like all Cornish miners, they had a pride in their industry and the part that Cornwall had played in it. 'Go where you will,' I have heard a man say, 'and I reckon you won't find a mine in any part of the world but what there will be a Cornishman at the bottom of 'en.' There was not one who did not want to go back to work underground. 'Above ground is all right for they that is reared to it, but we're underground men,' they would say. 'There's more tin in Cornwall than has ever been taken out. Give us a chance and we'll raise it.' Every discussion came back to, 'Give us a chance to go back to the mine.' This was our problem. There was no escape from that challenge. Like Saul, who went out to look for his father's asses and found a kingdom awaiting him, we had started out with the intention of showing sympathy to the people in distress and found ourselves involved in the task of rebuilding an industry on a Christian basis.

Here was a people, who, unlike many industrial workers, had never lost faith in God. The fire that John

Wesley kindled was not altogether extinguished. They were a race with a tradition that fitted them for an undertaking such as we planned. From time immemorial they had worked their industries of fishing and mining on the share system. When I was at St. Ives there were over three hundred men on the fishing, none of whom, as far as I know, ever worked for a wage. Whether the fishing was for herring or mackerel, each man in the boat shared in the gettings. He put in so many nets and had his share, while the owner of the boat had in addition what was termed 'the Capstan share'. It was the same with mining in its early days. Sets were worked by a company of friends, on capital provided by another friend who had money to invest. Working on a system of sharing is in the Cornishman's blood.

We had come to these men and taught them of the Kingdom of God, a new way of life which would express itself in another and better industrial world. 'Hallelujah!' they said as they listened. 'When that day do come we'll make the old mine ring with the praise of God.'

By this time others had joined Arthur Jenkins, Gerard Collier and myself, men of varying types. Thomas Attlee, a brother of the present deputy leader of the Labour Party in the House of Commons, Russell Hoare, a Cambridge scholar, Frank Fincham, a Congregational Minister, and several others. As we went about the county preaching and holding meetings in the square at Camborne and the Bull Ring at St. Just we, no less than the miners, were upheld by thoughts of the coming of a new social order. The collapse at our doors of the age-long industry of mining had quickened our senses to the danger that threatened our civilization. The years following the signing of peace had brought no assurance of safety. The nation was beginning to arm afresh, the old industrial world was everywhere failing; the revolution in Russia had resulted in the setting up of an order destructive of religion; the war had shaken the foundations of society. Anything might happen. The Kingdom of God might be at hand, to bring the whole process of production and distribution under the influence of religion. As Gerard and I walked about the stricken area of West Cornwall it seemed to us that there could be no other alternative to the purely materialistic basis of society which now prevailed in Russia. A sense of immediacy seems to be bound up with any strong belief. Father Tyrrell says in *Lex Credendi*: 'At every period of religious revival, when men are looking and longing for the Kingdom of God, they are ready to be persuaded and to persuade themselves that it is near, even at the very gates; to translate the inward event to an outward one.' It was so with us at this time. The breaking up of our so-called 'Christian civilization' was imminent. We had reason to hasten as the time was short. Such was our state of mind.

This happened more than ten years ago; and yet, looking at the world to-day, with its disillusionment and loss of faith in itself and its institutions, I do not think that our estimate was altogether without foundation.

It was to the Church that we looked for the rescue of society. At the fall of the Roman Empire the Church had saved civilization, and she still had the power to infuse a new spirit into the failing industrial world. The Church whose Founder taught men to pray 'Thy kingdom come. Give us day by day our daily bread' could not be indifferent to the conditions under which they earned their daily bread. We planned therefore to make a beginning in Cornwall by founding an order, under the auspices of the Church, in which men might work for the glory of God and the good of their fellow-men. Since our intention was not merely to provide employment but to inspire industry with the spirit of giving, the workers were asked to surrender the surplus profits of their industry for the use of the whole community. Those who had capital over and above their immediate needs were asked to give, or loan it without interest, to provide tools, plant and machinery for the use of the workers.

In the Middle Ages men and women endowed cathedrals and parish churches for the glory of God and for the good of their fellow-men. The need to-day was for industry to be directed to the same end. Such a method of raising capital would not always be necessary, for, as the funds in the hands of such an industrial council as we proposed increased, the need for loans would disappear.

It was to 'The Church in Cornwall' and the many separated bodies of Christians that we made our appeal. I have a document commending this meeting, signed by Guy Warman, Bishop of Truro, Herbert Rider, Chairman of the Wesleyans in Cornwall, Rhys Harris, Secretary of the Congregational Union in Cornwall, J.R. Green, Baptist Minister, E.C. Lark, United Methodist Minister, William Bryant, Primitive Methodist Minister, and Arthur Jenkins of the Society of Friends. It was not the Catholic Church to which all might render their allegiance, but it represented a measure of unity and offered a hope that, struggling together to bring about some of the outward conditions of the Kingdom of God, we might find our way back to the unity of the Catholic Church.

We acquired a deserted mine near Scorrier that had not been worked for fifty years. This mine, like every mine in Cornwall, had a history handed down from father to son by men who had worked in her. 'The old men', as miners call them, will remember how at one time a mine 'cut rich' and under what conditions she was abandoned. They will talk of levels and adits that were cut before they were born, and are often able to make a plan of a mine that has been long deserted. This particular mine was well spoken of by 'the old men'. If I remember rightly, it had been worked for copper, at a time when the price of tin was low, and it might therefore be expected to contain tin at a sufficiently high level for economic working. Mr. William Hoskin, President of the Institute of Cornish Mining Engineers, who gave us his services, advised a survey, which involved the opening up of the old shaft and the clearing of certain levels to enable him to go down and make a further report.

Having begged sufficient capital to cover the cost of

this work, we fixed a date for the service of dedication which was to take place at the Friends' Meeting-House in Redruth. We had chosen a ring as a symbol of the marriage of men to industry under the blessing of the Church. This silver ring, large enough to encircle the finger of the great hand of a miner, was presented to the Bishop at the service of dedication with the following words: 'We wish to share with each other in our life and work and to do so under the guidance, protection and blessing of the Church of Christ in Cornwall. We bring you this ring as the symbol of our union with one another and of the union of the Church with work and life. We ask you to bless it and to bring into being the Communion of the Ring in Cornwall, into which any may be received who takes the ring, making publicly a solemn promise of service to God and man.'

After the blessing of the ring I watched fifty miners go up to where the Bishop and the Ministers of the different denominations were sitting and take the vow. 'I promise in the presence of God and of you, my brothers, that, while I share in the Communion of the Ring in Cornwall, I will work for the glory of God, for the love of Jesus and for my fellow-men.' Some spoke haltingly, as I had often heard men speak before the Altar at their marriage; others proudly, as if confident of themselves; but each in turn, from the oldest miner to the youth who had never been underground, spoke with the solemnity of men engaged in a great undertaking.

While I sat there watching them I thought of the Abbey Church the Monks of St. Benedict were building at Buckfast on the borders of Dartmoor. The great religious orders, the Benedictines, Franciscans and Dominicans, had been driven out of England, their lands confiscated and their buildings laid waste, but they were back again as a witness to the world that life without God has no meaning and that apart from religion all human activities are worthless and must come to an end.

I thought of how the industrial and economic systems of Europe had broken down, not because of the failure of national resources, the shortage of labour or the absence of technical skill. These were all present in abundance; what was lacking was the dynamic to start industry afresh, the power of the pure love of God and of our fellow-men. I felt that I was witnessing how this power could come into men's lives and fit them for service. These men, who had vowed that morning to work for the love of Jesus and for the good of their fellow-men, had been wage-earners working for a company whose methods they distrusted. Their incentive had been the weekly wage, but this was not enough. Their religion had no part in their working life. It was an emotion that had found no outlet other than at their prayer meetings. Their Hallelujahs and Amens could now come into their work. Each stroke of the pick might be a Hallelujah, for it was for the glory of God they were now going to work. All their earnings beyond their bare living would go to help other men to work in the same way as themselves. I turned from their eager faces to those who sat on the platform, the Bishop and Ministers of religion. They represented the greater part of the religious community in Cornwall, but they lacked cohesion and appeared, as they sat there on the platform to be a collection of individuals rather than a living organism. Were they aware, I wondered, of the revolutionary nature of the plan to which by their presence they had set their approval, and if so were they, as a body, courageous enough to lead the world back to a sacramental conception of industry?

Three months later the engineer sent in his report. The work of opening up the shaft and clearing the levels, he stated, was highly satisfactory and had been carried out at an exceptionally low cost. This was the first stage. If the mine was to be developed according to the engineer's recommendation, we needed a large capital sum amounting to many thousands of pounds. This we had foreseen and provided for by setting up a committee of people in London who had guaranteed to raise the sum required on condition that the scheme received the support of three important people in Cornwall whom they named, one of whom was the Bishop. He wrote commending the venture. The lady whose name had been chosen by the Committee had also written approvingly. Each morning I scanned the post for the third letter. After days of waiting I received a communication from the Bishop. 'Nothing can be done,' he said. 'I have consulted with the others concerned and they are of the same opinion. The letter enclosed will explain.' The letter to which he referred was signed by the man whose approval we sought. 'The Government,' he wrote, 'is preparing a scheme for road-making to relieve unemployment, and any rival scheme would be most inopportune.'

The Bishop was right in his estimation. Nothing could be done. If it had been possible for us to develop the mine, unaided by the support that had been promised us, it would have only been another scheme to assist unemployment.

What we had sought was the acceptance by the whole religious community of responsibility for the way men earned the daily bread. We had failed, and all that is left of the venture is a great silver ring and a proof copy of '*The Servants of the Church*. Plan and Constitution. Price one penny.'

17 A VISIT TO SPAIN

I have lately discovered a diary for the year 1923. It has many empty spaces, but against the date 27th April is the entry: 'Gerard died. Requiem aeternam dona ei, Domine.' This is followed by more empty spaces, the next entry being on 4th June, 'A. and I left home.'

Gerard had been away attending a Conference in Switzerland at the time we received the letter from the Bishop putting an end to our hopes for *The Servants of the Church*. He came home on Easter Eve and hurried up to see us. He was very strange that night. Whether this was due to the shadow of his approaching death, or dismay at what had happened in his absence, I do not know. In the midst of telling us of the people he had met he broke off suddenly and said, 'I see chasms opening before me.' The words were spoken in a way that made it impossible for us to inquire their meaning. We waited in silence for him to explain, but nothing further was said and we never knew for certain to what they referred. His ever-increasing sense of responsibility for the welfare of the Community was a burden too heavy for his sensitive soul. The war, the trouble in Ireland, the Russian famine, and now our failure to achieve what, to his mind, might have been the beginning of Christian Communism, had overwhelmed him. His death, which was due to a form of muscular paralysis, was unexpected. After being laid up for some weeks with an attack of influenza he was supposed to be sufficiently convalescent to come and stay with us. We had prepared my room where he could look out on to the garden; but on the day he was expected he sent a message for us to come to him instead. We found him lying very still, unable to move his hands or turn his head. He spoke some words that conveyed his love for us and that was all. We knew when we left him that his death was not far away. I went again that evening and took him the Last Sacraments, intending to stay the night with him, but by midnight he was gone. As I walked home on that still April night I was conscious of an overwhelming loss. A friendship such as we had never known before had gone from us.

Gerard and I had lived through so much during the years of the war and later, as we went about Cornwall together making plans for the reconstruction of its industries, that his death left a great gap in my life, a gap that no one could fill. What I needed was to go away and look at life afresh. This is the explanation of the entry in my diary for the fourth of June. On our way to the station I remember being held up in the narrow street of Marazion by a long cavalcade of shows and roundabouts that was on the road after Corpus Christi Fair. We nearly lost our train through the delay, but we took it as a good omen that we should meet others like ourselves who were moving on to some fresh adventure. We spent the following day in London, staying with Laura and Harold Knight. Munnings came to dinner, after a day at Epsom, and tried to persuade me to stay another night and go to the Derby with him. 'There are some rare people there, Walke,' he said. 'You would like to meet them. I was talking to-day to an old couple who were setting up an 'accommodation'. Forty Derbys, they told me, they had been to with the same old accommodation. What a life!' said A.J. 'You had better come up with me to-morrow and meet them.'

At Victoria Station the next morning we saw the royal train waiting to take the King to the Derby, and I thought of His Majesty and the man with the 'accommodation' enjoying their day on the Downs and rather regretted that we were not going to join them. But when the boat-train labelled Newhaven and Dieppe drew alongside the platform I was glad that we were going to France and not to the Derby.

It was ten years since we had been abroad, our last visit having been to Capri before the war. Nothing appeared to have changed in those years. The great crucifix still guarded the entrance to the harbour of Dieppe to bless all who passed in or out. The walk from the customs across the rails to the train for Paris, the frantic farewells of French families, the slow progress of the train along the sea front, were all as I remembered them. In these familiar scenes I forgot the tragedy of the war, when Dieppe was a port of embarkation for the wounded, and my own struggles and disappointments during those years; crossing the channel had changed my mental outlook; I was as I had been before the war. We arrived in Paris that afternoon and went on the same night to Bordeaux and from there to a village in the Pyrenees.

The only event that I especially remember during our stay in this village is my visit to Lourdes. On my way there, at Pau station, among a crowd of fashionably dressed people I noticed an old peasant woman sitting alone on a bench. In the midst of the excitement that prevailed on the arrival of the train for Paris, while porters struggled with trunks and dressing-cases and passengers rushed up and down looking for corner seats, this old woman sat quietly by the side of her bundle. I judged by her appearance that her home was a Breton fishing village. I had seen many such faces as hers at St. Ives, faces of women worn and grown old with anxiety and privation. But the face of this old woman, while it was like, was also strangely different from those. It held a serenity such as I have only seen on the faces of the dead. As on the faces of the dead the ravages of age had become softened; it was still the face of an old woman, but its expression was that or a child. Her rosary had dropped from her fingers and lay on her lap. I doubt if I have ever looked on one who appeared so quiet as this old woman. Her attitude as she sat there on that crowded platform, waiting for a train to take her home, was that of one who had ceased to take any part in the activities which go to make up the life of ordinary people. She was returning home after having completed a pilgrimage to Lourdes. I knew this much by the badge she was wearing. What had happened to her I did not know. Probably if I had inquired she would have said, 'I have been to our dear Lady's Shrine.' That was enough. Her old eyes had looked at the place to which the Queen of Heaven had come to visit the child Bernadette; her lips had touched the rock on which Her feet had rested; she had lighted a candle and had joined in the procession of the Blessed Sacrament, made her confession and received communion and was now returning with medals and rosaries for those at home. The train for Paris left; another came and went; the local train that was to take me to Lourdes was waiting. Before I took my place in this train I walked down the platform again. There she was, sitting by the side of her bundle as calm and beautiful as when I first saw her.

After my visit to Lourdes we left the village of Sauveterre and motored to Saint-Jean-Pied-de-Port at the foot of the Pyrenees, where we stayed the night after having dined with Robert and Eleanor Hughes, friends of ours from Lamorna. On the following day we went to Pamplona by the motor-bus that crosses the Pyrenees. At the Spanish frontier, where a bridge crosses a stream, we produced our passports. 'Annie Walke, Artist. Yes, I understand,' said the customs' officer. 'Bernard Walke, Clerk in Holy Orders.' He read it again. What could this strange profession be? The commandant was called and came out of a hut, buckling on his sword. 'Clerk in Holy Orders,' he said. 'What does that mean?' 'Clergyman,' I said. 'Vicar of St. Hilary.' This was still more confusing. They continued to sample the words, each time with greater suspicion, until Annie Walke intervened with,' Monsieur le Curé.' 'Ah, I see,' said the commandant, 'with Madame. Very good.' Giving a wink to Annie Walke that wrinkled one side of his nose to the level of his eye, he patted me on the shoulder and waved the driver on. We went up and up through forests of chestnut trees, round hairpin bends where the whole of the world seemed below us, to some sawmills at the summit of the pass; here we waited for the engines to cool. The rest of the journey was down a pleasant incline to the village of Hoiz, where there was a train to Pamplona.

It was in defending this town of Pamplona against the French that Ignatius Loyola received the wound which was eventually to lead him to the cave of Manresa and the founding of the Society of Jesus. We were several weeks in this place. We stayed at the Hotel Maisonave, and spent our mornings hearing Mass in one or other of the many churches and sitting outside cafes in the square. Each afternoon we went by the steam-tram to some village in the country, where Annie Walke painted (having developed a passion for this austere landscape) and I wandered about the country, looking at churches and talking to peasants. After a time it grew very hot and we had a longing for the sea. I had once walked along the coast of Biscay and knew of many delightful villages there. Our difficulty lay in making a choice. We have always had an inhibition about decisions of this kind and have often been driven to absurd lengths to avoid them. On this occasion we arrived at a compromise; we would go to San Sebastian and take the train that runs between there and Bilbao, leaving the train when we came to what looked an attractive place. In our carriage was a young Spaniard who became aware of our plan. 'Zumaya,' he said, 'very beautiful for artists, and very good hotel.' By the time he had written down the name of the hotel at which he advised us to stay, the train drew up at a station. 'Zumaya,' said our friend, and disappeared. I bear him no ill-will for capturing us and placing us in an hotel of which, as we discovered later, he was the proprietor. Zumaya was beautiful, as he had said, and we were very happy there.

At sunset on the day of our arrival the bells in the church started a wild clanging which heralded a procession of dancing children; these were followed by grotesque figures with heads of wolves and bears, who carried inflated bladders with which to beat the children and any one else who came within their reach. Then came a Basque band of three musicians, playing a kind of flageolet with one hand and beating a drum with the other, and a giant and giantess, twenty feet high, who danced with mincing steps in time to the music. The giants had come to announce the advent of the Feast and appeared again three days later to proclaim its end.

After Mass on the day of the Feast, a golden St. Peter was carried in triumph round the village, wearing gloves that hung loosely from his fingers and a jewelled tiara that constantly needed adjusting as the procession moved unevenly over the cobbled streets. As an image it was a more grotesque figure than the giants themselves, but it evoked great devotion from the fishermen of Zumaya who surged around it clamouring, 'Beate Petre, beate Petre, ora pro nobis.'

At our table that morning were four men dressed in loud clothes and shiny patent-leather boots; particularly disagreeable-looking men we thought them as they leaned across the table picking their teeth. After lunch, while we sat drinking coffee on the veranda, an ancient carriage drove up, drawn by two old white horses decked with coloured ribbons. There was a stir in the hotel as these four men came down the steps bowing and blowing kisses to the maids who thronged the doorway. They were resplendent now in tight-fitting costumes of embroidered satin and all the panoply of the bull-ring. They were the proprietors and the leading characters of a bull-fight which all the village had gone out to watch. I believe the old priest, whom we met later in the village, and we ourselves were the only people in Zumaya who were not present in the bull-ring meadow.

In the evening we saw our four friends again; they were at dinner, but no longer sat at the best table by the window. Their smiles and simpers met with no response from the maids who waited on them. Children left their parents to go and look at them and then ran away giggling. There they sat picking their teeth savagely, while children laughed in their faces and jibes were hurled at them from every table in that crowded room. They had refused to kill the bull and were now being taunted for cowardice - a charge probably quite undeserved. It was rather greed than cowardice they were guilty of. The bull was their private property, their stock-in-trade, as it were, and they hoped to bring him out again at another fiesta in a neighbouring village. After a pretence of toasting each other, they rose from the table. Like the bull, they were escaping, but not without some show of spirit, for as the crowd in the room greeted their departure with ironical clapping of hands and cries of 'Brava' they turned, and standing in the doorway bowed their acknowledgements.

Strange men were constantly arriving at this hotel. They always came late at night and were admitted at a door leading into the garden. What their business was we never discovered; possibly they were smugglers of French brandy with which the hotel was well supplied. A Belgian, who knew Zumaya well, and with whom we became friendly, was persistent in his questions as to our business and what had led us to stay in this hotel. 'Have you been here before?' he inquired. We told him 'No'. 'Then why are you here now?' he asked. He evidently knew more than we did about these nightly visitors and was anxious to discover our connexion with them.

This little man was a travelling photographer who specialized in lovers. Bashful couples crowded round his camera while he posed them two by two in alluring attitudes. One afternoon when business was slack, he offered to take us to call on the Spanish painter Zuloaga who had a villa in the neighbourhood. However, he was not at home and we never saw him. What we did see, however, was worthy of a journey into Spain. In his private chapel among other pictures were six El Grecos, including the massive picture of the Temptation of St. Antony. I have never been so conscious of the passionate romanticism of Spain as when I came on these pictures by El Greco in that obscure village.

After having been away for six weeks it was a joy to be back at St. Hilary. In my absence Canon Rogers had been in charge of the parish. Canon Rogers, or Father Rogers, as he was always known, was a Cornishman, his family having lived at Penrose for centuries, but in appearance and manner he might have been a Monsignor at Seville Cathedral. He was now eighty and had some years before resigned the living of Penzance where he had been a notable figure. Dressed in a cassock, without a hat in all weathers and, in summer-time, with a large green umbrella, he used to amble slowly from one end of the town to the other. There were so many people who wanted to speak to him and so many children clinging on to his cassock that his progress was always slow. This saintly old man who was now living at the Manor Cottage in Goldsithney and who, to the day of his death, climbed the hill to St. Hilary to say his daily Mass, was as much loved here as he had been at Penzance. The day we returned he was at the church waiting to tell me of all that had happened during my absence.

There were others who heard of our return. My old tramps (the 'regulars' as our maid Emma calls them) knew within a few days that we were home. Some of them apologized for not having come before to welcome us. 'Should have been here sooner, mister, if we'd known,' they said. A number of tramps drift down from the north, much in the same way as the birds do in cold weather. It is warmer in Cornwall and so they come from Manchester and as far away as Glasgow to spend the winter here. The 'regulars' are different. They are here winter and summer and keep to their beat, usually between Truro and the Land's End. A queer procession they would make if they could be seen all together, musicians who play on whistle-pipes or accordions, men with trays of needles and thread, others without trays who carry their meagre stock in their hands; some are without a leg and others without arms. I knew them all. There is 'our Will' who always quotes Shakespeare and asks for a loan, and Jimmy who cuts out pipe-racks and photograph frames with a fret-saw. Each Christmas this little man presents me with a robin supporting a calendar on his very red breast. I have a number of these robins stowed in my drawer. Jimmy is a cheerful little person whose only complaint against life is that his wife has too long a tongue. 'Don't you never marry a nagging woman,' he advises me each time he calls.

My two most regular 'regulars', Camborne Jack and Old Williams, I have known for the whole twenty years that I have been at St. Hilary. Camborne Jack makes no pretence of looking for work or even carrying bootlaces for sale. I have never seen him in any other clothes than corduroy trousers tied up with string below the knee, several waistcoats, an over-large coat and a red handkerchief round his neck. He leans against the doorpost when he comes, and says, 'Here, Mister. Have 'e got a vest or a shirt you can give me?' He then takes off his coat and exhibits a torn shirt or unbuttons his various waistcoats and exposes a hairy chest. There is no avoiding him, for he will stand about the door for hours. If I am out and he catches Annie Walke, he bullies her into giving him a pair of socks or one of my shirts and then lies in wait for me. 'What good are these things,' he says, 'to a man with an empty belly and no money for his lodge? You know better than to let me go away like that.' There is no satisfying him. 'What's the good of tobacco to me,' he says, 'if I have no pipe to smoke it in?' He will even demand a box of matches after all his other wants have been satisfied. His mouth is always drawn down and he never smiles or says 'Thank you'. Only once have I seen any expression on his ravaged old face beyond that of the professional tramp. This was after I had been ill and had not seen him for several months. There he was leaning against the doorpost, but instead of his usual demand he offered me his hand and said, 'I'm glad to see you, Mister.'

Old Williams was of a different type and had to be treated with greater ceremony. When he called he was always shown up into my room and introduced to any one who happened to be there. I met him first in the old churchyard, looking for the graves of his father and mother. It was only later that I heard his story. How his people, who owned a farm at Germoe, had sent him to Oxford with the intention of his becoming a clergyman. Whether he did not favour this idea or whether it was something else, I do not know - something happened that led to his leaving Oxford and never returning home. Now, as an old man, he had come back to the district he had known as a boy. I bought him a pedlar's licence and set him up with a stock of picture postcards with which to gain his livelihood. I renewed his licence each year, but I never purchased any more postcards. Those I bought him twenty years before were still in his possession, very faded and greasy, on the night of his death. Old Williams had a distinguished appearance and most courteous manners. I have watched him in Penzance on market days hurrying up the street, waving his hand to his clients as one friend does to another. 'Coming to see you soon,' he would call out to them as he passed. He was a Roman Catholic and on saying good-bye to me it was his custom to add, 'It is all right, Father, as long as we get to purgatory.' I do not know if he often attended Mass. He certainly never forgot that he was a Catholic and always carried a rosary. I saw him come into church one Christmas for the midnight Mass, dressed in a frock-coat that he must have hired for the occasion from an old-clothes shop. I was very annoyed at the suppressed laughter which greeted him and must have shown my displeasure, for the old man, thinking that my frowns were directed against himself came up to me and, after balancing himself on his toes to test his sobriety, whispered, 'I've had a little drop, as you can see, Father, but it's all right. I've been to my duties and got my absolution.' When he turned to go back to his seat I discovered that it was not the tall hat and the frock-coat that had been the cause of the laughter, but a bottle of whisky sticking out of his coat-tails.

The last time he called was the Christmas before I left home. I was ill at the time and Laura told him that I was not seeing any one. 'Give the Father this Christmas card,' he said, 'and tell him it will be all right if we can get to purgatory.' That same night on his way home from St. Hilary to his 'lodge' in Penzance he walked into the water of the harbour, where his body was found the next morning. He was nearly blind and growing very old. I think that it was better for him to find his way to purgatory through the waters of the harbour than from a bed in a common lodging-house.

Shortly after our return from Spain we were out on Perran Downs and came across a young donkey on a span. I have often noticed on young animals the same look that distinguishes children from grown-up people. Chickens and ducklings, young bull calves and little pigs, colts and young donkeys, all have the appearance of being of another race. 'God's little creation,' as a man at St. Hilary once spoke of it to me, 'is very good at this time.' It is the little creation of which Blake wrote in *The Songs of Innocence*. This world of innocence soon passes. I have looked into a nest of half-fledged birds and seen five extended heads with gaping mouths waiting for this strange creature, whom they looked on for the first time, to provide them with food. On my next visit, five little naked bodies were huddled together in fear. Their mother had told them that all was not well with the world.

I once watched a donkey a few hours old after having explored the moor where he was born, come back and assure his mother by his antics that it was an excellent moor and a good world for a donkey to come into, while the mother shook her head much in the same way as an old woman does, after listening to the babblings of a child.

The donkey I discovered on Perran Downs had passed this age of innocence. He looked sad at having to submit to the chain on his fore-leg and was distressed at being unable to get at a clump of young furze that grew beyond the reach of his span. All my love for donkeys came back to me as I stood and watched his efforts to reach that bit of furze. On my way home I held forth to Annie Walke on the pleasures of keeping donkeys and how unwise I had been in getting rid of ours. A few days later, on an afternoon when the country was shrouded in a sea mist, Laura, our maid, came to tell me that I was wanted at the door. 'You're wanted most particular,' she said. 'Who is it?' I inquired. 'A lady, who says she knows you very well but that she can't come in,' said Laura. I got up unwillingly from the fire and went out to see this lady who wanted me 'most particular'. At the door stood Annie Walke, with the donkey I had admired on Perran Downs. She had been down that afternoon and bought the donkey, harness and shay. 'My birthday present,' she said, 'only I could not wait until next week to give it to you.' At that moment I knew that I did not want a donkey, that I was too old to return to driving about the country in a donkey shay. I admired the donkey and examined the harness and shay, but Annie Walke knew me too well to be deceived by my exclamation of surprise and happiness. 'Never mind,' she said, 'wait for a fine day before you take him out.' I could not unharness the donkey and go back to sit over the fire as if nothing had happened. The only thing to do was to get up in the shay and go for a drive. It was not a happy drive as, apart from my dejection at my own ungraciousness, the donkey had not been properly broken and would not answer to the rein. I was constantly getting down from the shay to prevent him climbing banks or burrowing into hedges. Donkeys have a way of always walking by the side of the road. I had lately seen them in Spain trotting along the dusty roads with bundles of grass on their backs, always by the side and never in the middle of the road where a horse would go. It is their nature to want to pass unobserved; but this donkey, not content to walk by the side of the road, attempted to climb hedges to escape the tiresome business of drawing a cart. As I wandered on in the drizzling rain, wondering what I could say to Annie Walke on my return, I thought of the old man at Sennen who said to me, 'They motors have spoilt the road for donkeys'; and now I said to myself: 'They've spoilt you for donkeys.' This was my last ride in a donkey shay.

We kept this donkey, whom we called Ignatius, for

several years until he mysteriously disappeared. I had been away from home and on returning found no Ignatius in the fields. Some days later I met a child who said to me, 'Mr. Laity of Trevabyn has sold your donkey, Father.'

'Sold my donkey! What do you mean?' I said.

'He's sold 'en, Father,' the child answered. 'I seed Mr. Laity drive him out of the field. He said that he'd get rid of the old thing while the Parson was away.'

I went to Trevabyn that morning and found the family at dinner. 'What is this story, John,' I said 'of your having sold my donkey while I was away?'

'My dear Father Walke,' said John, getting up from the table with the carving knife and fork in his hands 'whatever tales have you been listening to? Sell your donkey! My gracious me! Whatever next will they be saying!'

'Don't you believe him,' said Rachel, the youngest daughter. 'I told father that you would be vexed with him.'

'I am vexed,' I said. 'You'll go and buy him back this morning.'

'I've never sold him,' said John obstinately, 'and you ought to bc ashamed, Rachel, at taking your father's character away as you are doing. Seeing you weren't at home,' he continued, 'I lent him to a friend who keeps the White Hart at Hayle. A good home he's got there, too,' he added as if he had done us both a service. John Laity was right, he had a good home at the White Hart and there I let him stay. He is the last donkey I shall ever own.

18 THE JOLLY TINNERS

There are houses, like people, that attract at a first meeting. It was so with the Jolly Tinners as we passed it on the first day we came to St. Hilary. I did not know the history of this square house, built of blocks of granite with a wide doorway opening on to the road, that seemed to invite passers-by to enter.

It was a friendly house; its windows held no peeping eyes and looked out on to the world without evil intent. I learnt later that it had been an inn. It was a house, I was told, that had always kept good company in the days when the mines in the district were working and the population of St. Hilary was treble what it is to-day.

The old vicarage where I was born was another such house. 'The Black Dog', it was called, before it became a vicarage. Often, when we were children, a stranger would open the door of the hall where we were playing and call for 'a pint of beer'. Unlike the house of my childhood, the Jolly Tinners had remained unchanged. There was the bar, over which many landlords had presided, and the shelves that had once held rows of shining glasses. The kitchen had a stone floor and an old-fashioned Cornish slab round which stood a high settle. Upstairs four bedrooms overlooking the road were separated by folding doors, that when these stood open the four bedrooms became one long room. This was the old club-room where the miners would meet at Feast and other holiday times. Everything in that house was as it had been when the last landlord closed its doors. The sign of The Jolly Tinners had gone, but it had not lost its air of good company.

Whenever I passed that way I regretted that this building, which had once been possessed by laughter and jollity, should stand empty and forlorn. I thought of many things for which it might be used, a house for an order of preaching friars, who could sing the offices in the church, or a place where we might lodge the wayfarers who were constantly calling. I had many plans, but none materialized, and the old house stood waiting for the children who eventually came to it.

Their first coming was brought about without my intervention. Some lady, unknown to me, who had never been to St. Hilary, rented the place and established four children there under the charge of Grace Costin, a friend of ours. After two years the lady, who had founded the home, tired of her experiment and proposed to break up the establishment and place the children in different institutions. This happened soon after our return from Spain. There was the old house, and there were the four children, Clara, a beautiful wild creature, Billy, a shy boy of twelve, Bill, the burglar, who was on two years' probation, and Elizabeth, a little girl of eight who had no parents or any relatives we ever heard of. Here they were, and here I felt they must remain. With the help of Father Rogers and Mrs. Bolitho I founded the home afresh.

I proposed having ten children, five boys and five girls. This would be a large family, but not so large as to be an institution. Institutions for children may be inevitable under the present conditions of society but they can never meet the children's need for a home. Fifty boys or fifty girls, all of the same age under one roof, are as little like a family as it is possible to be. The herding of so many children of the same sex together is unnatural and necessitates a discipline alien to home life.

The Jolly Tinners was to be a home for boys and girls until they were old enough to earn their living. Such a home would cost a considerable sum of money each year if the children were to be taught a suitable trade or profession. Except for a gift of a hundred pounds from the original benefactress we had no funds. It was a venture of faith which I have never regretted. The money has always come; often unexpectedly to meet some urgent need.

It was Clarke Hall (Sir William Clarke Hall, he became later), the Magistrate of Old Street Police Court, who introduced me to a sad world of children, a world where home is often an evil place that it were better for children not to know.

I have at times attended Clarke Hall's Juvenile Court, which used to be held on Friday afternoons in the Shoreditch Town Hall. It was free from the ugly surroundings of the Police Court with its prisoners' dock and shameful associations. The police here were in plain clothes, although I doubt if the children had any illusions about them. It was Clarke Hall himself, sitting in an arm-chair at the head of the table, who gave confidence to the little creatures who came stumbling in, often blinded by tears. His hair was so white and his face so smooth and rosy, that no child could be embarrassed for long in his presence. 'Come here, my child,' he would say, 'and you shall tell me about it' I do not remember his talking very much. His examination reminded me of the story of the Catholic Priest listening to a man in the confessional who had confessed to the sin of murder. 'More than once, my son?' said the voice behind the grille. 'No, Father, only once,' came the answer. 'Your mother?' said the Priest.

Under Clarke Hall's examination the child was made to feel that although he had set fire to the shavings in the workshop, or stolen a shilling from the till of the sweet-shop round the corner, he might have done much worse. There were probation officers and women magistrates sitting round the table, but the old man and the child who sat on his knee or played with his watch-chain appeared to be as little aware of their presence as they were of the portraits of past Mayors of Shoreditch looking down on them from the walls. Clarke Hall must have heard many strange stories from children on those Friday afternoons, tales of cruelty and horror, of arson, theft and immorality. He listened to them all with the same unhurried air, debating with himself how he could best help each particular child.

Some of these children he sent to the Jolly Tinners, having committed them to my care until they were sixteen, under an order of the Court. One of the first, I remember, was a little girl whose father was a Chinaman and whose mother was English, a woman of mixed tastes as regards husbands. Her first venture had been an Indian, whom she married and left after a child was born. She then lived with a Chinaman, a good man according to the report of the neighbourhood. The Chinaman was a sailor and on one of his voyages to Australia this woman with whom he had been living married a negro. Len Wou, her child by the Chinaman, was now eight years old and apparently did not approve of this exchange of fathers. According to the evidence given by her mother at the Police Court, she was beyond her control, remaining in bed all day powdering and painting her face. I believed at the time that the charges against the child were brought with the intention of getting rid of her. However, as she was evidently unhappy in her home, I consented to have her at St. Hilary. This led to further complications, as the Chinese population in Limehouse became suspicious. 'What has the white woman done with the Chinaman's child?' they asked. And I was sent for to explain that the child was happy and in a good home. My arrival in a powerful car, such as is rarely seen in Limehouse, caused a sensation among the river-side population. Every one 'in the narrow street where Len Wou had lived came out of the doors and crowded round the car. They all seemed to know why I was there. 'Very good car,' they said. 'Very rich man, very good man, adopted Chinaman's child.'

After explaining that it was not my car and that I was not a very rich man nor had I adopted the China-man's child but that she was in a good home, I went into the house and saw Len Wou's mother. There was a black baby in a cradle by the fire. 'He's going to be a priest,' his mother said as she put a teat into his mouth to stop his crying. 'His father is a good man and would like to have a priest for a son.' From her history it was evident that she favoured good men irrespective of their colour. We had Len Wou with us for several years and then her mother came and kidnapped her and we never saw her again.

I have found the parents of these children to be very haphazard in their relationship to them. Under the conditions in which they exist, life is so fierce a struggle that it is difficult to remember children who are absent. A mother, after being unconcerned for years as to what has happened to her child, will write a letter full of affection and quite possibly never write again. It is not so with the children. However much they love the home here and however many ties bind them to the place, they miss the background of their own family. I have known children without any record of their own parentage invent a family of brothers and sisters and give a detailed account of the place where they lived and the things they did there. My experience has been that nothing ever completely compensates a child for the loss of a real home of its own.

As far as it is possible to provide a substitute, the Jolly Tinners is a home. If you were to ask the children about the Matron, they would not know of whom you were speaking. 'As your mother is not here,' she says to a new child, 'I am going to be your mother.' She is a mother in the understanding she has of children and the affection she bestows upon them. Most of us, as we grow older, forget how desperately important quite trivial things can be when we are young; but she never makes a mistake of this kind or forgets the likes and dislikes of any child, that comes under her charge.

I have a book in which all the available information about each child is recorded, date of birth, school certificate, report from Mr. Cyril Burt, the London County Council psychologist, and many other things. There is much information in this book on their history and characteristics, and yet, if ever I refer to it, what is written conveys little to me. It is not that I have altogether forgotten what they were like when they first came, but that they have so changed that it is difficult to associate them with their early records. The kind of things I remember best are little white faces searching the platform on their arrival at Penzance, grimy hands placed in mine as they arrive home, or how a very small boy ran down the church after Benediction and clasping my knees looked up to my face and said, 'I never want to leave this place, never. Look at the candles!' There is a child now in the home who has probably forgotten how, years ago, he went out of the house in a rage, and swearing never to return, climbed on to the roof of the church from whence he dared any one to come up after him. I shall always remember that queer little figure on the roof shouting, 'What is God, I should like to know?'

It is ten years since the Jolly Tinners opened its doors to these children. During this period I have had many anxious times, inevitable with any family of children, and especially with a family like ours. The streets round Shoreditch and Clerkenwell, where most of them come from, are not good places for children to spend the first years of their life.

The Church regards the 'age of innocence' as continuing up to the seventh year, but before this age is reached many London children are familiar with every form of vice and crime. The world they know is the world of the streets, their entertainments are gangster films and public-house brawls. St. Hilary, with its quiet ordered life, is another world to them.

'I'm in the fresh air, I'm in the fresh air,' I heard a child sing as she danced one night by herself in the garden. 'Can't sleep,' said another child who came from City Road. 'Can't sleep for the noise that goes on.' The clanging of trains, the shouts of stall-holders in the City Road were wont to pass unnoticed; here the song of birds, the cawing of rooks and the sound of an occasional footstep in the road kept him from sleep.

After a long experience I am convinced that it is environment and not heredity that is the determining factor in a child's life; he may inherit a moral weakness such as a tendency to steal, as he may be born with a liability to tuberculosis, but the character of the child can be strengthened to resist this tendency just as his body can be built up to resist the ravages of disease.

'Give me a child up to seven and the world can do with him what it will,' said St. Ignatius. He was probably right in his estimate of the importance of those early years; modern psychology is on his side and would suggest that the unconscious, which so largely dominates our life, is built up in infancy. And yet those other years, from seven to fourteen, with which I have been mostly concerned, must have their share in determining the child's future. The character of a little girl earning a living for a dissolute father by dancing in the streets, or of a boy who has never known a home and has lived, as a stray cat or dog lives, by picking up what he can from the streets, cannot fail to be affected by the years lived at St. Hilary. In the streets where the children at the Jolly Tinners have spent the first years of their life, nothing grew, no flowers or trees, only hard pavements and brick walls. There was nothing to correspond to their growing life except perhaps a sickly kitten.

Such celebrated cases as the deaf-mute girls, Laura Bridgeman and Rose Kellerman, indicate that the soul of a child is awakened to a sense of God and itself by its impact with a sensible world. How difficult it must be for a child to grow up in surroundings that make no provision for its needs.

In the Friends' Meeting-House with the lovely name of 'Come-to-Good' in the valley of the Fal, half-way between Truro and Falmouth, are the smallest benches I have ever seen, so small are they that a child no more than three years of age can sit at ease with feet resting on the floor. The early Friends who built 'Come-to-Good' in the days of George Fox made provision there for children.

The Catholic Church has done the same. Her faith and worship never fail to make an appeal to the minds of children. She provides for all their needs. In confession their souls are restored to innocency and made fit for

Communion with Him who became a child for their sakes. His presence is never far away, for above the altar is a white light burning to tell them that Jesus is there to listen to their prayers. There is no need of little benches like those at 'Come-to-Good', for there are many things for a child to do - prayers to be said and candles to be lit at the shrine of His Mother and before the image of St. Joseph.

The children at St. Hilary, when they grow up and go away, will possibly forget much that they learnt there; but whatever happens to them and however often they fail they will never forget the way back to God.

The Church to which they come every morning is set among things that are rightly the heritage of every child. There is the country where everything round them is going through the process of growing up, which they themselves often find so bewildering. There is protection and security, a place where dinner is always ready when they return from school and where there is some one who has time to stop and listen to their tales of what they have been doing. Add to this the long summer days spent on the beach at Perran, and winter evenings round the slab in the kitchen, and you will have some kind of picture of the life that goes on at the Jolly Tinners, a house that has 'a good name and keeps good company'.

19 BROADCASTING FROM ST. HILARY

Each year this church dedicated to St. Hilary is visited by thousands of people who have listened to the Christmas Play. There have been other plays, but it is *Bethlehem* that draws them to St. Hilary. They stand in the tower, where the angel Gabriel delivers his message to the shepherds, and reconstruct the drama they have heard so often. 'Where was the home of the Family?' they say. 'And was it in that chapel over there that the children danced before the infant in the manger?' They never fail to mention that they heard the steps of the children and the jingling bells round their ankles; the sound of the children's feet on the stone floor conveys to them the spirit of rejoicing more completely than any spoken word.

In the Middle Ages, crowds travelled from all parts of England along the 'pilgrims' way' that passes through St. Hilary to the shrine of the Archangel on St. Michael's Mount. They come now by the same road to visit the church that owes its foundation to the Benedictines who were guardians of the shrine.

This was brought about through a chance meeting with Filson Young, twelve years ago. Shortly afterwards I had a slight accident, followed by an attack of neuritis and insomnia. Filson, who was then staying at Carbis Bay, used to motor over and take me for drives at night, when I would lie back and shut my eyes while 'Prudence' was driven very fast over the moors beyond Zennor and home by St. Ives or the Land's End. It was on these nightly drives that our friendship began, a friendship that has deepened each year as we have worked together in producing my plays.

One morning that autumn, he came over and found me revising the Christmas Play. I read him one of the scenes and he inquired, on leaving, if I would consider broadcasting the play. I said that I did not think it was suitable for broadcasting, since its merit lay in the devotion of the players. At the time I could not conceive how this could be conveyed to listeners. The play was intimate, a part of our life at St. Hilary, and I feared that in the publicity of a broadcast it would lose its value. However, Filson was persistent, and when I finally received an offer from him on behalf of the British Broadcasting Corporation, together with permission for him to make an appeal at the end of the play for my 'Cornish Home for London Children', which was in need of funds, I rather reluctantly consented to the play being broadcast.

It was a great venture for Filson Young who stood sponsor for its success, for myself who was to produce and teach the players to speak in a way that could be heard by listeners, and for the engineers who had to encounter a number of technical difficulties. There being no telephone line near the church, and the exchange at Marazion being three miles away, it was proposed that transmission should be made through a wireless link, although to deal with three hundred miles of land line, on which a defect at any one point would ruin the transmission, seemed risk enough without the added uncertainty of a wireless link. Eventually a line was set up between the church and Trevabyn Farm where there was a telephone, a line that hung on trees and trailed along hedges, and at any moment during the transmission might have been interfered with by one of the Trevabyn bullocks.

The players sang the Rosary as they came through the churchyard, but their voices were lost in the sound of the gale that now roared in the roof and beat against the church tower until it seemed to us as if listeners would hear nothing else.

The church was a strange place to enter that night. In the Chapel of the Dead were piled rows of batteries. Alongside the Roman milestone with the inscription to the Divine Caesar was a table with a switchboard, round which stood a number of men, line engineers and others from

Savoy Hill. Telephone bells were constantly ringing and men calling, 'one, two, three, four, five, six, seven, eight, nine, ten, Sunday, Monday, Tuesday, Wednesday, Thursday, Friday, Saturday, Hullo, Hullo, Hullo, St. Hilary calling, Truro, Plymouth, Gloucester, London.' Wires stretched from end to end of the church, suspending microphones in the tower for the shepherds, in the Chapel of the Sacred Heart - which had become the home of the Family to whom the shepherds came - and in the straw of the crib round which they all gather to worship the Holy Child.

I looked at the players - how unfamiliar and strange they were in this setting: Peters struggling to throw my old Spanish cloak round his shoulders, Tom Rowe, always a realist, lighting a candle in the lantern he carried, and the children sitting very quietly in a row, as they had been told, lest the bells on their garters should break in on the opening scenes. We had said some prayers invoking the help of Our Lady and were now waiting for the signal to begin. I was filled with anxiety as to what might happen.

'Stand by, every one,' said the engineer, taking off his earphones. 'Look out for the red light. They are making the announcement from London.'

Filson was walking up and down the aisle holding a flash-light, glancing at a manuscript from which he was to read his introduction to the play. There were a few moments of silence and when I looked again there was a red light burning overhead and I heard Filson's voice from the Chapel of the Sacred Heart, saying, 'St. Hilary calling.'

I walked down to the belfry and waited. There were the six ringers with their coats off, with the bells set ready for ringing. The captain of the tower gave me a nod of his head, as if he would say, 'Don't be afeared, Parson, depend upon it, we'll ring a proper peal.' They were waiting for my signal, and as I raised my hand, 'She's gone,' said the Captain of the tower, and the treble bell, followed by the other bells, proclaimed their message of the Nativity.

From that moment I had no feeling of anxiety, only

a sense of exultation as I heard the bells ring out above the roaring of the gale. Never at any other time have I been so conscious of the wonder of the world. Over the High Altar burned a white light proclaiming the presence of the Incarnate God whose Nativity we were celebrating, while above our heads was another light burning red, warning the players that any sounds within the church were at that moment being transmitted over the face of the earth.

The strangeness of the church with the batteries, engineers from London and overhead wires had gone. There remained the angel who was standing beneath the arch of the tower looking very lovely with gold and silver wings and uplifted hand waiting to proclaim the news of man's salvation, and Peters on his knees in the straw, with my cloak now fallen from his shoulders and his old hands uplifted in supplication. Time had fled and left me with the angel Gabriel and an old shepherd somewhere on the plains near Bethlehem.

The voices of the children returning home from Bethlehem, as they told of how they had met 'an old man and a maiden' and how the whole world was full of glory when they looked into the maiden's face, possessed a quality that no art could equal. Words were mumbled and never heard, inflections were often laid on the wrong syllables, but these things did not matter; this is the way that shepherds round Bethlehem would have told the news; it is the way men and women of all ages speak who come off the land.

I was there to prompt and direct them, but I did nothing that night but follow silently after them as they moved from the tower to the Chapel of the Sacred Heart and from there across the church to the crib in the Lady Chapel. They were children at their prayers whom none would venture to correct for their lack of diction. This is, I believe, the secret of the play *Bethlehem*, of which, after nine years, listeners are not tired.

After the players had left the church and were having supper, a message came through from Sir John Reith, the director of Broadcasting House, saying that Mr. Ramsay MacDonald had been dining with him and that they had listened to the play together and wished to thank the players for their beautiful presentation of the Nativity. This was a very thoughtful act, as my experience has been that the strain and excitement of broadcasting is always followed by a reaction. There is no means of knowing how the play has been received. Letters may come later, but what is needed at the time is to have the assurance that some one person has listened and cared for your work, which for the moment you feel to be of supreme importance.

Letters did come in response to the appeal made by Filson on behalf of my Home for London Children. A few hundreds at first, written and posted the night of the broadcast, each enclosing a gift for the children, but these few hundreds did not prepare me for what was to follow, when the postman called to say that there were several sacks of letters waiting for me at the post office and that they were hiring a horse and cart to bring them up. Each post brought a fresh relay and for days my room was stacked with unopened letters. It was weeks before I had sorted out and acknowledged the thousands that arrived. Many of those who wrote have never forgotten the children and after each succeeding broadcast they have written and sent a contribution.

Our next venture was *The Western Land*. The chief character was played by a man named Hocking, who farmed Penberthy in St. Hilary parish, with a farm-place down in the dew where you may pick a bunch of primroses in February month. Hocking is a great lumbering man with a voice and a laugh that can be heard more than two fields away. He had twelve children - six boys and six maidens as he called them. There is a photograph over the mantelpiece, in the parlour at Penberthy, of the twelve children all sitting astride of one of his great cart-horses. He is a powerfully made man and on one occasion when I called at the farm and told him of the trouble that I had been having to get a pony to jump a small brook on the Relubbus Moors - 'Damn 'ee,' he said, 'if I had knowed of it I would have carried the both of 'ee across,' and, looking at his heavy shoulders and great arms, I would not have been surprised if he had done so.

It was in the autumn, at the end of harvest, that I started rehearsing him in his part; I would ride up to the farm about sundown and be told by one of the boys that 'Father is up to the higher meadow looking at the cattle. If he isn't there he's down on the moors.' When I eventually found him, often on the other side of the farm from where I was told he was likely to be, I would lead the pony and we would walk very slowly towards the house, stopping to look at a hedge that wanted repairing or to encourage his spaniel who was hunting a rabbit in a furze bank. On our arrival at the farm, after stabling the pony and further talk, usually about a little mare with which his eldest daughter had won a number of prizes for jumping, he would say, 'Sit down, Parson, and the missus will fit us a cup of tea,' and begin to take off his boots. I have never known a man who could unlace his boots and take off his gaiters with so much leisure. 'You are always in a hurry,' he would say when, after tea, I would suggest that it was getting late and time for us to begin rehearsing. 'One of the maids will light a fire in the parlour and then we can sit down and have a comfortable time.'

'Now then,' I would begin, when after what seemed hours of delay we had arrived at the parlour. 'This is what I have written.' 'Stop a minute and we will come to that later,' was always his answer, 'I have got something here to show 'ee.' I could have enjoyed every moment of his conversation if I had not been anxious about the part he was to play in the coming broadcast, but after the first evening, I discovered that there was no way of hurrying Hocking, he would go on taking his time in whatever he was saying or doing, much in the same way as he would start ploughing a ten-acre field.

The man whom I had chosen to take the part of the flower grower, was a Scillonian from St. Agnes, who had lately come from the islands and was now growing daffodils in St. Hilary parish. I knew nothing of the island dialect and had written his part to be spoken in the rhythm and intonation that the Cornishman uses in his speech. In doing this I had made a mistake, the Scillonian prides himself on speaking pure Elizabethan English without a suspicion of Cornish dialect.

'Do you think my husband could say "Where are you to?" Oh, no,' said Mrs. Hicks, 'he knows better. We don't speak like that on the islands.'

'They will be listening to me at St. Agnes,' said Mr. Hicks, 'and I would be ashamed to go back there if I were to talk in that kind of way.'

With Mrs. Hicks sitting at the table waiting to trip me up in a Cornish colloquialism, I had the feelings of a boy at school with the form-master on the look-out for a false quantity in a line of Virgil, but after that first reading I began to enjoy our encounter, as I took an equal delight in pointing out grammatical errors in her proposed revision of my script. His voice and manner of speech were not suitable for broadcasting, but there was that in his child-like personality that went well with his talk of planting bulbs and picking daffodils in the spring, while his pedantic way of speaking was a foil to the farmer, who laughed and spoke before the microphone with the unconcern with which he shouted at a team of horses.

The miner and the fisherman were men who had played in *Bethlehem* and they presented no difficulties - Robert, the fisherman, is something of an artist, the only man among the players at St. Hilary who is capable of creating a part for himself. On the first night of a revival of this broadcast which, owing to my illness, was under the direction of Filson Young, the players waited for the farmer to arrive while a boy was sent to watch at the end of the avenue for the car that was to bring him. The engineer sent word from the control-room to say that they were changing over. In less than two minutes the play was due to begin. Seeing there was no farmer, Filson said to the fisherman, 'Can you play both parts, Robert?' 'Give me a minute to concentrate and I'll have a go at it,' said Robert.

Away at Penberthy Hocking was walking up and down the farm-place muttering, 'Where the devil is that motor-car? What does he mean by it?'

As he stopped to listen for the sound of the car his son came out and shouted, 'You'm too late, father, they'm started up to St. Hilary.'

'And dam'ee,' said Hocking, 'the boy was right, for when I come into our kitchen there was myself speaking out of the old wireless box. I scarcely knew what to make of it, whether I were in the kitchen or up with they at St. Hilary. They'm telling that it were Robert Carnell. If 'tis true, he made a darned good job of it.'

On the night of this first broadcast, however, the farmer, the fisherman, the flower grower and the miner were all in my room half an hour before eight o'clock.

'Now,' I said, putting a bottle of sherry on the table, 'this will make your voices sound pleasant. We are going to have a good time - whatever they may think of us up in London.'

'Come on, boys' said Hocking, 'we'll drink Parson's health and a good time for all of us.'

It was more like a party than a broadcast, and when Hocking slipped up and forgot his words the fisherman broke in with, 'Farmer has made a mistake and forgot his piece.' The laugh that followed from the farmer was, I was told at Broadcasting House, a recovery that any actor might have been proud of.

The Little Ass - our next broadcast - resulted from a few words I had with John Laity who farms the glebe as his father and grandfather did before him. John is one of my oldest and most loyal friends at St. Hilary. The only time that we have ever quarrelled is when we have talked about donkeys. He does not like donkeys; he never did - nasty creatures, he calls them, and says that 'it's a shame on the parish to see a parson driving round with one of them'. I was always receiving complaints from him about my donkeys, whom he charged with opening gates, breaking down hedges and leading his horses astray, and finally with biting off the ears of his calves. The morning that John Laity rode up with this last accusation I told him that every one should know of the things that had been said about my donkeys. 'I'll broadcast it,' I shouted at him, and went in and started to write *The Little Ass*.

It was to be a pastoral comedy in which the fate of two lovers depends on the finding of the little ass.

Nicholas Peters was to play the part of the donkey's owner; a little old man whose sole love it was; the farmer, the enemy of the donkey, I had modelled on Hocking of Penberthy, hoping that he would play the part, but at the last moment it proved too much for him and I undertook to play it myself.

Now Nicholas Peters has a great affection for me, so to threaten to send Father Walke up the line to Bodmin Jail and to call him 'a nasty spiteful old toad' did not seem right to Peters. Nothing that I said would induce him to put any spirit into his lines. He spoke the words under protest until one night, at rehearsal, I took to teasing him while the other members of the cast looked on and laughed. This was too much for Peters; the look of an angry bird came into his eyes and his voice rang out with bitterness: 'You spiteful old toad,' he said, with such conviction, thrusting his face close to mine, that we all laughed, and the more we laughed the more realistic became his abuse.

Rachel, the daughter of John Laity who provoked the play, was the heroine, and Robert Carnell the young lover. They both have the soft musical voices characteristic of the Cornish people, and gave an admirable presentation of two country lovers. Unfortunately the first production was not a success owing to a faulty transmission. But considering the length of land-line, it is greatly to the credit of the engineer and post-office linesmen that, in sixteen broadcasts, we have had only one breakdown.

Our next play, *The Eve of All Souls*, was concerned with the old superstition that on All Hallowe'en the souls of the dead come back to visit the places they have known.

In England death, except that of the King or some notable personage, is an individual concern; anniversaries are kept or forgotten by families, but there is no one day on which the village, the town or the nation thinks of its dead. In Catholic countries All Souls' Day is sacred to the dead. A catafalque is set up in every church to represent them, cemeteries are thronged with mourning figures and the churches crowded with worshippers who have come to share in the offering of the Holy Sacrifice on behalf of the souls of the departed. Except for those who fell in the war, England no longer publicly commemorates her dead, but they are not altogether forgotten. In the villages the bodies of those who lie round the church belong to the parish as much as if they were alive. I was most conscious of their presence on that first day I visited St. Hilary. They were so great a company, outnumbering the living by many thousands. They all came from the parish and 'belonged to we' as Mary says in the play. It was this nearness of the dead which led me to write *The Eve of All Souls*.

On the evening of the first broadcast I had sung Vespers of the Dead in the church, where stood a catafalque round which four yellow candles were burning; the Altar was vested in black, the church are in mourning for the dead. I came from there to our dining-room that had been transformed into a studio. The ceiling was draped and the walls hung with heavy curtains to deaden sound. It was a very dark and gloomy room to enter, with no furniture except a Cromwellian table on which the microphones stood, and the old grandfather clock that strikes the hour of ten in the play, as Mary and John close the door of their cottage on their way to the church.

Only a few of those taking part in the broadcast were here with me. Others were waiting in the church. A red light flickered and one or other of the company spoke their words. The light disappeared and we waited in silence. Another red light was signalling in the church for the wedding-march to begin, for the choir to sing or the ringers to start the bells. While the play is going on there were men high up in the belfry, climbing about among the bells to put on the mufflers for the peal of the dead, with nothing but a candle in their hand to light them. It is dangerous work, for a man might lose his footing or misjudge the distance and come crashing down among the bells.

In our house there is a tower, built by a former vicar who wished to escape from the noise of his household. The voices of the dead come from a lonely room high up in this tower, where there is only a microphone to listen. There is no one near. The engineer at the controls presses a knob and the voices of the dead from that lonely room start on their journey to millions of listeners. Sitting with the players in that other curtained room, while we waited for the flick of red light, I felt very eerie, as if I had actually entered into a world of the dead. The room is oppressive with its heavy curtains and draperies; no sound reaches us beyond the muffled voices of the players; it is a place from which I am glad to escape. The red light goes off for the last time. That is the end and the players look at me.

'Was it all right, Father?'

'Very good,' I say, 'and now we'll all have supper.'

This is where the evening begins. There are two long tables laid out in our great kitchen. The men sit at one and the women at the other. The pleasantries of social intercourse must wait until the men have been fed. Some of them are going on to work a night shift in the mine at Germoe, and anyway what is a supper for, if it is not to enjoy the food? Conversation, songs and drinking of healths will all come later. As I listen to the songs and laughter that follow, I am tempted to broadcast *The Supper after the Play*, but like many of the best things in life it is too intimate to be shared by any but friends.

20 THE LAND AND ITS PEOPLE

I am writing this chapter from an hotel in the mountains of Gran Canaria, where I am spending the winter. The scene from the window at which I now sit has no resemblance to the scene on which I looked when I lay in bed in the sanatorium writing the first chapter. In place of the stone walls and wind-swept trees of Cornwall I now look on a hillside scarlet with the bloom of geranium, on orange plantations and tall palm trees. Peasants walk slowly before oxen which draw single-handled ploughs; camels walk still more slowly, bearing baskets of earth or crates of bananas; women spend the day knee-deep in water, for ever washing clothes on flat stones, while children play at carting earth and building terraces.

There is nothing here to remind me of Cornwall, and yet when I meet these men and women on narrow pathways and listen to their quiet greetings I recognize that they are akin to the men and women I know at St. Hilary. Their language, their ways of life and methods of agriculture are all different, but the land unites them in a common service. They are all engaged in the same struggle.

A Newlyn woman once said to me, 'The barrenness of the land is nothing compared to the barrenness of the sea; and yet the sea isn't barren altogether, it is the old elements that are always against the fisherman.' It is the same with farming. The 'old elements' are always against the farmer. There are times when spring is late and a man can't get on to the land, when the hay is lying out in the fields as wet as dung, when the wind lays the corn so that a reaper and binder can't touch it, or when there is nothing but rain at harvest-time. Life on a farm is a struggle with the old elements from Lady Day to Michaelmas and Michaelmas to Lady Day; a struggle in which a man must act with cunning and forethought, must know how to wait and how to be in haste.

A farmer at St. Hilary will go out of a morning and know that the time has come for spring ploughing. He will need no calendar to remind him of the day of the month. The spring has touched him, as it will reach wine laid up for years in deep cellars away from the sunlight; like the wine that becomes cloudy at its approach, he will respond to the touch and, before the dew is off the grass, a plough will cut the first furrow of the year.

There is no scent so redolent of spring as the newly turned earth. I have watched men at Trevabyn, after having taken out the horses at dinner-time, lean against the handle of the plough and look back over the steaming earth and freshly turned furrows, while the horses stamp and fret at being kept from their stable. I know what the men are thinking of, for my ancestry is of a people who lived and worked on the land; the same feeling comes to me at times especially at the spring and fall of the year, when I want to go out and dig and take the earth in my hands and smell its fragrance.

There is little time to spare on a farm in the spring, so fast does one event follow another. Soon after Christmas comes the lambing season, when the shepherd is about all night attending to the ewes and the young lambs, followed by spring ploughing, sowing the roots and harrowing the pasture land that has been set up for hay. Everything is growing and must be attended to until, by midsummer, the grass is standing high arid ready for cutting.

I remember as a boy what a delight it was to walk over fields that had been lately mown and were now strewn with swathes of grass and moon-daisies. Here was a country forbidden us while the grass was growing. During these months we were unable to reach our favourite stream or find the nest of the corncrake whose 'crake, crake' was always close at hand. To walk in this newly acquired country brought with it each year some fresh discovery. One spring a partridge had nested there and the mowers left a patch of grass round the nest, where the mother bird sat and hatched her eggs while we tossed the hay round her. Another year a wild duck hatched a brood on the banks of the stream and we caught some of the ducklings and put them in charge of a hen, but they escaped and returned to the stream where we never saw them again.

The happiest days of my childhood were spent riding in empty wagons strewn with hay-seeds, climbing on to the rick where our feet and legs sank deep into the hay, and drinking cider from a great stone jar that had been kept cool on the shady side of the rick. These and many other joys of the same nature are known to those who work on the land, long after the days of childhood are past.

Here on this island I meet with men who sit between sacks of corn on the backs of mules, riding so proudly that they might be kings on their way to their coronation. I have seen the same proud look on the faces of men in Cornwall taking a team of horses to drink at the pond or riding on a wagon loaded with hay.

There is an old man at St. Hilary, long passed the age at which men go to work, who in the last years of his life reclaimed a small piece of land by the roadside that was overgrown with furze and bramble bushes. His strength was failing and the land was stubborn, but he worked fiercely, as children will in a garden that is their own. 'It is the way of old men,' a passer-by said to me. 'I reckon he knows his time is short.' He had not much strength left, but what there was he gave to that piece of waste land. The Parish Council disputed his ownership, but on an appeal to the County Council he won the right to the land he had enclosed. Whenever I rode by, at all times and in all weathers he was walking round that patch of ground. 'Come and have a look, Parson,' he would say; 'before I tackled 'en there was nothing but furze bushes.' His time is short, but that is no matter. He has tamed that rough bit of land.

I have heard farm labourers, earning thirty-two shillings a week, speak with the same pride on looking over a field of wheat or a rick-yard filled with stacks of corn. There is a hook, high up in the roof of St. Hilary Church, from which in old days, so farmers I have told me, was hung the last sheaf of the wheat harvest. When this sheaf was cut the reapers fought for its possession and ran with it, crying 'A neck, a neck', to the farm-place, where they were entertained by the farmer. There are no public rejoicings at harvest-time to-day. The custom died out before I came to St. Hilary, and yet the oldest of all joys, 'the joy of the harvest', still lingers.

After harvest, the coming of the threshing machine is a day always to be looked forward to on a farm. I am never able to resist its attraction. Whenever I hear its humming I go and watch the crowd at work pitching the sheaves and building the rick as the straw comes from the elevator. I sit with the old men, fathers and grandfathers of those at work, and watch the sheaves passing into the drum and the grain falling into sacks that men take on their backs and run with to the granary, where millions of grains are piled on the floor. They laugh as they work, with their faces and bodies grimed with sweat and dust from the machines. When at eleven o'clock the whistle sounds for what is termed 'a bit of croust' - heavy cake and a drink of cider - they sit with their backs against the rick and boast of the morning's work. 'Pretty work,' they say, 'when things are going like they are this morning, Captain.' They are mostly workmen hired for the day, yet it is often they who are most concerned as to the length of the straw or whether the grain is clean. It is the workmen and not the farmer who experience the finer joys of the artist: the farmer is engaged in selling and buying; he regards his stock and the crops on the farm as so much capital, and in pursuit of grosser things he will often lose the more subtle pleasures of the man who works for no other profit than his weekly wage.

The last work of the year is in the nature of a giant burial. There is little more to be done; the wheat is sown, the earth is dormant and must wait for the spring to awaken it; all that remains is to bring in the roots. A pit is made and lined with bracken or straw, and for weeks men are working in the wet fields, pulling and trimming swedes and mangolds. Heavy carts plough through mud that at times reaches to the axle, until the field is cleared and the pit has grown to a high mound covered with straw and hedge-clippings. When the winter has settled on the land and feed is short, the pit is opened and the gold swedes are tipped round the fields for the cattle. The circle of the year is completed with the housing of the roots. The land and the men who work on it must wait for the coming of another spring.

What are the men like whose lives are spent in this fashion? I know many, and can tell you their names, where they live and the numbers of their families. But with men who have no experience in translating their thoughts into words, and for whom speech is chiefly concerned with what they have done and things they have seen, it is difficult to enter the inner recesses of their minds and to discover how far they are influenced by other and less material things.

At funerals, when half St. Hilary have followed a body to the grave, I have watched the black figures, walking two and two, stream into church as I waited before beginning the psalm in the Burial Office. The bearers, after having placed the body on the stools at the entrance to the church, sit through the service as if their work was finished and only to be resumed when, the service ended, they would be required to carry the body to the grave.

The faces of the chief mourners are hidden as they sit crouched in an attitude of woe resembling the figures in Blake's illustration of the *Book of Job*. Behind them are rows and rows of men and women whose faces are as much a part of their funeral garb as their 'Sunday black'. I scarcely know them in their white collars and unaccustomed clothes, and as I read the lesson from the fifteenth chapter of Corinthians I have often wondered what thoughts are passing through their minds. 'That which thou sowest, thou sowest not that body that shall be, but bare grain, it may chance of wheat, or of some other grain: but God giveth it a body, as it hath pleased him, and to every seed his own body.' They are familiar words. The sowing of bare grain, 'it may chance of wheat or of some other grain', which breaks through the earth in the spring, they understand; but what of the body they have come to place beneath the earth in the churchyard?

I look again as I read the triumphant words of a final victory over death with which the lesson ends, and I fancy these black figures are more alive than when they streamed two and two into church; a look of recognition has come into their faces; they are stirred as standing corn is stirred by a passing wind. When they rise to sing, as they sometimes will,

> *Rock of Ages, cleft for me,*
> *Let me hide myself in Thee,*

their bodies sway to the rhythm of the hymn and their voices attain a poignancy that betrays their longing for some life other than the one they know. It is a passing emotion, for when I look again, as we stand round the grave while men prepare to lower the body, the look has gone. Their voices come uncertainly as they attempt another hymn. The words 'Earth to earth' are too final to be dwelt on long. When the last words of the service are spoken they hurry away as men who have no concern with the scene they have witnessed.

Passing the groups of mourners on my way back to the church I hear scraps of conversation: 'Have 'e tealed your taters?' 'Bullocks are fetching a poor price.' They are back again to the life they know. Their religion offers little to sustain their flickering faith.

Here on this more southern island, the men whom I pass carrying baskets of earth or sitting on the hillside herding goats, live in a country where the Mother of God reigns in the splendour of the golden Retablo above the High Altar. On the feast of Christmas, a happy crowd streams up the aisles of the church to the Altar, where the priest sits, holding in his arms the Holy Child whom he has taken from the crib. Each in turn will kneel to kiss the feet and the hands of this infant. On Good Friday the same crowd will come to kiss His feet now nailed to the cross. I am told that many of the men never go to communion and rarely attend Mass except on the great Feasts, but that there are few who will not send for the priest at the hour of their death and receive the last sacraments. It is possible that their faith is a mingling of fear and superstition, but it is faith of some kind, an acceptance of another order of life than that in which they labour. The land is there to be treasured and tended as the first claim on their life, but in the background is God, His Mother, the saints and angels, a hierarchy to which they seek admittance, greater than all the kingdoms of the world.

In the Catholic form of Baptism, the priest at the door of the church inquires, 'What dost thou ask of the Church of God?' and the answer is 'Faith'. Again he asks, 'What does faith bring thee?' and the answer is 'Eternal life'.

Few at St. Hilary have arrived at that simplicity which leads men into so close and tender a relationship to God that they can kneel and kiss the feet of the little figure in the arms of the priest. It is not that they are without the faith that brings eternal life, but, shorn of any but the most meagre expression, their faith is individual, fitful and dependent on the emotion of the moment.

An old man said to me one morning as we were standing together looking over the fields above Chynoweth heavy with may-blossom, 'When I look on the may in bloom I'm not afeared to ask God for eternal life.' This old man looked on the world with the eyes of a poet and saw in the abundance of the may an assurance of the love of God. Whether there are many like him, I do not know; they are a secret people and rarely disclose their thoughts.

I can think of others who have attained to the same relationship with God as the men of this island who kneel and kiss the feet of the Infant Jesus. Such a one was George Crebo. I had known him for years before I learnt the kind of man he was, my only dealings with him being the purchase of a donkey shay when I first started keeping donkeys. During the war he was charged with assaulting a member of the Military Tribunal and was sent to prison for three months with hard labour. The evidence as to who was responsible for the quarrel was conflicting and there were many who thought the sentence hard and unjust. He was a proud man, and I feared the effect such a sentence might have on him. On hearing of his discharge from prison I went to Plain-an-Gwarry to see him. He was not at home. 'Gone to his work,' his wife told me. When I inquired how he had got on in prison his wife said, 'He's looking very well. Says he was very happy there. He's never a great one for talking and we haven't inquired further.'

Some years after, hearing that he was ill, I went to visit him. Knowing the nature of his illness and that his death was not far away, I spoke to him of being willing to forgive his enemies and offered to convey a message to the man who had been the cause of his imprisonment.

'Forgive Alfred!' he said, and laughed. 'I've done that long ago. I learnt to love him in prison. I had Jesus with me there and He taught me to love Alfred. I had always loved Jesus,' he went on, 'and now I am going to tell you something. When our first boy was born, (he had six great sons) I wanted to call 'en Jesus, but I daren't say it. If I had faced up to it and called 'en Jesus it might have been better for me. But there,' he went on, 'Jesus do know all about it, for I've told Him many times. Some great talks we've had together when I was in prison.' He had a small copy of St. John's Gospel which he read constantly. 'Don't want to know anything more than that,' he would say. 'It's like water from Relubbus that comes out of the living rock.' George was not a Catholic, but he had learnt to kiss the feet of the Infant Jesus.

I have known others whose faith was of the same nature as that of the farmer I met one Sunday evening riding round his fields. 'Good evening, Parson,' he said. 'Everything is looking handsome, and I don't forget to praise God for it all - the weather, the crops and every blessed thing that is. I shan't be always here to look on them,' he continued. 'Every poor devil has got to die!' Then raising himself in his stirrups and pointing his whip at the fields, 'But they'll be here,' he said, 'and my boys will be here. I have taught them all I know about the farm, and they'll be here to tend it when I am buried up in the churchyard.' Such was the faith of the patriarchs, that their seed might be prolonged and that they might possess the land. I am not sure that it is not the faith of many who tend the land to-day.

There is another quality in the faith of these people that I suspect rather than know, a going back to their early ancestry, something in their nature that links them to the cromlechs and stone-circles; but of these things it is difficult to write. Although I have lived among them for over twenty years I am still a stranger at St. Hilary, so much is there in their lives that remains as secret as the land they serve.

21 HOLIDAYS IN LONDON

Many of our friends from Newlyn and Lamorna were now living in London. Harold Harvey and Lamorna Birch are the only two painters who remain of those who were our friends when we first came to St. Hilary. We rarely go to Lamorna now. The line of rails from Penzance to the main arrival platform at Paddington links us to our friends. This line to the West has always attracted me. Many years ago when I was working in the East End of London I would go sometimes to Paddington Station and watch the 10 a.m. - this was before the days of the Riviera - start on her journey to the West - Exeter, Plymouth, Falmouth and Penzance. The names of these places were familiar to me from the days of my childhood. I often listened to stories from my father and mother, who both came from the West Country, of days before the railway reached Cornwall, and how they travelled to Plymouth by coach or steam packet from Falmouth when they visited London. I am now familiar with every mile of that line; villages, stations whose names I have never succeeded in reading, churches, clumps of trees and farm-places are so well known to me that I notice when a tree has been cut down or a new house built.

To motor to London, as I have done several times with Filson Young, is a different experience, more intimate and personal. You go through villages and for a few moments share the life there, meet men going and returning from work, cross county boundaries and end the day with crowded impressions of people and places passed on the road. To go by rail from Penzance to London has none of these experiences to offer; the scenes from the window are there to be looked at but not to be shared; if people wave from the fields it is the train they are saluting and not you, as they do on the road when you slow down to pass a herd of cows or inquire the way. And yet there are places I never fail to look at, as one turns to certain passages in a much read book - Saltash Bridge, with the ships below, Exeter Cathedral, where my father was ordained, Glastonbury Tor, the White Horse, the trout hatcheries at Hungerford, and Windsor Castle beyond Slough. I must have gone up and down this line some hundreds of times during the years I have lived in Cornwall and yet I still regard it as a pleasant although a familiar adventure.

The return journey is still more pleasant; to hear Cornish talk and see friendly faces on Paddington Station, to be told by Nichols, or whoever is in charge of the train, what has been happening and what kind of weather they have been having in Penzance, never fails to give me a thrill at the thought of returning to Cornwall.

Among our friends from Cornwall now living in London are Harold and Laura Knight, who have a studio in St. John's Wood, where I always stay when I am in London. Dame Laura is a fitting title for a woman who is a Rubens among modern painters. I can only think of one other that would suit her better, a title I learnt from a macaw who lived in the courtyard of a Spanish hotel where I once stayed, and who was constantly calling 'Laura Real' (Royal Laura). Dame Laura is excellent but Royal Laura is better.

During the war, at a time when she had failed to apply for the necessary permit for painting out of doors, I went with her to the Corpus Christi Fair in Penzance and kept a look-out for the police while Laura made sketches in a note-book. After the first day Laura was known to every one on the plot. Showmen, fat women, contortionists and mountebanks were all willing to be her models and anxious to serve her. When the fair ended and it became known that the picture was not finished, they invited her to travel with them and one of the women she had been drawing offered to share a wagon with her - a rare compliment, for these people are shy at inviting a stranger to take the road with them. It has always been like that with 'Laura Real';

fishermen at Mousehole, showmen, circus people and members of the Russian ballet welcome her as one of themselves. At Aldershot where, during the war, she was painting a picture of a boxing competition, stout sergeants and young corporals would run and carry her easel and offer to clean her palette and brushes. After her return from this visit to Aldershot there was nothing that she did not know about the technique of the prize-ring. 'Everything depends on your footwork,' she would say as she danced on her toes round the studio, giving an exhibition of the feints and the clinches of Joe Beckett or whoever was heavy-weight champion at the time.

Soon boxing was abandoned for dancing. It was the season of the Russian ballet and, night after night, Laura would hurry away to the theatre at 6 p.m. and not return until close on midnight with a sketch-book full to the last page with drawings of dancers in the wings, dancers in their dressing-rooms and on the stage, scene-shifters and dressers. There was nothing about the ballet that did not concern her; its history and tradition, its music and technique were all of absorbing interest.

One night she had arranged to present Harold and myself to Lydia Lopokova. It was the first night of a new ballet and Laura was to take us to the great dancer's dressing-room. 'Remember, Harold,' she said, 'when you enter, to say "Brava, Brava, Brava"'

'Remember to say what?' said Harold.

'To clap your hands,' said Laura, 'and say "Brava" three times.'

'Oh, all right,' said Harold.

We watched the ballet from the stalls and at its conclusion, when the theatre had emptied and there seemed no longer any place for us there, we found our way to the stage and waited. There was no going any further, for we did not know where to go, and there was no one of whom we could ask the way. The stage, which a few minutes before had been a place of brilliant life and activity, was now in semi-darkness. It was as if Harold and I had wandered into a deserted world in which we were the only two living beings. Into this world came Laura across the stage, her eyes sparkling with excitement.

'Wasn't Lopokova wonderful?' she said as she led us along stone passages and up stairways. 'Don't forget what I told you to say, Harold. Clap your hands and say "Brava" three times.' But when we arrived at the dressing-room where Lydia Lopokova sat triumphantly receiving bouquets and congratulations, Harold merely said, 'How do you do?....' not a clap of the hand or one single "Brava". Laura looked at him as if to say, 'Now, Harold, now.' But Harold would not be told.

After the ballet, Laura lost her heart to the circus. No child, visiting the circus for the first time, ever surrendered more completely to its charms than Laura. For months she lived and worked 'on the plot'. Blackpool, Margate, Broadstairs, Middlesbrough, Huddersfield, became the most desirable places to live in; and fried fish and chips, cheese and onions eaten late at night, accompanied by cocoa, the most delectable food. None of her friends ever saw Laura at this time. We only knew that she was 'somewhere in the north' with the circus. When this particular circus came to an end and Laura returned to St. John's Wood she brought Joe and Allie with her, two of her dearest circus friends. I was staying with Laura and Harold at the time and met these two artistes. Joe was a tumbling clown, and often when I was lying half asleep on a couch in the studio I would hear a soft patter on the floor and look up to discover Joe, with the sad smile peculiar to clowns, practising 'flip flaps' down the length of the studio.

Joe and Allie were contemplating the purchase of an elephant to be trained as a single act, to stand on a tub, to dance and play football and do all the things elephants do in circuses. To buy an elephant in London seemed to me to be fantastic, but I was assured by Joe, who knows, that there are places where you can buy an elephant as easily as you can buy a dormouse at Selfridge's. While I was there, we talked of nothing but the elephant. If I went out to lunch or dinner at night, I hurried back, eager for the news of its purchase. I had become almost a partner in the concern, for, hearing that they would need a place in the country for his training, I had offered Joe and Allie the glebe barn at St. Hilary. It would be very amusing, I thought, to go out and see an elephant taking his morning exercise up and down the avenue. This happened more than two years ago and as yet I have had no word of the coming of that elephant; possibly it is as well, for I have since been told that they have 'nerves', and will often stampede at the sight of a mouse. Seeing that the glebe barn is full of mice, it is difficult to forecast what might have happened if this elephant had come to St. Hilary.

On one of my visits to the Knights I remember going with Harold to a dinner given by A.J. Munnings at the Garrick Club in honour of Lamorna Birch when he was elected an Associate of the Royal Academy. The dinner was everything that a dinner should be - good food, good wine and good company: the only thing lacking was the presence of the guest of the evening. Lamorna Birch had gone that night to a dinner at the Chelsea Arts Club. A.J. had invited all his friends but had forgotten to send an invitation to Birch until it was too late.

I sat next to Gerald Kelly, a great talker. I do not know how it came about, but our conversation throughout the dinner was on the subject of prayer. The Church of England, he maintained, was a school of literature and not of prayer. 'Where,' he said, 'but in the Old Testament are such stories to be found as that of Sampson and Delilah, or of the prophet who mocked the priests of Baal and girded his Loins and ran before the chariots of Ahab at the sound of the coming of rain? A people who have had these stories read to them from their childhood,' he continued, 'are likely to have a crude idea of God but a very sound judgment on literature. Listen,' he said, and began to recite lines that occur in the Song of Deborah and Barak. '"The kings came and fought, they fought the Kings of Canaan in Taanach by the waters of Megiddo; they took no gain of money. They fought from heaven; the stars in their courses fought against Sisera. The river of Kishon swept them away, that ancient river, the river Kishon. O my soul, thou hast trodden down strength! Then were the horse-hoofs broken by the means of the prancings, the prancings of their mighty ones."'

'Any love that I have for literature,' he added, 'I owe to reading the lessons in church for my father when I was a boy.'

We passed from the subject of literature to prayer as expressed in the lives of some of the mystics. Before leaving the table I promised to send him a copy of *Revelations of Divine Love*, by Mother Julian, an anchoress who passed her life enclosed in two rooms adjoining the church that goes by her name in the city of Norwich. I have never met Gerald Kelly since, and sometimes wonder if he has ever read those 'Revelations' and if he was as attracted as I was to her interpretation of the universe. In this revelation she says, 'He showed me a little thing, the quantity of a hazel-nut, lying in the palm of my hand, as me seemed; and it was as round as a ball. I looked thereon with the eie of my understanding and thought, "What may this be?" And it was answered generally thus: "It is all that is made." I marvelled how it might last; for me thought it might sodenlie have fallen to naught for littleness. And I was answered in my understanding, "It lasteth, and for ever shall: for God loveth it. And so hath all things being, by the love of God."'

It was close on midnight when we got up from the table and walked round the great dining-room, and looked at the many portraits of distinguished men who had once sat at the long table from which we had risen, while A.J. recounted their history as one who had lived in their period, taken wine and talked intimately with them. After we had wandered into the smoking-room down the stairway trodden by Thackeray, Garrick and Dickens, we returned to the dining-room. 'Now,' said A.J., as if we had come from a long journey, 'we will sit down and have something to eat.' And we all sat down again to the table and ate sausages and mashed potatoes and drank Guinness out of pewter tankards. 'Better than being at home snoring in our beds,' as Harold Knight remarked on our return journey in the taxi.

We had drunk Lamorna Birch's health and extolled his merits as a landscape painter, we had looked at a great collection of English painting and A.J. had recited his hunting ballad *Antony Bell*, in itself a memorable event. I have heard that ballad several times, always on some such occasion, when the company was agreeable and the wine on the table; but, making all allowance for the time and the company, I never fail to be moved by its freshness and beauty. When I once suggested to A.J. the possibility of his broadcasting it, he looked at me and said, 'What! Broadcast *Antony Bell*? There are a d... sight too many people listening!'

Before we left that night, A.J. invited the company to lunch next day, or rather the same morning, for it was now 2 a.m. 'We will have Lamorna with us if we have to carry him here,' he added. We all arrived and sat down, the same company, but this time with Lamorna Birch, who was as gay as a child at his birthday party. After lunch we drove away in four taxis across the bridge of Southwark to the home of Charles Dickens, walked down the street where he had lived, and looked at the fanlights over doors he must often have entered; then to the 'George', the starting place of coaches in Pickwick. Here, in the bar hung with way-bills, pistols and time-tables of coaches for Rochester, Dover and the Great North Road, sat the landlady. Before her on the counter was a bowl of cowslips, so fresh that they might have been picked that morning and brought by the coach arriving from the West. When Lamorna Birch was presented to her as the newly elected Academician, she said, 'I am pleased to see you, sir, and to know that they will have so pleasant a gentleman at the Royal Academy'; and when Lamorna admired the cowslips she picked out the finest and placed them in his button-hole. Her voice had the sound of tinkling glass as she shook her ringlets and said, 'I am sorry, gentlemen, but I cannot serve drinks during closing-time. You gentlemen ought to have lived in coaching days when there were no closing hours.'

What would Mr. Pickwick have thought and what would he have said if he had arrived from Rochester and been told that he must wait until 6 p.m. for his hot brandy and water? Of one thing I am certain, he would have behaved very gallantly to the charming hostess of the 'George'.

After all this worship of Dickens I proposed that we should go to the Church of St. Bartholomew the Great in Smithfield, the only Norman Church in London, and visit the shrine of Rahere, the founder of St. Bartholomew's Hospital. Fresh taxis were called and we drove to Smithfield, through the meat-market to the door of Rahere's church, where there was a notice posted saying that the church was closed to visitors after 6 p.m. We knocked at the door round the corner, where we were told that the caretaker lived, and a little man appeared and informed us that it was too late for visitors. 'You must let us in,' I said, 'we have with us' - pointing to A.J. - 'the future president of the Royal Academy.'

'Can't help it,' said the man; 'the church is in darkness and he couldn't see anything if he were the king of England.'

'Look here,' said A.J., 'this gentleman who is talking to you is the Bishop of Cornwall.'

'Never heard of him,' said the man.

'That shows your ignorance of religion,' said A.J.; 'but I think you are a good fellow all the same and that you would not like us to go away without seeing your church.'

Flattered by the cajoleries of A.J., he opened the door and we wandered beneath the great Norman arches of the nave into the chapel of Our Lady, behind the High Altar, which was then only partially restored. This part of the church was used as stables not long ago, the caretaker told us. 'You need not tell me that, I can smell them,' said A.J.' sniffing the air. I have visited St. Bartholomew several times since, but never has it looked so noble as it did that night, lit with nothing more than a flash-light borrowed from the caretaker.

At one of our rare meetings in London some years later A.J. happened to inquire how I spent my time at St. Hilary. 'I ride round the country on a pony,' I answered.

'A pony,' he said. 'What do your parishioners think of their parson riding round the parish on a pony? That's a poor example to set them. Why, I will give you a horse if you want one,' he continued.

So many people have talked of giving me things, that I said 'Thank you' and thought no more about that horse until a year later when I was in London and A.J. rang me up to invite me to dine with him.

'I can't come to dinner,' I answered, 'but if you are going to Dedham for the week-end I will come down with you and get my horse.'

'What horse is that?' he inquired.

'Why, the horse you gave me,' I shouted into the phone. There was a silence and then I heard A.J. laugh before he answered, 'If I gave you a horse, Walke, you must come down and get him. Meet me at Liverpool Street to-morrow at eleven and we will go down together.'

Mrs. Munnings was remaining in town for that weekend and A.J. and I were alone. Coming away from the stables after looking at the horses that were being got ready for the hunting season, A.J. said, 'You must have that horse, Walke. Can you see the chestnut running there in the meadow? He's just the little horse to suit you. Your parishioners will be proud of their parson when they see him on a horse like that.' He cracked a whip and the horses threw up their heads and started to gallop into a farther field, the chestnut leading. It was all that I saw of that horse until, a fortnight later, I had a wire: 'Meet horse at Marazion Station.' A letter came the next morning saying, 'Take care of the little horse, Walke. I would not let any one but you have him. When I saw him go out of the yard I felt as if I were sending a son away.' That is just how I should feel if ever I had to part with him.

After dinner on the evening of my visit I lay back in an arm-chair over the fire and listened to A.J. reading from a collection of ghost stories, very terrifying some of them. It grew late and every now and then A.J. would say, 'What do you feel like, Walke? Can you face the stairs with nothing but a candle in your hand, or do you think we had better stay here with another bottle of port?'

I thought it wiser to remain where we were round a the fire than to face that dimly lit hall before we needed, and so we sat on until an empty wood-basket and a dying fire drove us to bed.

Father Wason was also living in London at this time. He had bought an old-established church publishing firm, Cope and Fenwick, and rented premises in Old Burlington Street, where, in addition to liturgies, also sold 'pieties'. It was probably the name 'Cope and Fenwick' that first attracted him. 'Most distinguished,' he said, 'and bound to bring customers.' He had very few customers, however, and those who did venture to enter the shop were never encouraged to buy anything. 'What do you want?' he would say, looking up from his breviary. 'Nothing here. All rubbish,' and return to his offices. At other times he would adopt the manner of a business man and sit at the telephone calling up booksellers all over London to inquire if they had some rare book or other in stock. It always gave him pleasure to speak of himself as 'Cope and Fenwick'. He had no customers for these rare editions but, as he explained, it gave a good impression to 'the trade'. If ever I tried to persuade him from this mad venture of book-selling he fell back on some mysterious virtue of being in the trade. 'You are not in the trade and it is impossible for you to understand the business,' he would say.

At one period of his shop-keeping career he prevailed on Laura Knight to let him have a number of her etchings for exhibition. The 'pieties' were banished, a carpet and curtains were bought and the shop transformed into a miniature picture gallery. In this adventure he was assisted by a Mrs. Miriam Plichta, with whom, when he was not saying his offices, he would play chess. During one of these games the exhibition was visited by a very distinguished lady, a patron of the arts, who, after going round the walls examining the etchings through her lorgnette, approached the table where the two were sitting over the chess-board.

'Catalogues,' said Wason, pointing to the desk; 'plenty of catalogues.' Not to be recognized at a picture show was unusual and slightly disconcerting to the lady, who, after waiting some moments in silence, ventured to remark, 'Chess is a very absorbing game.'

'Very, check,' said Father Wason to Madame Plichta.

After a time, he moved from Old Burlington Street to Duke Street, Piccadilly, with the Coptic and Syrian liturgies and a slightly diminished store of 'pieties'. It was during the Duke Street period that the business of Cope and Fenwick was bought by two friends of Father Wason who appointed him Managing Director and published his novel *Palafox*.

The last time I saw him before I left England for the Canary Islands was when I invited him to lunch with Filson and me at a restaurant in the Strand. He was late and we sat at one of the tables at the far end of the room waiting for him. The circular door swung round and I saw him enter as if uncertain how he had come or why he was there. The door continued to swing and people hurried by and took their places at tables, while he remained where the swing-door had left him. He did not appear to be concerned to find us; he had come into the room as a leaf might have entered and was now waiting for a fresh wind to carry him elsewhere.

I did not go to meet him. He looked so distinguished, so saintly and apart from all these hungry people, that I was content to sit and watch him. A waiter was directing him to a vacant table and, as if here was the impulse needed to carry him farther, he drifted round the room and arrived where we were sitting.

'Why do you come here to lunch? Dreadful place,' he said as he sat down.

'Cheap,' I answered. 'What will you drink, Wason?'

'Can you get anything in this place fit to drink?' he muttered, all the time fumbling in an attaché case with loose sheets of manuscript which he discarded and threw on the floor. 'I have some poems here,' he went on, 'and the first chapter of a novel which I will read you.' A waiter was now picking up the loose sheets Wason was throwing on the floor, and placing them on the table while Wason, unconscious of what was happening, was taking them up and throwing them down on the other side of his chair.

Looking back over the years since I first met Father Wason as an undergraduate, I regard him as not only the most original but one of the most rare personalities that I have ever known. In these pages I have tried to recall some few incidents in which he has figured during my years at St. Hilary. They are nothing more than incidents and in some cases a mere record of a mannerism adopted to conceal, from all but his most intimate friends, a nature too shy and at the same time too intolerant of the commonplace to meet with the world's approval.

Filson Young is another friend from Cornwall whom I always visit in London. I have rarely been to London for the past ten years without being taken by him to lunch at the St. James's Club, and have grown very fond of its stately rooms and the quiet decorum which forbids members to be seen smoking at its windows.

Filson has the rare charm so few cicerones have, of investing quite ordinary things with the glamour of an adventure. Though I had worked for some time in the East End of London and fancied I knew something of the West End, when Filson began motoring me about I felt like a provincial visiting London. He is the last person in the world to go 'sight-seeing' and yet, whether we drove north, south, east or west, we would arrive somewhere and find entertainment provided for us. If we drove to Twickenham on a summer day, intending to sit and watch the ferry, the fisherman on the bank would land a dace. When on a Sunday afternoon we drove round the London Docks and the empty City, we saw Dean Inge come out of that dark house which is the Deanery and walk up the steps of his cathedral. Ludgate Hill was deserted; there was no one in sight but this solitary figure going up the steps of that great Cathedral to read the second Lesson.

I have started out on many drives with Filson in 'Prudence' but never returned without happening on a pleasant inn and a bottle of wine. On one occasion we motored from London and spent the weekend at Downside Abbey, where we were received, not as guests at an inn, but according to the rule of St. Benedict that lays down: 'Let all guests that come be received as Christ Himself.'

22 PASSING YEARS

Nothing arouses me more to a sense of the passing years than to find a young couple, whom I have known as infants, waiting some evening to see me. 'What do you want?' I say. It is usually the girl who speaks. 'We thought, Parson, we would like you to put up our banns on Sunday.' This boy and girl who now want to get married do not even remember my coming to St. Hilary. 'Been here some time. Can't tell how long,' they would say if any one were to inquire of them the number of years I had been in the parish. To the generation that has grown up since I have been at St. Hilary I must appear as one of the old stones in the fields that mark a boundary; a stone which has been there so long that no one stops to inquire into its history.

In our hall there is a space of white wall which has pencilled lines on it with a date to each line. It is the height of our Austrian children from the first day of their arrival to their last visit. Eddy, the little boy with the strange sailor suit, is eventually marked as being six feet and two inches in height. Then come the names of Marion and Zdenko some inches below. I look at these records and think of the children who came to us so short a time ago. Eddy's wife, a beautiful Viennese girl whom we have never seen, has written her first English letter to her Liebe Süsse Mrs. Walke.

Marion and Zdenko have been several times to St. Hilary within the last few years. On these visits Marion, who is very popular with every one, spends his days at the farm across the road with the Osborne family. You will remember Tom, the man who drove the robin from his room. Tom and Marion are well matched and great friends. 'They are waiting for me,' Marion says at breakfast, 'to start the reaper and binder in the big field,' or, 'I am going to Helston Market with Tom this morning.' Nothing on the farm is without interest to him.

He notices how, if he is hoeing turnips, the men working on either side of him will hoe part of his row when they think he is not looking, to save him the shame of being left behind. The thought of this courtesy will delight him for the whole day. At night, he hurries across to the farm to put some of the animals to bed and returns with a detailed account of how the ferrets curled themselves up in the straw when he had given them their supper, or the way the young calves licked his hand after he had bedded them down for the night. He has many engagements to tea with his friends in the village, but the Osbornes have the first place in his affection. 'I could sit in the kitchen and watch that family all day,' he says. 'They are so lovely.'

While Marion abandons himself to each passing moment Zdenko is introspective and occupied with his own thoughts. They both, in different ways, have the Slav nature, which they inherit through their Czech parentage; Marion in his gaiety and willingness to entertain each new friendship as it comes, Zdenko in his longing for an intimacy which is his very own. The charm of his little speech, 'Please I have come,' when he arrived on the doorstep with Gerard Collier, has never left him. His letters are full of the time when he will come to England and be always near us. He is occupied now, and is happy, in his work in Teheran, but on his long rides across the mountains of Persia his thoughts are never far away from his friends at St. Hilary.

The years in which these children have returned to us have passed very quietly and swiftly with little to record. Each spring I have gone to the same places to look for the earliest flowers. In the wilderness, a small copse beyond the garden, there is a clump of snowdrops, so small a company and so hidden that I doubt if anyone but myself knows of their presence in the wood. I found them the first spring I came to St. Hilary, and each February I have gone to the wilderness to look for them. There have been times when I have mistaken the tree under which they grow, and have thought that they must have died out, for they were such very frail snowdrops; but when I looked again I discovered they were still there, as secret and demure as when I first found them.

On any day throughout the winter a primrose may be found in bloom somewhere in the garden; they are pale and wan, with wizened faces, and look bewildered at the coldness of the world into which they have come. I pick them out of compassion and place them in a glass bowl as fragile as themselves, a bowl that Annie Walke bought in Dresden as a child and has treasured ever since. The first real primroses are found in the rick-yard of the Glebe farm. Here, in March month, the bank looking towards the south has more primroses than a child could hold in both its hands. Like the farmer with his sowing, I know the exact day when I may expect to find them in bloom

More than snowdrops and primroses I look forward to the flowering of the celandines. There is a waste piece in the garden they have taken for themselves. Nothing else grows there except a fig tree that never bears any fruit; there is no room for anything else since the celandines have taken possession. Each spring when the sun is shining the ground beneath the fig tree glows with patches of burnished gold. How this golden flower loves the sun! I have watched its buds open and extend themselves in ecstasy, when every petal stands apart, sensitive to its touch.

I look forward with the same expectancy to certain trees coming into leaf. There is a sycamore in the wilderness whose sticky buds open into crumpled leaves while other trees show no sign of spring, and a beech, the loveliest of trees, in the lower meadow that breaks into green a full week before her sister trees have opened their buds.

And yet it is the measured approach of autumn I most enjoy. The days have shortened but as yet there is no sign of winter; St. Michael's and St. Martin's little summers are yet to come.

During those first years at St. Hilary I was engaged each autumn in the garden planting bulbs and cutting down timber. The glebe is heavily wooded with trees planted a hundred years ago which have now passed their prime and need felling. There are ash trees, beech and sycamore. I have learnt the nature of each and how best to fell them and under what conditions they will make good burning. The elm is a bitter tree whose wood is only fit for making coffins, and must be stored for two or even three years before it burns freely. The beech has a bright flame, its smoke is clear and has a pleasant smell but, like the sycamore, it burns quickly and needs constant feeding. Of all the trees the ash provides the best burning. The green log from a tree felled the day before burns with a gay flame that leaps from log to log and leaves a white ash on the hearth.

In my room, from which one morning in revolt at its ugliness I tore away a fumed oak mantelpiece and converted the grate into an open hearth, the fire is kindled each day from a smouldering log.

The autumn felling, which until a few years ago I did myself with the help of a hired labourer, lasted into November month. It was a work I enjoyed, although at times when a tree fell I experienced regret at what seemed so great a destruction. After several hours of work on a big tree, when the cut begins to open I know that we are nearing the end; but as yet the tree gives no sign. We bend again to the saw and after a few strokes there comes a sound of breaking from the heart of the tree. A tremor runs through its branches - 'Stand clear,' I call to the man, 'she's going.' The last fibre is broken and the tree sways, uncertain which way to fall. She is going now and will fall where I had planned. Slowly the tree bows its head as if in farewell. The crash is coming. Each twig, as it is borne forward, beats the air and gives a sharp cry that is lost in the sound of rending and breaking as the tree plunges downward and buries its tallest branches in the earth.

For over a hundred years this tree has stood upright, decorating itself each spring with fresh green leaves, swaying to autumn gales that I have never known, and now it lies on the ground bruised and broken.

I fell no trees now. The gale six years ago blew down enough timber to provide us with firing for many winters. Before the last of the trees was sawn into logs my days of felling timber were ended. I am content each autumn to sit in the garden and watch its glories. Late flowers are still in bloom and the belladonna lilies, 'naked ladies' they are called in Cornwall, are still to come. I watch each rose-tipped spike pierce the earth and count them jealously. A hundred and eighty-five 'naked ladies' I counted one year in the south border.

Other flowers which I associate with the garden in autumn are dwarf cyclamens which grow beneath the beech trees. I discover these each autumn with the same surprise as the celandines in spring. Like the belladonna lilies, they have no leaves to obscure their loveliness; they spring out of a carpet of ivy and look for all the world like a company of angels with folded wings.

Birds are more friendly at this season than in the spring when they are busy about their own affairs. A Jenny wren chatters and scolds from the bush close at hand. A nestful of young robins, who were hatched in the garden, come and stare as if they would say, 'Since we are spending the winter with you, it is as well to be friendly.' Each day they become more impudent, lighting on my foot and taking ants from the stone seat where I am sitting. The rooks have returned to their nests and gather each evening to talk over the events of the day.

I am aware of the increased friendliness among all living things. The children congregate in flocks. I hear their voices on their way home from school as they stop to gather masts from under the beech trees in the avenue. Men returning from work linger over gateways and talk with passers-by of the harvest and the year which is drawing to a close, while I sit on the stone bench and watch the first falling leaves.

When the sun begins to lose its power I wander to

the Wilderness, and gather an armful of kindling wood. I look for dried twigs broken from the eucalyptus tree growing there, withered branches of bay and other sweet-scented trees that will give a fragrant smoke. The wood is dry and when I have laid it on the hearth a single match will kindle it into a flame. No event of the year gives me more pleasure than these early fires of autumn.

These things happen each year. Nothing has changed. The flowers, the birds, the rustling of the rooks in the trees and the voices of the children have been the same every autumn of the twenty years that I have been at St. Hilary.

23 THE END OF TWENTY YEARS

CROWBAR RAID ON A CHURCH
THE KENSITITES AT ST. HILARY
ORNAMENTS SMASHED AND CARRIED OFF
VICAR A PRISONER

Such was the headline of a London daily paper on August 10, 1932. The same paper, describing the scene, says:

The beautiful reredos at the back of the Altar, designed by Ernest Procter, A.R.A., was destroyed, and the canopy torn down. Two tabernacles were removed, the Venetian bracket supporting the image of St. Joseph was dug out of the wall and the images of St. Anne and Our Lady removed. The fifteenth-century font was smashed and the plinth at the foot of the memorial to Canon Rogers, a former Vicar of Penzance, was broken.

According to this report 'the raiders had arrived at Marazion in two private motor-cars and two motor-coaches, their forces having been first concentrated at Plymouth'.

Whether they came from Plymouth or no, they were all men whom I had never seen before; only one face was familiar to me, that of a woman who, some months before, had obtained a judgment in the Consistory Court to remove a number of articles from the church. Now the court under which this judgment was given is, in many ways, a strange court. It retains the name, it employs the language and to some degree the forms of the old spiritual court, but these are merely camouflage, since its continuity with the old court was broken and its spiritual nature lost on the day it allowed an appeal to a secular court on matters spiritual.

It was no hasty decision that led me to refuse to plead before or accept the judgment of such a court on matters spiritual. As a citizen I regretted having to place myself in conflict with the law of the land, but as a Catholic priest I felt bound to defend to the best of my ability the rights of the Church.

On entering St. Hilary Church one morning, some weeks before the date appointed for the hearing of this case, I discovered a stranger there whom I recognized later as the Chancellor of the diocese, Sir Philip Baker Wilbraham, K.C., the man whose court I had already notified my inability to attend; a charming person I found him to be. After walking round the church together, we happened to sit down on a bench facing the altar of St. Joan.

'I wish you could see your way, Mr. Walke,' he said, 'to attend my court.'

'I regret being unable to,' I answered, 'but, as so often happens in cases of divided loyalty, decisions have to be made which are not always pleasant.'

I looked up at the picture of St. Joan and smiled, and so did he. 'I hope you won't burn me as they did Joan,' I added.

During the early days of this spring, I was pursued by writs in connexion with the proceedings. These writs must be served in person and, as I happened never to be at home when the officer arrived, he made many journeys to St. Hilary. I had three horses at the time who were constantly needing exercise - A.J., the chestnut given me by Munnings, Don, a young horse Annie Walke had bought from the farmer John Laity, and the pony, Aladdin.

A man called John Paul James looked after them in his spare time. John Paul had lived in the parish for some years, but I knew nothing of him until I took to keeping horses. He appeared in one of the glebe meadows, the morning A.J. arrived, a complete horseman in breeches and gaiters, bowler hat and check coat. The horses took to him at once and recognized him as a man who, in his own phrase, 'treated them with discretion'.

John Paul had two passions: horses and hymn-singing. When he rode with me, as he often did when I was visiting in the parish, he sang Moody and Sankey hymns he had learnt as a boy. He also set great store on a volume of Spurgeon's sermons which he was constantly offering to lend me.

'That's a wonderful thought,' he used to say after quoting one of the sermons; but, as I never listened, these thoughts were lost on me. When he was not singing or quoting from Spurgeon's sermons, he would hold forth on A.J. 'Look at his quarters! What shoulders and what a head he's got on him,' he would chant as if repeating a line of one of his hymns. Visitors to the church were entrapped and taken to see the 'Parson's horse', whose sire, according to John Paul, had won all the classic races.

On my leaving St. Hilary, when A.J. was sent to a friend at St. Agnes, John Paul stood at the end of the avenue, bowler hat in hand, waving his farewell, while tears, I am told, streamed down his face. He had stood bare-headed while I was taken away in a car to the sanatorium at Tehidy, but there were no tears then; they were saved for the horse who left a few days later.

'Never is a moment spent on a horse wasted,' wrote Winston Churchill in one of his books. I agree with him. Never does the country look so well as seen from the back of a horse. You are above the hedges and can watch what is going on in your neighbour's fields, what crops they have sown and how they are looking. You see many things that would pass unnoticed were you not in his company; a lark gets up under his feet, another horse neighs from a field or a rabbit bolts across the path and you are alive to all that is happening around you.

St. Hilary has many bridle-paths, some of which lead to the top of Tregonning Hill, whence, on a fine day, you can look half over Cornwall, from the Land's End to Bodmin Moor. There is no better place to be, on a spring morning, than on Tregonning Hill with a horse. In its keen air, vexing thoughts of little men with writs summoning me to appear at Westminster were blown away across the moor. The donkey tethered there, cropping the furze bushes, the old mine-workings and the man cutting turf are part of the natural order; donkeys have roamed the hill, men have cut turf and worked the mines there for centuries, and will continue to do so when the writs and consistory courts have been long forgotten. So I went often to Tregonning Hill and found in the wild spot an escape from the troubles which were vexing St. Hilary.

On the morning of the raid with which this chapter opens, I had saddled one of the horses, intending to ride there. A few minutes before I was to start, a woman rushed into my room exclaiming, 'They've come, Father, and Captain Hopes is locked up with them.' Hurrying across to the church, I met Norman Peters, a bell-ringer who lives close by. Together we tried to open the south door but found it locked. It was a strange experience to be standing knocking outside the door whose key had been entrusted to me at my induction more than twenty years before.

'We'll try the priest's door,' I said to Norman (this is a doorway leading into the chapel of Our Lady). After repeated knockings, the door was opened a few inches; stooping down - for the entrance is very low and narrow - I could see a number of strange men gathered there. I called to them through the opening that I was the vicar of the parish and demanded admission. The door was then opened a little wider and we crept through. Norman Peters made a dash for the belfry to ring for help, but was overpowered. The three of us imprisoned there, an old man, a youth and myself, could do nothing against the forty or fifty men assembled. I attempted to withdraw into myself, to say my prayers and to repeat as much of the offices of the breviary as I knew by heart. I thought of Tregonning Hill where I might have been and the old donkey nibbling the tops of the furze bushes. But however much I tried, I could not escape from what was going on round me. I might shut my eyes, but I still saw men standing on the holy altar, hacking at the reredos or carrying away the image of Our

Lady. I could not close my ears to the sounds of hammering which now filled the church.

I have not yet escaped from the scenes I witnessed that day and possibly never shall: whenever I enter an old country church and see the signs of destruction wrought there in the sixteenth century, I can hear the sounds of hammering and the crash of falling images. The men working this havoc have in my imagination the same faces as those who invaded St. Hilary that morning in August. The old church, quiet and peaceful when I entered, is filled with the phantoms I have conjured up. I see them tearing down the figure of Christ upon the Rood and casting out the Mother from the House of her Son. Often on leaving, my eyes will rest on the broken face of a once-smiling cherub, a witness to all that happened there, and I am glad to escape...

There are two tabernacles in the church at St. Hilary: one on the High Altar, condemned by the Chancellor; the other above the Chapel of the Sacred Heart, on which the Court had pronounced no judgment, since it was not there at the time of the hearing. In this tabernacle the Holy Sacrament was reserved. Now the guardianship of the Blessed Sacrament is part of the priest's office; the two men with me realized as fully as I did that the Holy Sacrament must be defended against profanation. While we were conferring together, a man who appeared to be in charge, approached me and suggested that if I surrendered the monstrance, now locked in the safe, he would be willing for me to remove the Sacrament. I could make no terms with him. Seeing that we were preparing to defend the Sacrament at all costs, he consented to my demands and allowed me to carry It to a place of safety. On my way to the house to fetch the key of the tabernacle, I spoke hurriedly to the people who had gathered outside and told them to procure candles. I returned and after vesting went to the altar and, opening the door of the tabernacle, took out the Sanctissimum.

Outside the church were a number of people who live close by - Johns, Hopes, Peters, Jenkins and their wives, a crowd of children returning from school and a few young labourers from the farm at Trevabyn. As I came from the little doorway of the Lady Chapel carrying the Holy Sacrament, I found them all on their knees lining the pathway through the churchyard, with lighted candles in their hands.

I had passed from the noise and tumult of passion to a quiet world of faith.

That night there was a service of reparation, when the Holy Sacrament was borne back to the church. All along the roadway from house to church were rows of people with bowed heads; as the procession passed slowly by they sang the hymn of St. Thomas:

> *Bow we then in adoration,*
> *This great Sacrament revere:*

words in which the summit of man's faith is reached. Never had I so realized the God-given quality of faith as on that night when, together with this company of people, I entered the dismantled church.

During the week people were busy restoring the house of God; carpenters and masons were repairing the damage; other images were substituted for those carried off and the church made gay with many flowers; so that by Sunday it was fit for the offering of the Holy Sacrifice. Everything was as it had been; but the cycle of peace which we had enjoyed for the past ten years had come to an end.

St. Hilary was no longer hidden from the outside world by its circle of trees; its name appeared in newspaper head-lines; a sign-post was set up on the high-road pointing a finger to the Church-town; crowds came to visit the church and at times invaded our garden. The place had lost its old air of peace.

Every day now brought hundreds of letters of sympathy; many contained gifts of money, small pieces of jewellery or wedding-rings, towards the cost of restoring the church. I spent the remaining days of August and the greater part of September sitting in the garden writing letters of thanks to these people.

I was also rehearsing *The Eve of All Souls*, which was to be broadcast for the first time. On the night after its production, as I was returning from a supper for the players held in the old schoolroom, I sensed fresh trouble brewing for St. Hilary. This schoolroom is reached by a flight of stone steps, dark and dangerous in winter-time. Coming down these steps on the night of the supper, I was astonished to see a row of motors in the lane. Motors are rare in the Church-town on week-days, but at ten o'clock on a November night they are a phantasy. I called out to the owners of these cars, who were collected in the road-way, and inquired who they were and what was their business at that time of night, but got no answer. Later on, the bell-ringers and players who had finished supper confronted this party, now assembled outside the church doors, and taunted them with not knowing the difference between a.m. and p.m.

'Come to Mass on All Souls' Day, have 'ee, my dears?' said they. 'Don't 'ee know what a.m. do mean? Some one has been having you on a string, I reckon.' The notice on the church door read:

All Souls' Day. Requiem Mass, 10 a.m.

Confusing this with vespers, part of which had been sung at the broadcast the night before, they had arrived with the intention of attending the service of which they disapproved. Their plans had failed that night; but they came again on following Sundays and sang hymns against the singing of the congregation, and created so great a disturbance that no word of the Mass could be heard. The police being informed came over on the second Sunday of the disturbances and took the names of those present; some of whom were convicted later of brawling under an order from the Court of the King's Bench.

I was too ill with influenza on these Sundays to be present and other priests, including Canon Carr, the Vicar of Penzance, took my place at the altar. Annie Walke had done her best to conceal from me what had happened; it was only the constant ringing of the telephone bell that led me to suspect that something was being kept from me. By Christmas Day, I was well enough to say Mass, and Annie Walke, who had also been ill, was sufficiently recovered to come down to dinner, and we opened a bottle of champagne to celebrate Christmas and our recovery. The next morning, I had a sick call and took the last Sacraments to an old priest who lay dying. As I stumbled home along the lane by the church, I was overcome with weakness and misery. 'This is the end,' I thought.

For two months I lay in bed, too feeble to take interest in anything beyond what I saw from my window. During my previous illness, I had lain and watched Willie Laity plough the big grass field known as Parson's Meadow. I could see the horses at the turn and hear the voice of Willie, as he shouted to them, and the jingling of their harness as they started afresh. Each day the green strip of grass grew smaller until there was not a single green 'tub', as they say in Cornwall, to be seen. The field had been harrowed and sown and lay in its cold winter sleep.

But now, as I watched the gulls walking there, it appeared to have already awakened; while it was still December, spring had come to that field. I saw it first as a thin blue-green haze. Within a week, the haze had grown into long straight lines stretching from one end to the other. 'It's the new wheat!' I exclaimed. The worries of the past year, the misery of being ill fell away as I repeated the lovely lines from 'The Everlasting Mercy':

> *The young green corn divinely springing,*
> *The young green corn for ever singing.*

The End of Twenty Years

John Laity had always been a good friend to me, but never more so than when he laid down wheat that year in Parson's Meadow.

On one of these mornings Annie Walke came to say that she was going out for a ride. For weeks she had been grappling with clergymen, reporters, policemen, my illness, and the illness of our maid, as well as having chickenpox and influenza herself. There was spring in the air that morning as she started to ride out on to the moors where the early gorse would, I knew, be already in bloom. I was looking forward to her return and to hear of all she had seen and how the country was looking, when there was a knock at the door.

'The Doctor to see you,' said our maid, Emma. He came into the room and, nodding to me, began to warm his hands at the fire. While he talked, I was all the time waiting to hear what I already knew he had come to say.

'Well?' I said at last.

'I am sorry,' he began, 'to have to tell you that the test proved to be positive.'

'That means, I suppose, that I have got T.B.?' I said, raising myself on my pillow.

'I am afraid that is what it comes to,' he said.

I thought of Annie Walke on the moor among the early gorse bloom and wondered if I should ever ride there again.

'It's going to be a long business,' I ventured, anxious to gather the worst.

'That is impossible to say,' he answered, 'but I am afraid you will have to give up the thought of doing any work for at least a year.'

After the Doctor had left I sat up in bed and looked round the room.

It is a charming white room of which during this illness I had grown very fond; but now, since I had heard about this T.B., everything seemed to have changed; nothing I looked at offered any comfort; 'The young green corn,' that a few hours before had so delighted me, had become grey; the pictures I had treasured ceased to have any meaning for me. I could think of nothing but of how was

I to break this miserable news to Annie Walke when she returned from her ride? I thought of many reassuring phrases, but when she did come in, after what seemed to me hours of waiting, I blurted out, 'The Doctor has just been and says I have T.B.'

A few days later I was moved to the sanatorium at Tehidy. It was from my bed there in Hut Number 10, I began to write these memories.

EPILOGUE

The bells of St. Hilary had not deceived me. Perhaps you, my reader, will remember how, at my induction, over-eager to assure a long residence, I lost count of the number of strokes and was forced to begin counting afresh.

The twenty years I then rang for myself ended about the time I left St. Hilary for the sanatorium at Tehidy. After eighteen months I have returned to complete the unrecorded years. How many they were, I do not know.

It is enough that I am back again at St. Hilary.

INDEX

Index

Index

Index